East African Archaeology

East African Archaeology

Foragers, Potters, Smiths, and Traders

edited by

Chapurukha M. Kusimba and Sibel B. Kusimba

University of Pennsylvania Museum of Archaeology and Anthropology
Philadelphia

Library of Congress Cataloging-in-Publication Data

East African archaeology : foragers, potters, smiths, and traders /
edited by Chapurukha M. Kusimba and Sibel B. Kusimba.– 1st ed.
     p. cm.
Includes bibliographical references (p.) and index.
  ISBN 1-931707-61-8 (alk. paper)
  1. Africa, East–Antiquities. 2. Antiquities, Prehistoric–Africa,
East. 3. Prehistoric peoples–Africa, East. I. Kusimba, Chapurukha
Makokha. II. Kusimba, Sibel Barut, 1966-
DT365.3 .E23 2003
967.6'01–dc22   2003016364

Kathleen Ryan, consulting editor.
All illustrations in this volume were done by Lindsay Shafer.

∞ Printed in the United States of America on acid-free paper.

Contents

Figures and Tables

TABLES

Preface

East Africa has special meaning for us Homo sapiens. It is, as far as we know, the place where early humans first experimented with the technologies, social relationships, and food-getting strategies that eventually became the survival repertoire of modern people. East Africa, including the present countries of Tanzania, Kenya, and Uganda, is remarkable for its diversity of environments, languages, economic lifeways, and ethnic groups. How did East Africans shape this diversity over time? This volume's goal is to impart an appreciation of the many facets of East Africa's cultural and archaeological diversity over the last two thousand years. It brings together chapters on East African archaeology, many by African archaeologists, who review what is known, present new research, and pinpoint issues of debate and anomaly in the relatively poorly known prehistory of East Africa. In the last chapter, discussant Peter Mitchell, a South Africanist scholar, provides a broader perspective on East Africa by highlighting similarities and differences in problem and process faced by South African prehistorians and historians. Mitchell's chapter helps to contextualize East African prehistory by focusing it against one of the better-known and researched areas of the continent.

It would be difficult indeed to impose common research methods or goals on East Africa's four-million-year record of human settlement. Thus it is especially difficult to write a book that adequately addresses the region's research (Robertshaw 1995:55–56). Our volume attempts not to offer a synthesis of the region's prehistory but to provide examples of current research in later East African prehistory, ethnoarchaeology, and cultural resource management that point to future research directions. Many of these chapters began as papers that were presented in a symposium organized by Chapurukha Kusimba at the 95th annual meeting of the American Anthropological Association; several other chapters were solicited in order to provide a more rounded edited volume.

The contributions to this volume address five themes: later hunting and gathering groups (Chapters 1 and 2), ethnohistorical and ethnoarchaeological perspectives (Chapters 3 and 4), ironworking and ironworkers (Chapters

5 to 8), cultural resource management (Chapter 9), and the origins of social inequality (Chapters 5, 8, and 10). East Africa is one of few places in the world where foraging lifeways persisted well into the 20th century (Kent 1996). Ethnoarchaeological studies like Mabulla's work with the Hadzabe, presented here in Chapter 3, can provide testable hypotheses about Stone Age and historic hunter-gatherer adaptations, compared here in Chapter 1. Bower (1991) and Karega-Munene (1996; Chapter 2 here) have recently reexamined East Africa's complex Neolithic archaeology in the light of ethnoarchaeological work with present-day potters (Herbich 1987; Wandibba, Chapter 4 here).

Research into African ironworking has benefited from the intensive study of archaeomaterials as well as ethnoarchaeological study of technology's social role (Kusimba and Killick, Chapter 7 here). In light of the urgent need to conserve East Africa's cultural and wildlife resources, Musiba and Mabulla (Chapter 9 here) advocate better planning and management of cultural and wildlife resources at the community level, combined with the use of sustainable eco- and archaeo-tourism.

Investigation into urbanism on the East African coast and the rise of the precolonial kingdoms of the Great Lakes region has weathered a period of anti-colonialist writings and is now contributing to theoretical debates on state formation (Robertshaw 1990). Like the study of agricultural origins, that of state formation may be freed from the "red herring" (Robertshaw, Chapter 10 this volume) of questions of identity and begin focusing on questions of process, especially the role of social power. No longer can state formation in Africa be synonymous with external trade.

Early Africanists saw technological change as either an aid to chronology and seriation or the driving force behind culture change. Childs's (1994) volume on African technology announced that a new approach to technology would emphasize not its determining effects on other levels of culture but its embeddedness within both economic and ideological social domains. This more ethnographic understanding of technology's role in social life has inspired lithic studies emphasizing environmental adaptation and technological organization, archaeometallurgical approaches to artisanal and technological styles, and approaches to pottery analysis that examine the multitude of influences on pottery style, including social communication and trade relationships as well as ethnicity (Herbich 1987; Karega-Munene 1996). The contributors to this volume are participants in these ongoing revisions of method and theory.

East African archaeology bears the stamp of several generations of archaeological research, initiated by the drive and ambition of settler families like the Leakeys. The 21st century looks bright for East African archaeology with more opportunities for research than ever before. Until the mid-1980s, for example, only a handful of western universities provided doctorates in African archaeology. Today, no single program is the leader. Consequently, Africanist and non-Africanist archaeologists are exchanging ideas and approaches, and the work of the former is becoming increasingly visible in journals of world archaeology. At the same time, practitioners of East African archaeology are sophisticated, exploiting advanced scientific techniques (Childs 1994), revising theories and methods, and questioning basic anthropological concepts such as ethnicity. The varied chapters in this volume, many of them by East African-born scholars, show the diversity and dynamism of Stone Age, Neolithic, and Iron Age prehistory in East Africa today.

I

Comparing Prehistoric and Historic Hunter-Gatherer Mobility in Southern Kenya

Sibel B. Kusimba and Chapurukha M. Kusimba

This chapter compares the land-use patterns of prehistoric and historic hunter-gatherers of south-central Kenya. We examine hunter-gatherer mobility patterns during the Later Stone Age (LSA) based on lithic and faunal data from Lukenya Hill. We use similar data to examine mobility patterns of historic hunter-gatherers at Kisio Rock Shelter, Tsavo National Park, south-central Kenya. Tsavo's Iron Age hunter-gatherers coexisted with farmers and herders and possessed iron tools and pottery. A marked decrease in mobility characterizes the land-use patterns of historic hunter-gatherers of south-central Kenya as compared to Paleolithic hunter-gatherers of a similar environment. Such comparisons can increase our understanding of the particular histories of ethnographically and historically known hunter-gatherers and the appropriate uses of hunter-gatherer ethnographic analogy in archaeology.

Archaeologists have long used the ethnographic record of hunter-gatherer societies as a productive source of models of prehistoric hunter-gatherer cultures. Using information from societies like the !Kung San, Lee and DeVore (1968:11–12) assembled an empirical model of hunter-gatherer societies that emphasized high mobility, flexible social arrangements, and exchange and kinship alliances. This model was abundantly applied to prehistoric situations ranging from East African fossil hominids to late prehistoric groups in the northeastern United States (Shott 1992:846). Over time, however, a revisionist perspective has urged consideration of how local historical factors influence diversity in hunter-gatherer societies such as that of the !Kung San. Archaeologists are increasingly noting discrepancies between ethnographic and archaeological cases (Sealey and Pfeiffer 2000) and appreciating diversity rather than employing a single empirical model (Rowly-Conwy 2001). Archaeology has an important role to play in understanding hunter-gatherer diversity since many empirical cases are contained in historical and archaeological as well as ethnographic records (Mutundu 1999).

Africa has the world's longest history of hominid habitation. Furthermore, it may well have the world's longest history of habitation by behaviorally and physically modern hunter-gatherers who have possessed complex tools and language capabilities for as long as 50,000 years or more (McBrearty and Brooks 2000). Africa also has a rich ethnographic and historical record of hunter-gatherer cultures persisting into historic times and the present day (Lee and Daly 1999; Stiles 1992). Because of its long continuous history of hunter-gatherer societies, East Africa is an appropriate place to examine how they changed over time. One of the most important changes such societies underwent was the introduction of food production and food producing societies into their areas of habitation. In many cases, hunter-gatherers developed exchange relationships with food producers, and indeed survived because of, not in spite of, such relationships (Headland and Reid 1989). Nevertheless, food producers often politically dominated hunter-gatherers (Smith 1998; Thorp 1996; Wadley 1996; but see Cronk and Dickson 2001).

In this chapter, we use archaeological data from stratified sites at Lukenya Hill in the Athi Plains of Kenya to infer the site and land-use patterns of its late Pleistocene LSA inhabitants. Using similar data we examine site and land-use patterns from Kisio Rock Shelter in Tsavo, Kenya, where hunter-gatherers lived from 1000 CE to the mid-20th century (Fig. 1.1). Finally, we suggest reasons why Paleolithic hunter-gatherers in south-central Kenya appear to have been significantly more mobile than their historic counterparts.

Both the Lukenya and Kisio sites are in an *Acacia-Commiphora* bush-land typical of arid East Africa (White 1983). The Tsavo region is drier than the Athi Plains, receiving around 300 mm of rain per year compared to around 500 mm of rain per year in the Athi Plains. Significantly, it is also at a much lower altitude (200–600 m, compared to 1600–1800 m at Lukenya Hill) and very hot. Due to its poor soils and desert climate, it has an abundance of animals that need very little water and can tolerate poor-quality forage (Olindo, Douglas-Hamilton, and Hamilton 1988; Wijngaarden and van Engelen 1985). The present-day Tsavo fauna includes elephant, buffalo, Burchell's zebra, kudu, impala, warthog, dik-dik, and rock hyrax; large carnivores including lion, leopard, and spotted hyena; primates such as baboon and vervet monkey; and many species of insectivores, birds, reptiles, and amphibians. In faunal assemblages from Lukenya Hill, Marean found an extinct small alcelaphine, the extinct giant buffalo *Pelorovis antiquus*, oryx,

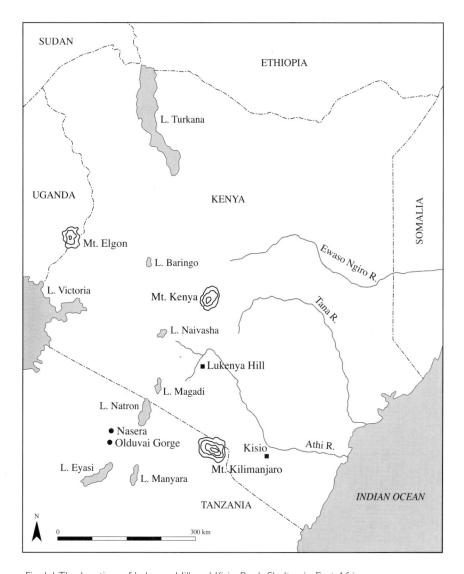

Fig. 1.1 The location of Lukenya Hill and Kisio Rock Shelter in East Africa.

Grevy's and Burchell's zebra, hartebeest, wildebeest, Grant's and Thompson's gazelle, and eland (Marean 1990:335–345; 1992). Many of these animals, such as oryx and Grevy's zebra, are today found in areas that receive less than 300 mm of rainfall (Marean and Gifford-Gonzalez 1991), demonstrating the greater aridity of the Lukenya Hill area during the Pleistocene.

3

Methods: Hunter-Gatherer Mobility and Lithic Analysis

We use data from lithic assemblages to infer LSA and historic hunter-gatherer land-use patterns. Many archaeologists have used lithic raw material proportions to infer hunter-gatherer mobility (Carr 1994; Nelson 1992). More sedentary groups can be expected to rely primarily on local raw materials and to use smaller amounts of nonlocal raw materials. More mobile hunter-gatherers, who have greater access to raw material, will be less likely to conserve their raw materials. Conservation is marked by a variety of behaviors, including greater reduction of raw materials, transport, caching and recycling, and the manufacture of formal tools (Nelson 1992). Holding raw material distributions constant, more sedentary groups, who have less access to raw material, should conserve nonlocal raw material more.

We also incorporate faunal data into our comparison. After all, the major reason why hunter-gatherers move is to find food, although social reasons such as marriage partner search also play a role (see Mabulla, this volume). Shifts in diet are some of the most important reasons why hunter-gatherer mobility strategies change. Sometimes these shifts in diet are conditioned by environmental change and consequent change in the plants and animals available. At other times, technological change spurs an enlargement or narrowing of the components of the diet. Over time, hunter-gatherers have come to focus increasingly on smaller food resources, using ever more complex technologies to allow them to hunt smaller animals and process nuts and seeds. Such changes have enabled hunter-gatherers to reduce their mobility (Stiner, Munro, and Surovell 2000). Finally, social change and social conflict can enlarge or reduce the food resources a group may find available.

The LSA: Land-Use Models and Ethnographic Analogies

The archaeology of the LSA in sub-Saharan Africa, from around 50,000 to 12,000 BP, is represented by very few sites (Brooks and Robertshaw 1990). Widespread aridity and low population densities are probably responsible for the scant archaeological traces of the time (Klein 1984, 1989). Paleoecological evidence demonstrates that much of tropical Africa was colder and more arid than today (Coetzee and Van Zinderen Bakker 1989; Elenga, Vincens, and Schwartz 1991, 1994; Perrott and Street-Perrott 1982). Few areas of Africa have a large enough number of sites to allow archaeologists to look reliably at land-use patterns. In South Africa, however, a highly mobile land-use pattern has been suggested for hunter-gatherers who produced the Robberg Industry, which dates from 22,000 to 12,000 years ago (Deacon and Deacon 1999). Robberg Industry sites appear to be ephemeral site occupations, always in rock shelters, and involve the manufacture of small tools, especially bladelets, often made from bipolar cores, and a reliance on large, migratory, grazing ungulates. Some have suggested that Robberg peoples were highly mobile "hunters of big game" similar in their land use and technology to Paleoindian hunters of the Americas (Mitchell 1992). H. J. Deacon (1993, 1995), however, argues that plant foods may have been just as important during the Robberg as they are ethnographically for African hunter-gatherers (see Mabulla, Chapter 3 this volume). Unfortunately, plant use evidence is rare for this time period (Opperman and Hydenrych 1990).

Pleistocene Hunter-Gatherers at Lukenya Hill, Kenya

Lukenya Hill in south-central Kenya (Fig. 1.1), an inselberg on the semiarid, *Acacia-Commiphora* grassland of the Athi Plains, has five archaeological sites dating to the Pleistocene and containing LSA assemblages: GvJm16, GvJm19, GvJm22, GvJm62, and GvJm46. Sources of lithic raw material in the area include abundant vein quartz sources and local obsidian and chert. Both these latter sources are less common than the vein quartz. The chert nodules are found in secondary deposits in stream channels throughout the Athi Plains, the closest being just 5 km from Lukenya Hill. Similarly, the local obsidian bombs outcrop in several areas, at a similar distance. Other obsidians in the Lukenya Hill assemblages have been sourced to the Central Rift Valley and the Kedong escarpment, 150 km and 60 km from Lukenya Hill, respectively. Both these areas are well within group territories for modern Kalahari hunter-gatherers (Hitchcock and Ebert 1989), indicating that direct procurement or trade were both possible means of accessing the Central Rift obsidians.

Lithic Assemblages from Lukenya Hill

Available radiocarbon dates for the Lukenya Hill sites are considered suspect but do provide a relative chronology for the sites that dates them to the late Upper Pleistocene. The GvJm46 and GvJm62 sites have the oldest components but overlap in age with the GvJm16 and GvJm22 sites. The GvJm19 site is the youngest with a terminal Pleistocene date. The analysis of the Lukenya assemblage shows that two groups of sites are discernible based on typology and raw material proportions (see S. Kusimba 1999, 2001, for a more complete discussion). The lithic assemblages from sites GvJm46, GvJm62, and GvJm19, the two oldest sites and the most recent site, are dominated by vein quartz raw material and scrapers, with very small numbers of microliths (Table 1.1). Quartz artifacts in the GvJm46, GvJm62, and GvJm19 assemblages have several characteristics of a simple, on-the-spot technology called "expedient" (Nelson 1992). Quartz cores appear in a wide variety of sizes, are less reduced than cores in other raw materials, and are often

Table 1.1   Percentages of Raw Materials and Tool Types in the Lukenya Hill
Assemblages

Site	% Quartz of All Lithic Artifacts	% Nonlocal Obsidian of All Lithic Artifacts	% Scrapers of Shaped Tools	% Microliths of Shaped Tools
GvJm46	92		67	15
GvJm62	75	30	69	13
GvJm22	68	46	20	48
GvJm16	46	73	25	66
GvJm19	85		60	23

reduced through bipolar reduction. Few quartz tools were manufactured at these sites. Those that were consisted mostly of simple scrapers.

At these sites, obsidian and chert, brought in from the surrounding Athi Plains and from the Central Rift Valley, were treated with conservational or curated strategies. Bipolar reduction predominates in the chert and obsidian cores. While in local materials, bipolar reduction is an expedient tool-producing technology, in nonlocal or less accessible materials, such a flaking method is often conservational (Parry and Kelly 1987).

The greater reduction of the chert and obsidian cores, coupled with use of bipolar flaking, is consistent with the intent to maintain these cores for future use; furthermore, Central Rift Valley obsidian tools and flakes were large and were often made into blades and blade segments (S. Kusimba 1999).

The second group of assemblages, from sites GvJm16 and GvJm22, contains primarily microliths rather than scrapers. The assemblages include higher proportions of chert and obsidian from both the local area and the Central Rift Valley. Furthermore, bipolar flaking is rare in these assemblages and chert and obsidian cores are more reduced. Even quartz cores from this second group of sites are significantly more reduced than quartz cores in the first group of sites.

The typological and raw material differences between the two groups of sites reflect differences in tool strategies and settlement patterns. Although all the Lukenya Hill hunter-gatherers had access to chert and obsidian from the surrounding Athi Plains and from the Central Rift Valley, the greater abundance of these raw materials at GvJm16 and GvJm22 indicates their inhabitants had more frequent contact with these dispersed sources; furthermore, they used the raw material in a less conservational way. These movements were presumably motivated by quests for food, social contacts, and the chert and obsidian lithic raw materials themselves, which they preferred for microlith manufacture.

Faunal Data from Lukenya Hill

Faunal remains from the Lukenya Hill sites are dominated by large, migratory grazers, such as extinct small alcelaphine, the extinct giant buffalo *Pelorovis antiquus*, oryx, Grevy's and Burchell's zebra, hartebeest, and wildebeest (Marean 1992b). There was very little evidence of hunting of local inselberg fauna, such as klipspringer and bush duiker (Marean 1990:335–345; 1992). Although some of this lack of local inselberg fauna might be due to preservational factors, the absence of local fauna is surely significant. Fauna at the GvJm46 site were overwhelmingly from one species, the small extinct alcelaphine, while the other sites had a diversity of migratory ungulate species.

GvJm46's position at the bottom of a steep cliff led Marean (1990:466) to suggest that the site was a drive site for herds of the extinct alcelaphine. Their teeth show a catastrophic mortality profile, except that older individuals are absent from the profile. Marean suggests that the kill site was used regularly after the long dry season, when many older animals would have died already. Marean suggests that LSA hunters combined opportunism with seasonal specialization (Marean 1997). From both the lithic and faunal data, it appears that groups who used Lukenya Hill did so as part of a seasonal round. Given the large amounts of Central Rift Valley artifacts, especially at GvJm22 and GvJm16, they spent a significant amount of time in other areas.

Historic Hunter-Gatherers of the Tsavo Area, Kenya

The Tsavo National Park is Kenya's oldest and largest national park. When it was gazetted in 1947, numerous human groups inside the park, who lived at least partly by hunting and gathering, were resettled around its outskirts (Hobley 1895; Stiles 1979, 1980). Many of these groups claimed descent from Wasanye and Waata hunter-gatherers of historical accounts. Waata or Wasanye foragers, pejoratively referred to by their neighbors as Walyankuru ("those who eat pig"), spoke a dialect of the Oromo language (Hobley 1895; Stiles 1982). The Waata were adept in the use of bows and poisoned arrows for hunting elephants and provided ivory to caravans heading to trade ports on the Kenya coast (Hobley 1895, 1912, 1929; Holis 1909). The Waata had patron-client relationships with their Oromo pastoralist overlords. "If they shoot an elephant one tusk is given to the Galla (Oromo) Chief" (Hobley 1895:557; 1929). Wataita agriculturalists from the Taita hills forged blood brotherhoods with Waata hunters for access to their secret

Table 1.2 Hypothesized Ecological and Economic Relationships among Iron Age Residents of the Tsavo Region

	Wasanye	Oromo	Wataita	Coastal Fishers/ Urbanites
Environment	scrub/thicket	arid grasslands	wetter hill slopes	coastal towns and cities
Mobility	high	seasonal	sedentism/low mobility	sedentism
Social organ- ization	egalitarian/ heterarchical	lineage/clan	lineage/clan	ranked/stratified hierarchical
Trade products	skins, meat, ivory, rhino horns, honey, beeswax, labor, ritual knowledge, medicines	milk, butter, meat, hides and skins, incense, domes- tic animals	crops, pottery, iron, rock crystal, finished tools	dried and/or smoked fish, beads, pottery, imported ceram- ics, metals, jewel- ry, tools, textiles
Ethic	egalitarian/ heterarchical	status-seeking, expansionist	status-seeking	status-seeking
Relationship with coast	diplomatic trade	diplomatic trade	trade controlled by coast	
Type of trade	individually contracted or person-to-person, symbiotic ex- change—utilitari- an or personal adornment	controlled by lineage/ethnic group or eld- ers—utilitarian and prestige goods	controlled by lineage/ethnic group or eld- ers—utilitarian and prestige goods	controlled by socioeconomic elites—utilitarian and prestige goods

knowledge of elephant hunting and, in turn, the lucrative ivory trade (Kusimba and Kusimba 1998–2000). In Tsavo, as in many parts of Africa, hunter-gatherers, pastoralists, and agriculturalists coexisted, bound by symbiotic relationships of exchange and intermarriage but also experiencing episodic conflicts (Table 1.2; Ambrose 1986; Mapunda, Chapter 5 this volume; Vansina 1990; Wilmsen 1989). Intergroup conflict over wealth-building resources such as cattle occurred in spite of alliances through which goods, information, and ritual power were exchanged (Merritt 1975; Kusimba and Kusimba 1998–2000).

Kisio Rock Shelter

Survey and excavation in Tsavo from 1998 to 2000 included excavation of Kisio Rock Shelter, a hunter-gatherer habitation dating to the last 1000 years and including several hundred pieces of pottery, 10,000 lithic artifacts, metal artifacts, more than 300 glass beads, and over 1,000 wild faunal remains (Fig. 1.1). The Kisio Rock Shelter is located in the Central Plains of Tsavo East, a flat peneplain of *Acacia-Commiphora* bushland dotted with small inselbergs. The immediate area of the site is a mixed habitat of open grassy areas and bushland on inselbergs. A small seasonal waterhole is nearby. Two radiocarbon dates bracket the occupation to between 100 and 1,000 radiocarbon years before present.

Lithic Assemblages from Kisio

The lithic assemblage at Kisio consists of 10,098 artifacts, which were examined by David Braun of Rutgers University. Ninety-seven percent of these artifacts were made of locally available vein quartz. Other raw materials in the assemblage include a fine-grained rhyolitic igneous rock, crypto-crystalline silica, and locally available obsidian (Table 1.3). Almost half the cores in the Kisio assemblage are bipolar, and 88 percent of the cores have three or fewer flake scars. There is very little retouch or platform preparation on the flakes, and only 1.4 percent of the artifacts are shaped tools (Table 1.4). Furthermore, very little recycling was employed at Kisio and only 1 of the 144 tools was a composite tool. These characteristics are similar to those of the quartz artifacts from GvJm46 and GvJm62 at Lukenya Hill and demonstrate that the majority of quartz artifacts were procured from the immediate

Table 1.3 Raw Material Types in the Kisio Rock Shelter Assemblages

Raw Material	Number
Quartz	3055
Chert	32
Lava	19
Obsidian	18
Chalcedony	4
Indurated sandstone	3
Quartzite	1
Magnetite	1
Total	3147

Table 1.4 Artifact Classes in the Kisio Rock Shelter Assemblages

Reduction stage	%
Debitage	85.4
Flakes	8.2
Cores	3.3
Tools	1.4

vicinity, flaked once or twice, then discarded. Unlike at Lukenya Hill, no component of the lithic assemblage shows a significant use of curated strategies, such as the transport of Rift Valley obsidian to the site, the use of conservational bipolar flaking or formal tool manufacture, or the manufacture of composite tools. At Kisio Rock Shelter, the lack of shaped tools or retouch and the lack of transport of nonlocal cores evidences an almost exclusive use of on-the-spot, simple technology as far as lithic artifacts are concerned.

Faunal Assemblages from Kisio

Kisio Rock Shelter's faunal assemblages were identified by Briana Pobiner of Rutgers University. The faunal assemblage was found in levels with abundant lithic material, pottery, iron artifacts, and beads. Furthermore, as none of the bones displayed any porcupine or carnivore tooth marks, we assume that humans were the main accumulators and modifiers of the Kisio bones.

Table 1.5 MNI/NISP of Fauna from Kisio Rock Shelter
Note: MNI and NISP were not calculated for any taxonomic levels above tribe.

Taxonomic Classification	Common Name	MNI	NISP
Class Aves			
Order Anseriformes			
Family Anatidae			
Anas hottentota	Hottentot teal	1	1
Order Columbiformes			
Family Columbidae			
Oena capensis	Namaqua dove	1	1
Order Coraciiformes			
Family Bucerotidae			
Tockus erythrorhynchus	Red-billed hornbill	8	62
Tockus flavirostris	Yellow-billed hornbill	4	18
Tockus sp. indet.	Hornbill	1	10
Order Galliformes			
Family Phasianidae			
Coturnix delegorguei	Harlequin quail	1	1
Class Mammalia			
Order Artiodactyla			
Family Bovidae			
Tribe Aepycerotini			
Aepyceros melampus	Impala	2	5
Tribe Alcelaphini			
sp. indet.		2	6
Tribe Bovini			
Syncerus caffer	Buffalo	1	1
Tribe Cephalophini			
cf. *Cephalophus harveyi*	Harvey's red duiker	1	2

Taxonomic Classification	Common Name	MNI	NISP
Tribe Neotragini			
Madoqua kirkii	Kirk's dik-dik	3	39
Tribe Tragelaphini			
Tragelaphus imberbis	Lesser kudu	I	I
Taurotragus oryx	Eland	I	3
sp. indet.		I	I
Family Suidae			
Phacochoerus africanus	Warthog	I	3
Order Hyracoidea			
Family Procaviidae			
Heterohyrax brucei	Bush/yellow-spotted hyrax	2	7
Order Lagomorpha			
Family Leporidae			
Lepus capensis	Cape hare	I	5
Order Macroscelidae			
Family Mascroscelididae			
Elephantulus sp. (*rufescens?*)	Elephant shrew	I	I
Order Perissodactyla			
Family Equidae			
Equus burchelli	Burchell's zebra	I	2
Order Primates			
Family Hominidae			
Homo sapiens	Human	I	I6
Order Rodentia			
Family Cricetidae			
Cricetomys gambianus	Giant rat	I	I
Family Gerbillinae			
Tatera sp. indet.	Naked-soled gerbil	I	8
Taterillus emini	Gerbil	I	I
Class Reptilia			
Family Testudinidae			
Pelosios broadlyi	Freshwater terrapin	I	3
Order Squamata			
Family Varanidae			
Varanus exanthematicus	Monitor lizard	I	I0
Family Agamidae			
cf. *Agama agama*	Agama	I	5
Family Boidae			
Eryx colubrinus	Sand boa	I	3
Family Chamaeleonida			
Chamaeleo sp. indet.	Chameleon	I	2
Family Colubridae			
Rhamphiophis oxyrhynchus	Eastern brown-beaked snake	I	6
Psammophis sp. indet.	Sand snake	I	2
Family Viperidae			
Bitis arientans	Puff adder	I	6
Order Salientia			
Suborder Diplasiocoela			
sp. indet.	Frog	0	344

At Lukenya Hill, Marean (1990, 1992b, 1997) described faunal assemblages based almost exclusively on migratory grazers. At Kisio, by contrast, the faunal remains are dominated by small nonmigratory animals (Table 1.5). In terms of MNI (minimum number of individuals), the most common animals found were red and yellow hornbills, dik-dik, and hyrax, and in terms of NISP (number of identified species), small bovids dominate over large ones. In addition, over 17 kg of land snail remains were recovered from Kisio. There were no domestic animals found at Kisio. Most of the species present—including the bovids, zebra, warthog, birds, hyrax, terrapin, frogs, chameleons, snakes, elephant shrews, rats, and gerbils—could have been food resources for humans. Hyrax, land snails, and hornbills are easily hunted, common food sources around Tsavo according to local informants (see also Kingdon 1982; Mehlman 1989). Indeed, other historic hunter-gatherers of Africa are known to have focused on similar small animal resources (Sampson 1998; Henshilwood 1997; Mutundu 1999). Ideally, taphonomic studies should be done to confirm that Kisio's small faunal remains were eaten by humans (Henshilwood 1997; Sampson 2000). Because no permanent water is nearby, the Kisio shelter was most likely occupied briefly and sporadically. During these periods, local fauna were procured and processed with the aid of expedient local tools.

Other classes of artifacts at Kisio show even more dramatic changes in historic hunter-gatherer lifeways compared to those of the Paleolithic at Lukenya Hill. The Kisio group was unmistakably linked through trade with surrounding peoples. First, over 200 European glass beads were found at Kisio; these were one of the most common trade items in East Africa in the mid to late Iron Age. Second, several metal artifacts were recovered, including an arrowhead made of sheet metal, first introduced to East Africa by the British in the early 19th century. Plain and incised decorated pottery was also found, although no evidence of pottery or metal production was found at Kisio. The metal tools, then, unlike the lithic artifacts, were almost certainly a curated technology. Thorbahn (1979), after excavating similar rock shelter sites with wild fauna and trade items, attributed them to hunting and gathering peoples who, as the ivory trade grew, began to specialize in elephant hunting and in providing caravans and other Tsavo groups with ivory in exchange for blankets, grains, and milk products. Certainly, the Kisio occupation was a brief seasonal one, given the lack of permanent water nearby. One cannot rule out, however, that Kisio's inhabitants may have pursued a variety of subsistence practices at other periods or perhaps seasonally, such as herding and farming on a sporadic and seasonal basis; they may have lived in longer-term settlements at other times of the year, perhaps providing labor to an agricultural settlement (Wadley 1996). Intriguingly, Thorbahn (1979) reports on rock shelter occupations with domestic faunal remains, although these excavated assemblages have not been located. More sites need to be excavated before an exclusive "hunter-gatherer" economy can be attributed to the inhabitants of Kisio; by the same token, more evidence of interaction is needed to demonstrate what kinds of social linkages may have brought beadwork and metals to the Kisio people.

Discussion

Lukenya Hill and Kisio Rock Shelter demonstrate the profound changes in hunter-gatherer lifeways that occurred after the invention of food production. Hunting and gathering went from being the only economic system available to being one of many strategies that enabled some African societies to participate in increasingly complex local and international trade routes. From a perspective of hunter-gatherer land use and hunting, one effect may have been to constrain hunter-gatherer mobility. Lukenya Hill was one of many points on an essentially open landscape that hunter-gatherers could occupy. Here, hunters chose to concentrate on large, mobile fauna, which presumably offered larger caloric returns than small mammals, especially if drive hunting was practiced. During the Neolithic period, however, hunter-gatherers were no longer the only occupants of the landscape; rather, they shared it with other groups, who practiced food production to varying extents.

According to Smith (1998), political relationships between pastoralists and food producers generally placed hunter-gatherers as political inferiors who were dependent to varying degrees on pastoralists or farmers to supplement their diet in return for labor or forest products. At Kisio, hunter-gatherers may have been tethered to rock shelters and their resources by Oromo and Maasai pastoralists, who were also their political superiors and probably controlled the open plains. As a result only small mammals may have been available for hunting (Hobley 1929).

The above hypothesis, however, must be tested by gleaning more evidence regarding what kinds of social groups lived in Tsavo and how they interacted. Although Smith (1998) and Wilmsen (1989) emphasize the political subordination of hunters who live alongside food producers, others have painted the hunter-farmer/herder relationship as an egalitarian one, based on economic and ecological symbiosis (Ambrose 1986). In East Africa, hunters hold political advantages and maintain economic autonomy as suppliers of valued honey and as holders of ritual knowledge (Cronk and Dickson 2001).

Historic Mukogodo hunter-gatherers of central Kenya offer a point of comparison with the hunter-gatherer occupants of Tsavo. These highland, former hunter-gatherers of north-central Kenya originally spoke a Cushitic language, but today speak Maa like their Maasai neighbors. Over the course of the 20th century they developed increasingly close relationships with Maasai, which culminated in their transition to a pastoralist way of life (Cronk 1991). Whereas the Tsavo area is mostly hot, dry lowland bushland, the area occupied by the Mukogodo is variable in altitude (900–2100 m) and higher in rainfall (600 mm/year). It includes many hills and valleys and has bushy woodland and forest as its main form of vegetation. Although little is known about the Mukogodo, Mutundu's excavations at Shurmai shelter doc-

Table 1.6 Proportions of Identifiable Fauna from Kisio Rock Shelter, Tsavo, and Shurmai Shelter, Mukogodo, Compared. (At Shurmai, hyrax NISP included both *Heterohyrax* and *Procavia*; at Tsavo, hyrax NISP included *Heterohyrax brucei* only.)

	Shurmai		Kisio	
Animal size 1 (<20 kg)	NISP	% of NISP	NISP	% of NISP
Taxa				
Hyrax	1514	68.4	7	1.2
Dik-dik	409	18.5	36	6.4
Sheep/Goat	118	5.3	0	0
Duiker	78	3.5	2	0.4
Rodent	9	0.4	10	1.8
Bird	4	0.2	93	16.5
Reptile	2	0.15	37	6.6
Frog	0	0.00	343	61.0
Cape hare	0	0	5	9
Elephant shrew	0	0	1	0.1
Animal size 2–3 (>20 kg)				0
Cattle	24	1.1	0	0
Burchell's zebra	24	1.1	2	0.4
Warthog	13	0.6	3	0.5
Giraffe	4	0.2	0	0
Buffalo	3	0.15	1	0.2
Wildebeest	2	0.10	0	0
Grant's gazelle	2	0.10	0	0
Impala	2	0.10	5	0.9
Baboon	2	0.10	0	0
Lesser kudu	0	0	1	0.2
Eland	0	0	1	0.2
Human	1	0.05	16	2.8
Total	2211		563	

ument an early-20th-century occupation that provides a window into a transitional period of close association with pastoralists. The Shurmai fauna, unlike those at Kisio, include domestic sheep/goat and cow, documenting that the Mukogodo were acquiring domestic animals as part of their interaction with pastoralists (Table 1.6). Other faunal data reflect faunal community differences in the local habitats. However, both the Shurmai fauna and the Kisio fauna document a focus on small mammals: at Shurmai, these are mostly hyrax and dik-dik; at Kisio, the faunal assemblages are dominated by frogs, hornbills, dik-dik, hyrax, and reptiles.

In the Mukogodo case, the emphasis on hyrax hunting could be a result of territorial pressure from Maasai pastoralists—the Mukogodo could have been confined through political subordination to small rocky territories unsuitable for pasture. As a consequence they may have focused their hunting on what was locally available (Mutundu 1999). On the other hand, a focus on small mammals can also be explained as a sensible choice for groups who traded with pastoralists but also maintained political and economic autonomy, and advantageous for transitional hunter-gatherers like the Mukogodo who were beginning to acquire domestic stock. According to Mutundu, a focus on small mammals may have been a deliberate hunting choice because these resources are more abundant and reliable, and thus can be counted on as a supplement to an increasingly herding-dominated economy (Cronk and Dickson 2001). By the same token, the Kisio small mammal choice may have been an effective hunting strategy that merely supplemented elephant hunting or food production.

More needs to be known about the occupants of Kisio Rock Shelter in order to understand how hunting choices fit in to their economy. Is the lack of domestic stock there typical of all hunting occupations in Tsavo? Were at least some of Tsavo's hunter-gatherers part-time pastoralists or farmers? Were these groups in transition to food production, like the Mukogodo, or had they deliberately chosen to give up food production (on a seasonal basis, for example) to participate in trade? These questions are unanswered at present. However, even in its preliminary stages, the comparison of Paleolithic and historic hunter-gatherers in East Africa illustrates that, while individual cases of modern hunter-gatherers may make poor Paleolithic analogs, the compilation of historical and archaeological case studies about hunter-gatherer history is of utmost importance in understanding both the ecological and social context of hunter-gatherer societies. At this point, however, the missing pieces of the settlement puzzle are still poorly understood in both of the cases described here. To understand more about how both LSA and historic hunter-gatherers used the landscape, more excavations beg to be done.

Acknowledgments

This chapter is based on fieldwork carried out in Kenya with permission from the Republic of Kenya, Research Permit No. OP/13/001/25C86, and with support from the National Science Foundation (Dissertation Improvement Grant BNS SBR 93-20534 DISS and Archaeology Division grants 9024683 and 961529) and the Fulbright Program.

2

The East African Neolithic: A Historical Perspective

Karega-Munene

This chapter examines the historical development of Neolithic studies in East Africa. The early use of type artifacts to define the time period obscured much variation in the East African Neolithic, which was eventually better understood through study of the various pottery wares. Competing schemes to organize the wares in time and space are evaluated. None accommodate the existing data adequately. A new interpretation alleges a strong link between pottery ware distributions and ethnic group boundaries that obscures much of the cultural processes governing Neolithic pottery ware production and dispersal, which probably included individual and local potter styles as well as exchange.

The term "Neolithic" was first used in an archaeological context in East Africa by the geologist John Walter Gregory (1896, 1921) working in the Rift Valley system. The term was then used to describe obsidian artifacts found on the Athi Plains, Kikuyu Escarpment, and near Lake Baringo in present-day Kenya (Fig. 2.1). Subsequently, the word "Neolithic" was used to describe isolated finds of stone bowls, polished stone ax-heads, and bored stones or stone rings that were made in various parts of the country (Dobbs 1914, 1918; Hobley 1913). This definition was also used in European and Near Eastern archaeology, where it referred to cultures associated with polished stone artifacts (Lubbock 1872). Early in the 20th century the definition was expanded to include cultures with domestic animals and plants (Burkitt

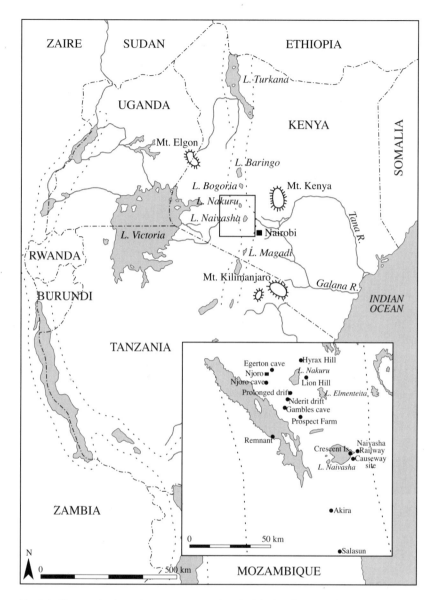

Fig. 2.1 Sites and other place-names associated with the Central African Neolithic.

1925; Childe 1953), and this definition was used in East Africa during the first half of the 20th century.

In the 1950s, the criteria identifying the East African Neolithic were expanded to include stone bowls and, in the mid-1970s, skeletal remains of domestic animals. This latter development resulted in the renaming of Neolithic cultures as Pastoral Neolithic. This term unduly emphasized herding as a subsistence strategy, relative to other food resources like plants, fish, and wild animals. In reality, the archaeological evidence for a more diversified subsistence base is overwhelming. Thus, I will use the term "Neolithic" to indicate food-producing cultures that possess domestic animals or crop cultivation. In the former French colonies, however, "Neolithic" still often denotes cultures characterized by polished stone tools and pottery (De Barros 1990; Shaw 1977).

Pioneer Research

Systematic research on the Neolithic started with Louis Leakey's 1931 expedition to the Lake Nakuru-Naivasha Basin in the Kenya Rift Valley (Fig. 2.1). Although the principal aim of that research was not to investigate the Neolithic, the presence of polished stone artifacts, stone bowls, human burials, and pottery indicated three Neolithic cultures. These were named Njoroan, after a farm near present-day Njoro township (Fig. 2.1), and Gumban A and Gumban B, after the mythical pygmy peoples whom the central Kenya Gikuyu knew as Gumba (L. Leakey 1931; Muriuki 1974). The three cultures were viewed as derivations of Kenya Wilton and Elmenteitan Mesolithic cultures, both of which were also identified in the research area (L. Leakey 1931).

Subsequent research failed to yield more sites with finds similar to those of the Njoroan culture; therefore, the term was dropped from the region's archaeological vocabulary. The research, however, revealed two more cultures in the Uganda and Kenya Lake Victoria basins, the Tumbian and Kenya Wilton C, which were then considered Neolithic cultures. The Tumbian culture was divided into four phases: Proto-, Lower, Middle, and Upper (L. Leakey 1936; Leakey and Owen 1945; O'Brien 1939). Subsequently, the Upper phase was renamed Lupemban and the older phases, Sangoan (Leakey and Cole 1952). However, because of inherent difficulties in separating the phases, they are now described as Sangoan-Lupemban and have been dated to the Middle Stone Age (McBrearty 1986). On the other hand, the term "Wilton" is inapplicable for the East Africa Neolithic (Nelson and Posnansky 1970), and the culture so named may belong only partly to the Neolithic (Ambrose 1984).

Chronological relationships among these cultures were explored through the pluvial/inter-pluvial theory, which suggested that prehistoric East Africa experienced climatic changes that could be reconstructed from beach deposits. As a result of the reconstructions, specific periods of wetness (pluvials), which were thought to have been separated by periods of aridity (inter-pluvials), were identified (Wayland 1924; L. Leakey 1931, 1936). Beginning with the oldest, the pluvials were named the Kamasian, Gamblian, Makalian, and Nakuran. The first two were regarded as belonging to the pre-

Holocene period, the latter two to the Holocene, that is, the last 10,000 years or so. Both the Mesolithic and Neolithic cultures were attributed to the Holocene. More specifically, the Makalian was presumed to date between about 12,000 BP and 4500 BP and the Nakuran from about 4500 BP to 2850 BP. The cultures that were attributed to the former period were the Elmenteitan, Kenya Wilton A, and Kenya Wilton B, while Kenya Wilton C, Njoroan, Gumban A, and Gumban B were placed in the Nakuran pluvial (L. Leakey 1931, 1936).

Research conducted in Uganda yielded three Neolithic cultures: Kageran, Wilton-Neolithic A, and Wilton-Neolithic B. The first of these was identified at a site located on the banks of River Kagera, and the other two at Nsongezi rock shelter and Chui Cave on the Uganda/Kenya border, respectively. The Kageran was characterized by choppers, scrapers, and flakes; Wilton A by pottery, backed blades, crescents, and scrapers; and Wilton B by crescents, burins, and scrapers (O'Brien 1939; Wayland 1934). Interestingly, unlike in Kenya, where polished stone artifacts, stone bowls, and pottery had been used to identify Neolithic cultures, the Ugandan cultures were so classified because they had thumbnail scrapers that were similar to those of Kenya Wilton. Existence of the Kageran was disproved by ensuing research (Nelson and Posnansky 1970) and use of the term "Wilton" discontinued.

Further research in Kenya led to the recognition of Gumban B and evolved Elmenteitan Neolithic cultures at Hyrax Hill and Njoro River Cave, respectively (M. Leakey 1945; Leakey and Leakey 1950). The naming of the Elmenteitan Neolithic culture at the latter site was based on the assumption that it had a generic relationship with the Mesolithic Elmenteitan culture (Leakey and Leakey 1950). More important, it was noted that stone bowls occurred in Mesolithic and Neolithic cultures, including evolved Elmenteitan. Thereupon, the cultures were grouped together and described as variants of the Stone Bowl cultures. This development elevated stone bowls to the status of Neolithic *fossiles directeurs*, thus making the identification and description of sites bearing such artifacts an important research pursuit. As a result, more stone bowls were reported from several locations in the region (Bower 1973; Brown 1966, 1969; Cohen 1970; Faugust and Sutton 1966; M. Leakey 1945, 1966; Leakey and Leakey 1950; Posnansky and Sikibengo 1959; Sassoon 1967, 1968; Soper 1971c). The chronology and associations of most of those artifacts remain uncertain, however, because they were either isolated finds or surface collections or finds from disturbed deposits.

Unlike in Europe and in the Near East, where direct evidence of food production in the form of remains of domestic animals and plants was increasingly employed in the identification of Neolithic cultures (Childe 1953; Mellaart 1965; Phillips 1980; Renfrew 1972; Thomas 1988, 1991), researchers in East Africa continued to rely on *fossiles directeurs*. It was reasoned that the absence of biological remains "was not particularly significant...because] the known characteristics of many [Neolithic] cultures...[in the region were] confined to the one-sided and incomplete evidence adduced at a few sites" (M. Leakey 1943:182).

Confutation of the Neolithic

The existence of the East African Neolithic, as demonstrated by the research conducted in the region during the first half of the 20th century, was not accepted by all scholars. Rather, some of them questioned and others dismissed its existence. It was argued, for instance, that the term "Neolithic" was inappropriate for the cultures concerned because of the absence of evidence of widespread stone-using settled agricultural societies (Posnansky 1967a:644). (Surprisingly, the only direct evidence of food production known at the time, namely, remains of cattle and sheep from Hyrax Hill, was ignored.) It was reasoned that the Neolithic could only be identified by the presence of domestic animals and plants (Clark 1967b). This was in contrast to previous observations that stone bowls and grinding stones strongly suggest some form of plant cultivation (Clark 1962:217).

Other writers argued that the Neolithic could be subsumed within the Later Stone Age (Sutton 1966). The Neolithic cultures in the Central Rift, for example, were regarded as creations of the remnants of the aquatic civilization of middle Africa (Sutton 1974, 1977, 1980). Although by definition a civilization that depended on aquatic resources for subsistence and other needs like transport is pre-Neolithic, its proponent intended it to be anti-Neolithic (Sutton 1980:322). Therefore, its material culture, which included bone harpoons and pottery, was to be found close to lakes, rivers, and swamps. The sites that were cited as belonging to this civilization in the Lakes Nakuru-Naivasha basin (where research on the Neolithic had been conducted) were Gamble's Cave II and Lion Hill. The extension of the aquatic civilization to the Central Rift Valley was unwarranted because at Gamble's Cave, for instance, it was represented by a fragment of a bone harpoon and a sherd of the so-called wavy-line pottery.

Other views seem to have arisen from the then-prevalent colonial attitude toward East Africans rather than from a genuine professional interest. It was reasoned, for example, that the ancestors of present black Africans were incapable of accomplishing ingenious feats such as making pottery, ironworking, and food production because they suffered mental stagnation attributable to climate and biology (Cole 1963:39). Further, the presence of domestic animals at Hyrax Hill was disputed not because the skeletal remains had been misidentified but rather because early food production in the region contradicted the general colonial mentality. However, although the very existence of the Neolithic was denied, it was grudgingly acknowledged that there were a few "indications of stock-keeping...before the Iron Age" (Cole 1963:49). That researchers then working in the region did not react to these racist sentiments suggests they considered the region's archaeology to be nothing more than an academic exercise, with little or no sociopolitical significance to the indigenous peoples who had been denied their past by colonialism.

Although these disputations reinforced use of the term "Stone Bowl cultures," no significant efforts were made to study the intended uses of stone bowls. Indeed, the only substantive study of the artifacts concerned morphology (Merrick 1973). Yet, given the contexts from which many of the artifacts have been recovered, it is likely they could have served one or more of the following purposes: preparation of wild or domestic cereals, ochre pulverization, or mortuary ritual. This notwithstanding, the expression "Stone Bowl cultures" continued to appeal to researchers, even at sites where the cultures were evidently associated with food production. Where used, Neolithic was enclosed in single quotation marks (Gramly 1975)—denoting a question of widespread validity—thus obscuring the Neolithic status of the cultures in question (Bower 1991).

Appreciation of the Neolithic was also impeded by researchers' failure to recognize the usefulness of biological remains as a source of evidence for food production. As a result, such remains were generally discarded in the field (e.g., Soper and Golden 1969) or treated casually: "Too often bones on a paleolithic site...[were] treated as sacrosanct and studied with care and attention as providing clues for relative dating and climatic indications whilst the humble domestic mammalia of a near modern site...[were] dropped hastily in a bag and either forgotten or only briefly described" (Posnansky 1962:273).

The few skeletal remains that were saved during excavation generally provided taxonomic lists, which were appended to reports on ceramics and stone artifacts (Chapman 1967; Pearce and Posnansky 1963; Soper and Golden 1969).

The Pastoral Neolithic

Considerable advancement in Neolithic studies in the 1970s confirmed the existence of pre–Iron Age food producers in southwestern Kenya and in the Central Rift Valley. These sites yielded *fossiles directeurs*, pottery, and faunal remains (Bower et al. 1977; Odner 1972; Onyango-Abuje 1977a, 1977b, 1980). Although the sites yielded remains of domestic animals, none of them produced remains of plants (whether wild or domestic), mainly because little effort was made to recover any. Use of circumstantial evidence of Neolithic crop cultivation in the form of polished artifacts and grinding stones continued. It was, for instance, argued that polished stone ax-heads were used for preparing land for cultivation and grinding stones for processing domestic grains for consumption (Onyango-Abuje 1976, 1977b), a supposition that is supported by ethnographic evidence (Harlan 1989).

In-depth faunal analyses, however, initiated a productive period of study of Neolithic herding. The Neolithic period was renamed Pastoral Neolithic. Pastoral Neolithic cultures used Later Stone Age technologies but relied economically on domestic cattle and sheep/goat (Bower et al. 1977:119). The coining of the term "Pastoral Neolithic" appears to have been influenced by three factors: the preponderance of cattle and sheep/goat in the faunal samples, the existence of the Maasai pastoral economy in the region, and the lack of plant remains.

Henceforth, the recovery of faunal remains became important. However, the new understanding of the Neolithic placed undue importance on animal husbandry. Plant remains do exist, but researchers have made very little effort to recover any. This notwithstanding, the majority of researchers continue to regard this negative evidence as evidence of absence (Gribbin and Cherfas 1982:48) in spite of evidence of plant remains recovered from East African Neolithic and other archaeological sites like Gogo Falls and Ngenyn (Hivernel 1978; Karega-Munene 1993, 1996; Lange 1991; Robertshaw and Wetterstrom 1989; Wetterstrom 1991).

Subsistence Activities

Current evidence places the appearance of domestic animals in Kenya from 5000 to 4000 BP (Table 2.1). In northern Kenya, domestic cattle and sheep/goat are dated to 4500 to 3400 BP at Ileret, Dongodien, and GaJi 2 on the eastern side of Lake Turkana (Fig. 2.1) (Barthelme 1984, 1985; Marshall, Stewart, and Barthelme 1984). Farther east, the appearance of domestic camel and sheep/goat is dated to between 6000 to 4000 BP at Ele Bor (Phillipson 1984b). The evidence from the western side of Lake Turkana places the appearance of cattle and sheep/goat at 2200 BP at Namoratunga (Lynch and Robbins 1979; Robbins 1984).

Knowledge about the appearance of domestic animals in the area between Lake Turkana and the Lakes Nakuru-Naivasha basin in the Central Rift is scanty; the area remains ill-explored. Evidence from Ngenyn and Maringishu places the appearance of cattle and sheep/goat at 2000 BP and 1600 BP, respectively (Bower et al. 1977; Hivernel 1978; Gifford-Gonzalez and

Table 2.1 Chronometric Dates on East African Neolithic Sites

Site Name	Site Type	Pottery	Date (BP)	Lab/Specimen No.	Material	Reference
Ileret	Open habitation	Ileret	4000 ± 140	GX-4643/A	Apatite	Barthelme 1985
Dongodien	Open habitation	Nderit	4580 ± 170	GX-4642-II-A	Apatite	Barthelme 1985
		Nderit	4100 ± 12	SUA-637-B	Charcoal	Barthelme 1985
		Nderit	3860 ± 60	P-2610	Charcoal	Barthelme 1985
		Nderit	3945 ± 135	SUA-637	Charcoal	Barthelme 1985
		Nderit	3405 ± 130	GX-4642-I-A	Charcoal	Barthelme 1985
Gaji 2	Open habitation	Nderit	4160 ± 110	SUA-634	Charcoal	Barthelme 1985
		Nderit	3970 ± 60	P-2609	Charcoal	Barthelme 1985
Lopoy	Open habitation	Turkwel	870 ± 80	UCLA-2124G	Burnt soil	Lynch and Robbins 1979
		Turkwel	950 ± 80	UCLA-2124J	Charcoal	Lynch and Robbins 1979
Apeget I	Open habitation	Turkwel	1800 ± 300	UCLA-2124K	Charcoal	Lynch and Robbins 1979
Kangatotha	Open habitation	Nderit	5020 ± 220	N-814	Burnt soil	Robbins 1972
Namoratunga	Burial	?Turkwel	2285 ± 165	GX-5042-A	Bone	Lynch and Robbins 1979
Ngenyn	Open habitation	?Turkwel	2080 ± 130	UCLA-1322	Collagen	Hivernel 1978
		?Turkwel	2020 ± 130	BIRM-770	Charcoal	Hivernel 1978
		?Turkwel	1970 ± 150	BIRM-767	Collagen	Hivernel 1978
Maringishu	Open habitation	Maringishu	1695 ± 105	GX-4466-A	Apatite	Bower et al. 1977
Njoro River Cave	Burial	Elmenteitan	2920 ± 80	Y-91	Charcoal	Barendsen et al. 1957
		Elmenteitan	2900 ± 75	Y-220	Charcoal	Merrick and Monaghan 1984
		Elmenteitan	3090 ± 65	Y-221	Charcoal	Merrick and Monaghan 1984
		Elmenteitan	3165 ± 100	Y-222	Charcoal	Merrick and Monaghan 1984
Keringet Cave	Burial	Elmenteitan	2910 ± 115	N-653	Charcoal	Cohen 1970
		Elmenteitan	2430 ± 110	N-654	Charcoal	Cohen 1970

Kimengich 1984). The majority of the dates from sites located in the Central Rift suggest that domestic stock appeared there between 3000 and 2000 BP (Ambrose 1985; Bower et al. 1977; Cohen 1970; Gifford, Isaac, and Nelson 1980; Gifford 1985; Gifford-Gonzalez and Kimengich 1984; Onyango-Abuje 1977b). Older dates have, however, been obtained at Enkapune ya Muto to the west of Lake Naivasha, where sheep/goat were present at 4000 BP (Marean 1992a), and at Salasun to the south of the lake, where cattle and sheep/goat are dated to 7200–6500 BP (Bower et al. 1977). The Salasun dates are suspect because they contradict conventional wisdom about the spread of pastoralism throughout Africa (Collett and Robertshaw 1983b:58). The dates may be unreliable because they are on bone apatite, which is subject to contamination.

The appearance of cattle and sheep/goat in the Lake Victoria basin to the west of the Rift is dated to 3400–2000 BP at Gogo Falls (Karega-Munene 1993, 1996, 2002; Marshall 1986) and in southwestern Kenya to 2700–2000 BP at Remnant (Bower et al. 1977), Narosura (Odner 1972), Lemek North-East, Sambo Ngige, and Ngamuriak (Marshall 1986, 1990a, 1990b). To the east of the Central Rift Valley, domestic fauna are dated to about 3300 BP at Lukenya Hill (Nelson and Kimengich 1984). Evidence from northern Tanzania is limited to Maua on the slopes of Kilimanjaro, where domestic fauna are dated to between 4200 BP and 1500 BP (Mturi 1986).

Thus, contrary to conventional wisdom, the chronometric evidence outlined above does not show a definite north-south trend for the appearance of domestic animals in East Africa. This hypothesis remains persuasive because it conforms to an assumed diffusion of food production from the Near East. Nevertheless, archaeological data to support or to refute it are lacking. Certainly the hypothesis needs rigorous testing through intensive research on pre-Neolithic and more Neolithic sites, including more complete recovery and dating of plant and animal samples.

Such research efforts should enable evaluation of the term "Pastoral Neolithic." While this term implies that pastoralism was the main economic activity during the Neolithic, faunal collection composition from virtually all sites indicates that animal husbandry was practiced alongside hunting and fishing (Barthelme 1984, 1985; Hivernel 1978; Karega-Munene 1993, 2002; Marshall 1986, 1991; Marshall, Stewart, and Barthelme 1984; Onyango-Abuje 1977a, 1977b; Phillipson 1984b; Robertshaw et al. 1983; Stewart 1991). The only exceptions are Maringishu in the Central Rift (Bower et al. 1977; Gifford-Gonzalez and Kimengich 1984) and Lemek North-East and Sambo Ngige in southwestern Kenya (Marshall 1986, 1990a, 1990b), where herding seems to have been the only subsistence strategy. The absence of wild animals, except for equid, in the faunal samples from Lemek North-East and Ngamuriak indicate the development of specialized pastoralism by 3000 BP (Marshall 1990). Even so, the temporal and regional extent of Neolithic specialized pastoralists is yet to be demonstrated.

Regional Syntheses

The first attempt to synthesize Neolithic cultures was made in the 1960s using pottery, rather than the artifacts that had served as *fossiles directeurs*. This resulted in the classification of the pottery into three categories— Classes A, B, and C (Sutton 1964). Class A consisted of Elmenteitan Ware pottery as represented at Gambles Cave II, Njoro River Cave, Naivasha Railway Rock Shelter and Long's Drift. Class B included Gumban and Hyrax Hill pottery, and Class C all roulette-decorated pottery, including Lanet Ware and some Gumban B pottery. Class A was considered the oldest because it was presumably created by hunter-gatherers, and Class C the youngest because of its apparent association with sedentary communities with ironworking knowledge (Sutton 1964).

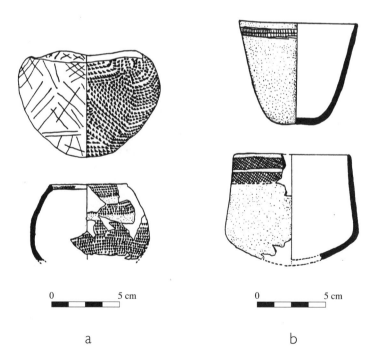

0 _____ 5 cm   0 _____ 5 cm

a   b

Fig. 2.2 a. Nderit Ware, b. Narosura Ware, c. Remnant (Elmenteitan), d. Maringishu Ware. (After Wandibba 1980; Bower et al. 1977; Karega-Munene 2002.)

Each of these classes encompassed much variation, thus rendering meaningful comparisons among them difficult. Although the majority of the pottery used in devising the classification was Neolithic, Iron Age Lanet Ware, first identified at Lanet near Nakuru town (Posnansky 1967b), was included. Thirdly, the chronological scheme that was proposed for the pottery—Class A being the oldest, followed by Class B, and Class C, in that order—was not based on chronometric evidence but on intuition. Although this approach may have been influenced by the dearth of radiometric determinations, it is noteworthy that no attempt was made to correlate the classes with any of the known dates like those from Njoro River Cave (Barendsen, Deevy, and Gralenski 1957).

In the 1970s another attempt was made to classify Neolithic pottery from southern Rift Valley sites. The study involved the examination of attributes like firing, decorative techniques and motifs, vessel shapes, and features like lugs, handles, spouts, and knobs (Wandibba 1977, 1980). This exercise resulted in the recognition of five wares that were named after their respective type sites: Nderit Ware, Narosura Ware, Remnant Ware (Elmenteitan), Maringishu Ware, and Akira Ware (Fig. 2.2 a–d).

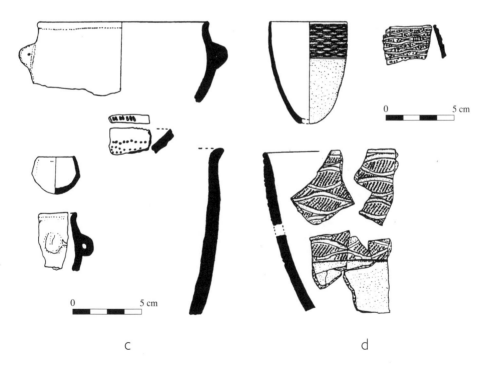

c

d

Fig. 2.2 (continued)

Nderit Ware encompasses the pottery that had originally been labeled Gumban and is characterized by carinated or narrow-mouthed bowls decorated on both surfaces. Decoration on the external surface is extensive and consists of closely set cuneiform impressions, and scores or grooves, line incisions, or jabs on the internal surface.

Narosura Ware is characterized by comb-stamping or line incisions, which are occasionally delimited with horizontal lines or divided by zigzag reserved bands on open- and narrow-mouthed bowls, bowls with slightly everted rims, and beaker-like vessels.

The typical vessel of Maringishu Ware is the ovoid beaker. Common decoration in this ware is broad, undulating horizontal ridges; the elliptical spaces between the ridges are filled with small linear impressions, punctations, or very fine cord roulette impressions.

Akira Ware is characterized by thin-walled vessels with highly burnished surfaces, the decoration consisting of panels of very fine incised lines. Narrow bands of applied decoration occur on some vessels.

Remnant (Elmenteitan) Ware is generally undecorated, but panels of punctations and irregular rim milling occur on some vessels. The common vessel types for the ware are open-mouthed bowls with slightly everted lips, large open-mouthed cauldron-like vessels, platters, and carinated cups. Other significant features include lugs, handles, and spouts on some vessels (Wandibba 1977, 1980).

In general, these wares are represented at several sites in northern and southwestern Kenya, the Kenyan Central Rift Valley, and northern Tanzania (see Fig. 2.1 and Table 2.1). The only exceptions are Akira Ware and Maringishu Ware, which have been found at a few sites only. Akira, for example, has been reported only at the eponymous site, Lukenya Hill, and Gogo Falls in Kenya (Bower et al. 1977; Gramly 1975; Karega-Munene 1993, 2002; Robertshaw 1991; Wandibba 1977, 1980); Seronera in Tanzania (Bower 1973a); and Karamoja in Uganda (Robbins 1972). Maringishu Ware, on the other hand, is reported only at the type site and Hyrax Hill (Bower et al. 1977; Wandibba 1977, 1980).

The wares have been ordered into three chronological sequences based on chronometric evidence. In the first of these, Nderit Ware is the oldest, followed by Narosura Ware, Remnant Ware (Elmenteitan), Akira Ware, and Maringishu Ware (Wandibba 1977, 1980).

The sequence in the second scheme was similar to the former, the only difference being that Akira Ware and Maringishu Ware were thought contemporaneous (Onyango-Abuje 1980).

The third scheme ordered the pottery as follows, beginning with the oldest: Nderit Ware, Kansyore Ware, Narosura Ware, Akira Ware, and Maringishu Ware (Bower et al. 1977).

Interestingly, the second scheme lumped Elmenteitan Ware (Remnant) pottery from Njoro River Cave with Narosura Ware pottery from the eponymous site because they dated to about the same period, and the third excluded Elmenteitan Ware without offering any reason (Bower et al. 1977). Further, the placement of Maringishu Ware in the schemes is suspect because the pottery's type site had only a single date.

The inclusion of Kansyore Ware, then the only pre–Iron Age pottery known outside the Rift Valley, in Bower et al.'s scheme is intriguing because the pottery was not only poorly defined (Wandibba 1990) but also poorly dated (Collett and Robertshaw 1980; Karega-Munene 1993, 2002). Unlike the wares discussed above, this pottery was defined solely on the basis of its surface treatment: gritty surface, poor firing, and decoration consisting of rounded shallow grooves, stab-and-drag grooves, and parallel lines of impressions (Chapman 1967). Although its geographical distribution appears to be restricted to the Lake Victoria basin and north-central Tanzania (Collett and Robertshaw 1983a; Karega-Munene 1993, 2002; Robertshaw et al. 1983), its reported presence at some of the sites has recently been questioned. The only sherd from Nsongezi rock shelter that was originally described as Kansyore (Pearce and Posnansky 1963) belongs to the Iron Age Urewe (Wandibba 1990). The sherds from Hippo Bay Rock Shelter and Karagwe in Uganda and Kitulu in Tanzania (Soper and Golden 1969) and Rangong, Radhore (Gabel 1969), and Lukenya (Bower et al. 1977) in Kenya that were originally attributed to Kansyore were reportedly misidentified (Wandibba 1990; Collett and Robertshaw 1980).

Other attempts at regional synthesis have involved regrouping the pottery using average link cluster of variables like decoration and vessel form, and examining the relationship between Neolithic sites in terms of their economy, chronology, pottery, lithic artifacts, and geographic distribution. The former attempt resulted in the recommendation of two changes in the pottery nomenclature: first, the replacement of the term "ware" with "tradition," because "a tradition cannot be recognized from a single type site" (Collett and Robertshaw 1983a:121; Robertshaw et al. 1983:34), and second, the renaming of the wares. Thus, Kansyore Ware has been renamed Oltome Tradition, Narosura Ware has been renamed Oldishi Tradition, and Maringishu Ware has been renamed Olmalenge Tradition. The new names are thought preferable to the letter (Sutton 1964) and ware (Wandibba 1977, 1980) systems. However, the names Nderit Ware, Narosura Ware, Maringishu Ware, Akira Ware, and Kansyore Ware are commonly used by all archaeologists working in East Africa (Ambrose 1982, 1984; Barthelme 1985; Bower 1984, 1991; Bower et al. 1977; Gifford-Gonzalez and Kimengich 1984; Hivernel 1978; Karega-Munene 1993, 2002; Marean 1992a; Marshall 1986, 1990, 1991; Mehlman 1977, 1979; Mturi 1986; Nelson and Kimengich 1984; Onyango-Abuje 1977a, 1977b, 1980; Wandibba 1977, 1980; cf. Robertshaw 1991; Schoenbrun 1990, 1993b).

Exploration of the relationships among chronology, material culture, and subsistence activities has resulted in the delineation of Neolithic sites into three broadly contemporaneous groups: the Savanna Pastoral Neolithic (SPN), Elmenteitan, and Eburran (Ambrose 1984). The SPN subgroups, Lowland SPN and Highland SPN, are distinguished by dating, geographic distribution, and elevation. Sites belonging to the former subgroup date to about 5200–3300 BP and are restricted to the low-lying areas of northern Kenya, while highland SPN sites are found in central Kenya and northern Tanzania, where they are dated to about 3300–1300 BP. The Eburran has five phases and is found in the Lakes Nakuru-Naivasha basin: the first phases are pre-Neolithic and date to ca. 12,000–6000 BP, while the Neolithic Phase 5 dates to ca. 2900–1900 BP. The Elmenteitan group is made up of sites that are restricted to the western side of the Rift Valley, the adjacent Mau Escarpment, and the Loita Plains to the west of the Mau Escarpment (Ambrose 1982, 1984).

Recent research demonstrates that strict adherence to this classification is unnecessary since the real extent of Neolithic sites in East Africa is unknown. To begin with, the classification is based on negative evidence which is largely due to the constraints of research. Secondly, the classification places Kansyore pottery wholly in the pre-Neolithic period, while it is now evident that the pottery was used by some Neolithic populations as well (Karega-Munene 1993, 2002). Thirdly, it is evident that sites are not restricted to the delineated areas; the Gogo Falls site contains Elmenteitan pottery but is well out of the outlined geographical zone (Karega-Munene 1993; Marshall 1986; Robertshaw 1985, 1991).

Interestingly, none of the chronological schemes or regional syntheses discussed above adequately summarizes the Neolithic in space and time. That two or more wares can be contemporaneous and are often found together in the same deposits begs explanation. At Seronera in Tanzania, for example, Kansyore Ware pottery was associated with Nderit Ware (Bower 1973); at Nyang'oma and Chole in the same country, Kansyore Ware was found in the same deposits with Iron Age pottery (Soper and Golden 1969); and at Gogo Falls in western Kenya Kansyore Ware was found in the same deposits with Elmenteitan Ware, Akira Ware, and Urewe Ware (Karega-Munene 1993, 2002; Robertshaw 1991). Conventionally, this phenomenon is explained as depositional mixing of deposits from successive site occupations by different linguistic and/or ethnic groups through time. Usually, the wares represent distinct cultural entities, which are then correlated with specific linguistic and/or ethnic groups. These associations are suggested by historical linguistic hypotheses about the movement of past populations in the region. The hypotheses suggest that the region was occupied by hunter-gatherers (ancestors of Southern African Khoisan speakers) during the pre-Neolithic period and that these groups were displaced or absorbed by southern Cushites (ancestors of the Alagwa, Aramanik, Asa, Burungi, Dahalo, Gorowa, and Iraqw of Kenya and Tanzania) who migrated there with their domestic animals from Ethiopia. Subsequent migrations to the region involved southern Nilotes who are also thought to have been food producers (Ehret 1967, 1968, 1971, 1974). The hunter-gatherers have been associated with Kansyore Ware; southern Cushites with Akira Ware, Narosura Ware, Nderit Ware, and Maringishu Ware; and southern Nilotes (ancestors of the Barabaig and Kalenjin of Tanzania and Kenya) with Elmenteitan Ware (Ambrose 1982, 1984).

These correlations are extremely tenuous for several reasons. First, skeletal remains of the pre-Neolithic human groups do not support the idea of Khoisan people in East Africa (Schepartz 1988). Second, stylistic differences among wares and their geographic patterning could be caused by style differences among artisans within a cultural or linguistic group, subcommunities within a community (Herbisch 1987), exchange patterns among neighboring groups, or vessel functions (see Wandibba, Chapter 4 this volume). Third, the association between pre-Neolithic hunter-gatherers and Kansyore Ware is disputed by findings at Gogo Falls in western Kenya, where the pottery was found with skeletal remains of sheep/goat and cattle in deposits dated to 3400 BP (Karega-Munene 1993, 2002). Fourth, although use of historical linguistics gives the archaeological data outlined above a narrative, it tends to further the pigeon-holing of ancient cultures into molds based on modern ethnic groups: "The attempt to attribute cultural remains to a particular linguistic group represents an archaeological cul-de-sac" (Stahl 1984:20). Fifth, the proposition that domestic animals were introduced in the region from the north is based on negative evidence and is yet to be archaeologically proved or disproved (Karega-Munene 1993, 2002).

The apparent coexistence of different pottery wares requires scientific investigation, not explanation through hunches. Instead of one pottery ware clearly succeeding another, they in fact overlapped in time and space (Table 2.1). Kansyore Ware dates, for instance, fall between 8200 and 2400 BP; those of Nderit Ware are from 7000 to 1500 BP; Narosura Ware dates from 2700 to 1400 BP; Maringishu Ware to 1700 BP; Remnant Ware (Elmenteitan) from 3300 to 1300 BP; and Akira Ware from 1900 to 1200 BP. Although these dates suggest that Kansyore is the earliest known Neolithic pottery and that it probably had the longest life span, they also indicate that Nderit, Narosura, and Elmenteitan Wares may have been created during its lifetime. Consequently, there is hardly any reason why Kansyore pottery should always be considered to be older than, say, Elmenteitan Ware, wherever they occur together. Additionally, one must not always assume that each group made their own pots (Karega-Munene 1993, 1996, 2002; Wandibba, Chapter

4 this volume). If the groups were capable of trading in obsidian, as provenience studies have demonstrated (Merrick and Brown 1984a, 1984b; Merrick, Brown, and Connelly 1990), they were also capable of trading in other goods.

Conclusion

Although the appearance of animals domesticated outside East Africa is reasonably dated by local standards, the dates do not conclusively tell us about the direction from which the animals reached the region. Similarly, the evidence currently available tells us hardly anything about the manner in which the animals were introduced or the process of change from foraging to food production. Although recovery of biological remains should be paramount in further research, at the same time, attempts should be made to explore other possible interpretations of the Neolithic phenomenon (Karega-Munene 1996).

The reexamination of Neolithic wares and their cultural, chronological, and economic contexts is crucial. Similarities and differences in material culture, like the ones that have been used to define the wares, are not only diagnostic of cultural or linguistic boundaries but are also reflections of dynamic relationships among the wares' producers and consumers (Karega-Munene 1993). Explanations of ceramic data in terms of large-scale migrations in situations where exchange patterns involving other goods existed ignores the complex interactions these groups shared (Karega-Munene 1996). An evaluation of all possible explanations, which is warranted by the data at hand, is vital for ongoing research. After all, it is new approaches and ideas that propel us forward in our search for knowledge.

Acknowledgments

Field research at the Gogo Falls site that produced the date of 3400 BP was made possible by funding from the L. S. B. Leakey Foundation (USA), Smuts Memorial Fund, Anthony Wilkin Fund and Bartle Frere Exhibition (University of Cambridge), Boise Fund (University of Oxford), and Dean's Committee of the University of Nairobi to whom the author is most grateful.

3

Archaeological Implications of Hadzabe Forager Land Use in the Eyasi Basin, Tanzania

Audax Mabulla

This chapter examines site and land-use patterns of Hadzabe hunter-gatherers in Northern Tanzania. It emphasizes seasonality, resources, and social processes as the major determinants of Hadzabe individual and group mobility. It offers a unique examination of rock shelter use ethnoarchaeology, including factors affecting rock shelter choice, times of occupation, group size, activities carried out, and discard patterns. The final section of this chapter makes a call to save the Hadzabe way of life and offers some directions for doing so.

Archaeological research has changed substantially since 1980. Ethnographic studies of forager land use, especially those that pertain to activities conducted away from perennial habitations (Binford 1980; Hitchcock 1982; Yellen 1977), have stimulated archaeologists to explore the interpretive potential of the full range of archaeological remains, including surface and low density artifact scatter. Contemporary forager land use was an important element of archaeological investigation in the 1990s (Gamble and Boismier 1991).

The study of contemporary forager land use provides a fruitful approach to understanding prehistoric landscape use and archaeological spatial patterning. An examination of Hadzabe land-use foraging patterns in the Eyasi Basin of northern Tanzania affords a better understanding of prehistoric forager adaptive strategies (Fig. 3.1). The major concern in studying Hadzabe

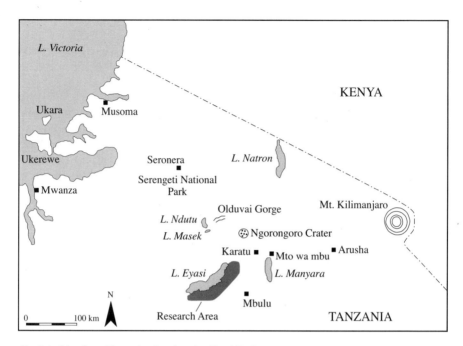

Fig. 3.1 Northern Tanzania, showing the Eyasi Basin.

foragers was to understand spatial use of the landscape and its resources in order to apply this understanding to archaeological patterning across space.

We shall consider several influences on Hadzabe mobility patterns, with the goal of using the Hadzabe pattern as a model for Middle Stone Age (MSA) and Later Stone Age (LSA) foragers in the Eyasi Basin. Hadzabe land-use patterns and their relationship to the archaeological record of the Eyasi Basin have not received sufficient attention. Ethnoarchaeology in the Eyasi Basin can be useful in evaluating the behavioral and spatial aspects of the archaeological record.

Hadzabe Forager Society

The foragers known today as the Hadzabe (had-za-bay) are referred to in the literature as "Tindiga," "Kangeju," "Kindiga," "Hadzapi," or "Hadza." The name Hadza is relatively recent in anthropological literature and is the shortest form of the name Hadzabe. Their language is "Hadzane." According to our informants, the names Tindiga, Kindiga, and Kangeju are nicknames derived from Bantu languages in the region and refer to Bantu tribesmen who fled colonial aggression and taxes to live with the Hadzabe in the bush. Through time, the name Tindiga has been used to refer to all people living in the bush and dependent on hunting and gathering. To the Hadzabe, their other names are derogatory and denote people who escaped village work and ran into forests due to laziness (see also Ndagala 1988). Nevertheless, food producers who live among the Hadzabe still refer to them as "Tindiga."

Although Hadzabe have long been in contact with other ethnic and cultural groups in the basin through trade, government settlement schemes, intermarriage, and labor, they still maintain a distinct ethnic and cultural identity. As far as language, political and social structures, customs, and economy are concerned, they still have little in common with their neighbors. Nonetheless, due to increasing interaction with their neighbors, some aspects of Hadzabe lifeways and cultural identity are changing as Hadzabe become more and more exposed to other worldviews.

The Hadzabe's nomadic lifestyle in a vast landscape, the fluid nature of their camps, and their habit of changing names has made population estimates difficult to obtain (Blurton-Jones et al. 1992). Early estimates put the Hadzabe at 400 or so individuals (Woodburn 1972). Recent demographic studies estimate the Hadzabe population to be about 600–800 (Blurton-Jones et al. 1992; Bunn, Bartram, and Kroll 1988; O'Connell and Hawkes 1988) or between 1,500 and 3,000 individuals (Kaare 1989; PMFPO 1992; Ndagala and Zengu 1989).

Traditionally, the Hadzabe are mobile, egalitarian, immediate-return foragers. However, in recent years the government of Tanzania has launched comprehensive development programs to settle them in permanent villages. Government settlement schemes lure the Hadzabe by providing them with free education and health services, beekeeping, and agricultural inputs (PMFPO 1992). Approximately one-fourth of the total Hadzabe population continues to practice full-time traditional hunting and gathering (Bunn, Bartram, and Kroll 1988; O'Connell and Hawkes 1988). The rest, through established government settlement schemes, have been semi-settled in Endamaghy, Munguli, Mwangeza, Yaeda Chini, and Mungo-wa-Mono villages in Mbulu District. Hadzabe stay at these villages only when food assistance from the government is available, but they often abandon these villages for foraging in the bush even when government foods are available. Semi-settled Hadzabe groups practice a combination of part-time traditional foraging and other production activities.

Aspects of Hadzabe Research

Since colonial times, governments, early missionaries, and international development planners have produced studies, policies, and projects aimed at transforming the Hadzabe's mobile, foraging lifestyle to one of permanent settlements and farming (Kaare 1989, 1993; Ndagala 1988; PMFPO 1990, 1992). Hadzabe social organization, economy, and ecology have been outlined by Woodburn (1968, 1972, 1980) and others (Kohl-Larsen and Kohl-Larsen 1958). Medical doctors and physical and cultural anthropologists have collaborated on biomedical studies of Hadzabe (Barnicot et al. 1972; Bennet et al. 1973). Anthropological research since the 1980s has been primarily concerned with subsistence studies, especially plant foods and their overall contributions to Hadzabe diet (Vincent 1985a, 1985b). Others have focused on Hadzabe perceptions of their past and their origin (Ndagala and Zengu 1989).

More recent researchers have focused on Hadzabe human ecology and demography (Blurton-Jones et al. 1992; Blurton-Jones, Hawkes, and Draper 1993) and the ecological, nutritional, and behavioral factors underlying Hadzabe bone-accumulating activities (Bunn, Bartram, and Kroll 1988; Hawkes, O'Connell, and Blurton-Jones 1991; O'Connell and Hawkes 1988). Hadzabe hunting and scavenging, carcass processing, consumption, and bone disposals have assisted the interpretation of early hominid subsistence behavior. Hadzabe hunting, scavenging, and carcass processing behavioral data and their archaeological consequences have been used either to formulate or to test propositions about early hominid behavior.

Hadzabe landscape use and its relationship to the archaeological record of Eyasi Basin foragers has not received sufficient attention. Woodburn (1972) examined Hadzabe residential arrangements in relation to economy and social organization at the scale of the camp ("site"). My study examines Hadzabe land use and resource exploitation and the influences of landscape ecology on individual and group behavior.

My archaeological landscape survey in the Eyasi Basin sought information on Hadzabe land use and the food quest. Why, when, and how do the Hadzabe move across the landscape? Who is involved in the movement? How do the Hadzabe perceive their landscape and its resources? What is the Hadzabe sense of the past, in terms of attachment to places and things found on the landscape? Presumably, the physical and cultural factors influencing Hadzabe movement influenced MSA and LSA Eyasi Basin foragers in a similar way. I collected data to generate testable hypotheses and to develop theoretically and empirically grounded expectations about the behavioral activities, land use, and resource utilization patterns of prehistoric Eyasi Basin foragers.

Factors Influencing Hadzabe Mobility

This study identified three major factors that influence Hadzabe use of the Eyasi Basin landscape: ecological, cultural, and economic (Fig. 3.2).

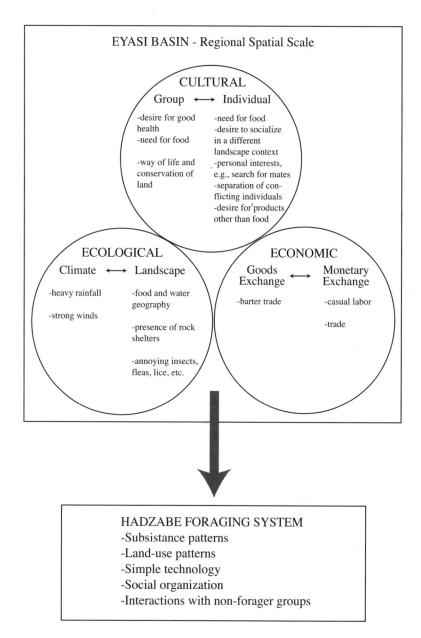

Fig. 3.2 Interrelated cultural, economic, and ecological effects on Hadzabe land use and social organization.

Ecological Factors

Distribution of Food Resources

Forager group movement is influenced primarily by the spatial distribution of food. Studies of the Hadzabe diet have shown that vegetable foods provide more of the resource base than mammal meat (Vincent 1985a, 1985b). The Eyasi Basin is a semiarid region with scarce to sufficient exploitable resources that are patchily distributed across the landscape. Water, plant, and animal foods are present in various habitats, and the differential availability of these resources is partly due to seasonal changes. Hadzabe land-use patterns are a response to this seasonally variable, patchy distribution of scarce to sufficient resources, usually plants (Bunn, Bartram, and Kroll 1988; O'Connell and Hawkes 1988; see Table 3.1), but other factors also influence mobility (see Fig. 3.2).

Presence of Insects at Base Camps

When obnoxious insects such as lice, fleas, and mosquitoes multiply due to accumulating garbage and human feces at or near Hadzabe camps, Hadzabe move to another place free of these insects (Woodburn 1972). Accumulating garbage and human feces can bring vermin such as scorpions, annoying and disease-carrying insects, and hence disease and plagues.

Search for Safe Refuge

Extreme weather presents significant risks to Hadzabe foragers. Heavy rainfall may penetrate grass-thatched huts, and strong whirlwinds may destroy Hadzabe base camps. In response, Hadzabe move to rock shelters or other sheltered locations (Woodburn 1972). During the wet seasons, the number of predators, such as lions, increases in the Eyasi Basin. Because of their relatively elevated positions, rock shelters are preferred by the Hadzabe because of the security they offer against predators. Also, rock shelters are warm and comfortable during the wet seasons.

Cultural Factors

Ecological conditions influence Hadzabe land-use patterns, but which cultural factors affect when, where, and how to move? More importantly, what is the relative influence of these factors at both the "group" and "individual" levels? To date, this study and that of Woodburn (1972) have identified a few of these influences.

Minimization of Impact on Landscape

According to Hadzabe, an area with rich and predictable exploitable food resources can be abandoned in favor of an area with patchy resources just because Hadzabe are tired of staying in one particular location. My

Table 3.1 The Spatiotemporal Distribution of Plant Food in the Eyasi Basin
Note: Adapted from MacDowell 1981.

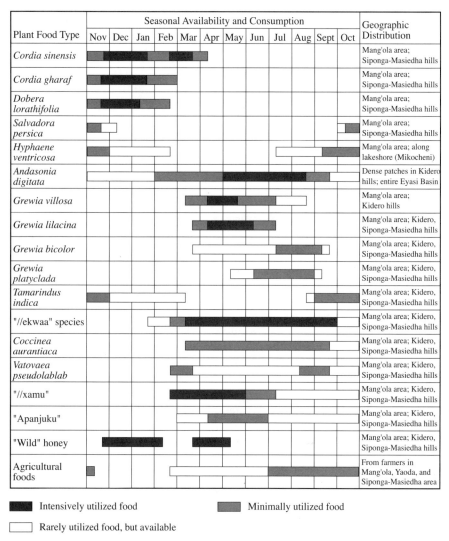

Plant Food Type	Seasonal Availability and Consumption												Geographic Distribution
	Nov	Dec	Jan	Feb	Mar	Apr	May	Jun	Jul	Aug	Sept	Oct	
Cordia sinensis													Mang'ola area; Siponga-Masiedha hills
Cordia gharaf													Mang'ola area; Siponga-Masiedha hills
Dobera lorathifolia													Mang'ola area; Siponga-Masiedha hills
Salvadora persica													Mang'ola area; Siponga-Masiedha hills
Hyphaene ventricosa													Mang'ola area; along lakeshore (Mikocheni)
Andasonia digitata													Dense patches in Kidero hills; entire Eyasi Basin
Grewia villosa													Mang'ola area; Kidero hills
Grewia lilacina													Mang'ola area; Kidero, Siponga-Masiedha hills
Grewia bicolor													Mang'ola area; Kidero, Siponga-Masiedha hills
Grewia platyclada													Mang'ola area; Kidero, Siponga-Masiedha hills
Tamarindus indica													Mang'ola area; Kidero, Siponga-Masiedha hills
"//ekwaa" species													Mang'ola area; Kidero, Siponga-Masiedha hills
Coccinea aurantiaca													Mang'ola area; Siponga-Masiedha hills
Vatovaea pseudolablab													Mang'ola area; Kidero, Siponga-Masiedha hills
"//xamu"													Mang'ola area; Kidero, Siponga-Masiedha hills
"Apanjuku"													Mang'ola area; Kidero, Siponga-Masiedha hills
"Wild" honey													Mang'ola area; Kidero, Siponga-Masiedha hills
Agricultural foods													From farmers in Mang'ola, Yaoda, and Siponga-Masiedha area

■ Intensively utilized food   ▨ Minimally utilized food

☐ Rarely utilized food, but available

observations, however, suggest that Hadzabe move to ensure that their activities have minimal impact on the landscape. Hadzabe value and conserve their landscape and its resources, and they are wise in land-use planning. Therefore, short occupations ensure that their impact on the landscape is minimal. On the other hand, long camp occupations can adversely affect

Hadzabe health. Accumulating camp garbage can attract disease-carrying flies and insects.

Appeal of Specific Food Items

An area with rich and predictable food resources can be deserted in favor of another with sparse but culturally and nutritionally preferred resources (see also Woodburn 1972). Once the preferred resources diminish, the group can return to the place with plentiful but less preferred food. Preferred and highly ranked resources include honey and meat. Bunn et al. (1988) and O'Connell et al. (1988) have, for example, noted Hadzabe hunters completely abandoning their hunting missions in favor of honey exploitation.

Appeal of Non-food Items

These may include stones for making tobacco pipes and trade goods such as tobacco, spearheads, clothes, shoes, and other items. Trade goods are usually obtained in Mang'ola on market day. Hadzabe groups and individuals attend market days in Mang'ola and other areas to purchase these products. The stones for making tobacco pipes are from mud tuffs on the northeastern shore of Lake Eyasi.

Attraction of Places to Socialize

Market days are not only considered selling and buying (trade) days, but also social gathering days which bring different social groups together. Hadzabe groups and individuals from the Masiedha-Siponga area, Mang'ola, and other places attend the market days to socialize, to feast, and to scavenge. The desire to socialize in a context away from a habitation location is not limited to market day but is also satisfied during other days when Hadzabe individuals or groups from one camp visit another camp. Mate search and conflict avoidance also encourage movement away from base camps.

Desire for Health

Hadzabe move when death, sickness, or terrifying nightmares visit in a habitation location (see Woodburn 1972). Hadzabe link sickness with the locations in which they occur; the best way to avoid sickness is to move away. Good health is seen as an attribute of regular frequent movement and failure to do so leads to illness (Woodburn 1972).

Economic Factors Other than Subsistence

Need for Money

Need for money has led some Hadzabe to seek casual labor in neighboring villages. During my eight-month stay in the area, I usually saw Hadzabe in

Mang'ola seeking casual labor a few days before the market day. This tendency influences Hadzabe mobility patterns, especially at the individual level.

Desire to Trade

The need for money to buy commodities also has led Hadzabe men to sell some of their material culture, particularly bows and arrows, to tourists in Mang'ola and to other local people.

Barter Trade

Hadzabe participate in exchange networks with non-forager Eyasi Basin groups. Hadzabe exchange goods include game meat, honey, and traditional medicines. In return the Hadzabe can receive money, arrowheads, tobacco, or other needed commodities. These exchanges necessitate Hadzabe movements and express social links.

Hadzabe Rock Shelter Use

The Eyasi Basin is known for its many rock shelters. The majority of the rock shelters are structurally controlled, free-standing rock slabs resulting from faulting. Most of them are found in high-lying basement hills. Here, the rock shelters gently dip to the east at an angle of about 40° with some local variations of about 5° (Fig. 3.3). These uplifted hanging blocks were affected by two erosional processes: exfoliation and wave action. Inland, exfoliation modified the western sides of the hanging blocks, creating considerable overhangs. This is why the majority of rock shelters have an opening with a westerly orientation. Along the eastern shore of Lake Eyasi, quarrying of the uplifted blocks by wave action and corrosion or chemical weathering by salt water created shelters and caves. This is demonstrated by the Mumba rock shelter. The host block is parallel to the shore line with a striking angle of 30°. At this angle, the overhang must have been too low for a shelter. Wave action during periods of high lake levels cut off the lower part of the hanging block, creating a shelter. Hence, faulting is a major force behind rock shelter formation in the Eyasi Basin. The rock shelter floors studied vary in size from 5.5 to about 218 m^2 (Table 3.2; Fig. 3.4).

Although the Hadzabe are homogeneous in terms of language, social organization, and lifeways, they prefer to identify themselves according to areas of origin or birth (Woodburn 1968). They identify themselves as people of Mang'ola (Mang'olanebe), people of Siponga (Siponganebe), people of the rocks (Harianebe), and people of the west (Tli'kanebe). Nevertheless, this does not mean that they live exclusively in these areas; rather these are areas where certain Hadzabe groups were born or prefer to live.

As already noted, the Hadzabe continue to make use of the rock shelters

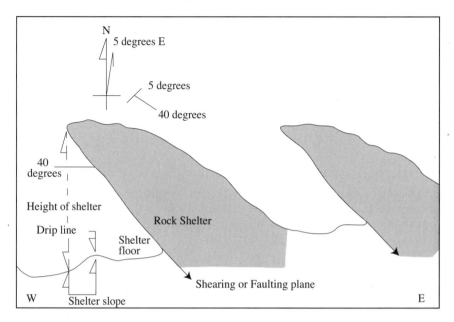

Fig. 3.3 An example of an overhang rock shelter.

in the Eyasi landscape as living places. Hadzabe call these large gneissic rock shelters *nyumba*, a Swahili word for "house." Hadzabe believe the *nyumba* are given to them by God. In the rock shelter survey I conducted, remains of baobab fruit barks and seeds, cereals (e.g., corn, millet), and animal bones were found on the floors of six rock shelters (Table 3.2).

Crafts, such as bead stringing, arrow haft shaving, and the hafting of feathers to arrow shafts, take place in rock shelters. Beadwork is undertaken by women and arrow preparation by men. Beads, bird feathers, wooden arrow shafts, fire sticks, wooden spoons, and wood shaving remains were found on many rock shelter floors (Fig. 3.5). Beads and arrow parts are generally found on separate parts of shelter floors, indicating gender differences in the use of a rock shelter's space. Studies of gender in Hadzabe rock shelter use will provide interesting avenues for future research.

In the occupied rock shelters, we observed food debris and items of Hadzabe material culture discarded around activity areas. Two dominant discard patterns were noted. Some debris was found within the rock shelter area; some was found outside the drip line, particularly on the talus slope. Most material, however, was located immediately outside the drip line (Fig. 3.5). Also, we observed prehistoric lithic material on shelter floors and on the slope of many rock shelters we studied. Hadzabe discard patterns of food debris, material culture, and rock shelter use may provide appropriate inferences for archaeologists.

Table 3.2 Studied Shelters of the Eyasi Basin (Y = Feature Present; N = Feature Absent)

Shelter Name	Paintings	Cultural Material	Recent Use	Shelter Floor Area (sq. m)
Gorfani-1	Y	Y	Y	
Gorfani-2	N	Y	Y	
Yoyomea-1	Y	Y	Y	
Yoyomea-2	Y	Y	Y	
Lushosho-1	Y	Y	N	
Lushosho-2	Y	N	N	52.00
Dhsadhsako-1	Y	Y	Y	
Dhsadhsako-2	Y	Y	Y	
Kaserenge-1	Y	Y	N	45.00
Kaserenge-2	Y	Y	N	
Endahakichandi-1	Y	N	N	58.24
Endahakichandi-2A	Y	N	N	86.00
Endahakichandi-2B	Y	Y	N	217.40
Endahakichandi-2C	Y	N	Y	58.80
Endahakichandi-3	Y	N	Y	107.80
Endahakichandi-4	Y	N	Y	47.60
Siponga-1	Y	N	Y	212.10
Siponga-2	Y	N	N	162.00
Siponga-3	Y	Y	N	107.80
Siponga-4	Y	N	N	101.50
!Qhadenaqwete-1	Y	Y	N	130.60
!Qhadenaqwete-2	Y	Y	Y	47.48
!Qhadenaqwete-3	Y	Y	Y	47.40
!Qhadenaqwete-4	Y	Y	Y	46.41
!Qhadenaqwete-5	Y	N	N	12.76
!Qhadenaqwete-6	Y	N	N	
!Qhadenaqwete-7	Y	Y	N	
!Qhadenaqwete-8	Y	Y	N	
!Qhadenaqwete-9	Y	Y	Y	26.00
Endanyawishi-1	Y	Y	N	20.80
Endanyawishi-2	Y	N	Y	21.00
Endanyawishi-3	Y	Y	Y	62.92
Ishea	Y	Y	N	
Pambasaibe	Y	Y	Y	44.00
!Qesasa	Y	Y	Y	
!Quandeki	Y	Y	Y	
Kambi ya Samaki-1	Y	Y	Y	
Kambi ya Samaki-2	Y	N	N	
Kambi ya Samaki-3	Y	N	N	5.50
Miqawu	Y	Y	N	
Mumba-1	Y	Y	N	
Mumba-2	Y	Y	N	

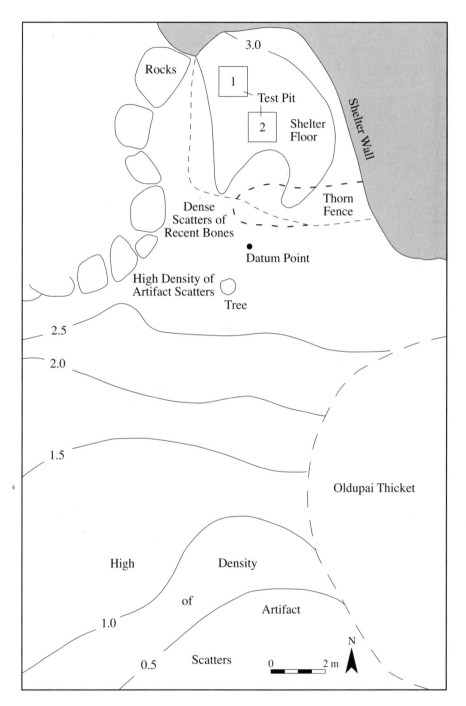

Fig. 3.4 Gorfani Rock Shelter-1, showing, among other things, a Hadzabe thorn fence.

Five of nineteen shelter floors with evidence of recent utilization were modified (Table 3.2). Three had simple thorn fence structures at the drip line (Fig. 3.5). Hadzabe say that these fence structures protect against predators and wind. Discrete sleeping units defined by roughly circular frameworks of branches were recorded at two rock shelters, and ethnographic details concerning the social composition of shelter occupants are available for one shelter. This latter rock shelter (!Qhadenaqwete-3; Fig. 3.5) was inhabited recently for about six months (December 1992–May 1993) during the wet to early dry season by a family composed of six individuals: father, mother, mother-in-law, two daughters, and a son. This shelter has a floor area of 47.4 m^2 (Table 3.2).

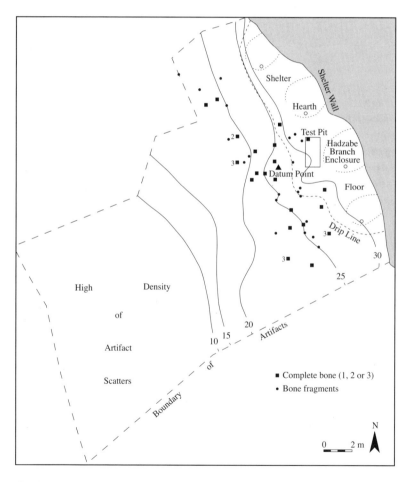

Fig. 3.5   !Qhadenaqwete Rock Shelter-3, showing, among other things, the Hadzabe enclosures and hearths on the shelter floor.

The four circular structures of branches demarcated four fenced sleeping units for father and mother (A), mother-in-law (B), daughters (C), and son (D). The sleeping unit for the couples was well fenced by tree branches to maintain privacy. The sleeping units were arranged in parallel and along the shelter wall, leaving a communal or working area in the center. Each of the four sleeping units had a fireplace or hearth located at the entrance (Fig. 3.5). Apart from cooking and roasting food, the fires are also used for keeping shelters warm and discouraging predators. Similar placement and spatial distribution of hearths in rock shelters has been found in European Upper Paleolithic sites, and at Big Elephant LSA site in Namibia (Clark and Walton 1962; Movius 1977).

At another rock shelter, we found wooden pegs driven into the shelter's floor for suspending arrows. According to our informants, arrows have to be placed on these wooden pegs when not in use so the poison on the arrowheads cannot be rendered weak by ground moisture. Menstruating women may weaken the arrows if they touch them. Also, married Hadzabe hunters do not hunt when their wives are menstruating, lest it bring bad luck. Unfortunately, such wooden pegs would rarely be preserved archaeologically.

We had the opportunity of observing Matina and his friend Nangai living in a shelter from December 30, 1992, through January 2, 1993. During the survey, we observed fire sticks, a wooden spoon, a hide finger ring, an arrow shaft fragment, rusted metal, a broken tobacco pipe, peas, a metal pot, a calabash, a goat hide, and remains of "magadi" soda (locally used as salt) on the floor of Gorfani Rock Shelter-2 (Fig. 3.4).

According to Matina, this shelter belongs to him and he occupies it during the wet season. When Matina and Nangai moved in during the rainy season of 1993, they brought with them a large bowl full of *Cordia gharaf* and *Salvadora persica* berries. These were consumed by the two men in two days. On the third day of our observation, Matina and Nangai caught a big tortoise 200 m from the shelter. It was brought to the shelter, where it was killed, then roasted to remove the carapace. These activities took place on the slope of the shelter, beyond the drip line. After removing the carapace, the meat weighed about 7 kg. This was consumed at once by the two men in a matter of 20 minutes. The cooking and consumption was done in the shelter and the bones were thrown off the slope of the shelter beyond the drip line.

According to our informants, the criterion influencing the choice of a particular shelter is the degree of protection that the rock provides from rain, sun, wind, and predators. Also, elevated rock shelters enable one to survey the landscape. The latter is crucial for spotting game animals for hunting. I call the factors that influence Hadzabe's choice of a particular rock shelter for occupation the "physical attributes" of rock shelters. My study, however, shows that not all rock shelters with desirable physical attributes are occupied by the Hadzabe. This suggests that Hadzabe cultural preferences are also involved in selecting rock shelters for occupation. I hypothesize that MSA and LSA foragers in the Eyasi Basin were also confronted by such choices in using rock shelters because not all rock shelters with desirable physical attributes are painted or have traces of past material culture.

About 48 percent of the rock shelters studied have evidence of recent use by Hadzabe. All have either rock paintings or archaeological deposits or both. Although the Hadzabe no longer paint, they claim that their ancestors were responsible for the rock art and other archaeological phenomena in the basin. Although these claims cannot be ascertained, nonetheless Hadzabe usage of rock shelters reveals elements of continuity. Hadzabe rock shelter usage is a long established tradition (Ndagala and Zengu 1989). The Hadzabe feel a sense of pride about rock paintings and are attached to past places found on their landscape. Hadzabe ritual and ceremonial activities may be performed exclusively in certain portions of the landscape.

Modeling Hadzabe Land Use in the Eyasi Basin

In this section, I construct a regional model of Hadzabe land use of the Eyasi landscape based on foraging strategies and social lifeways. As previously noted, the dominant element that influences Hadzabe mobility is the availability of resources. The Eyasi Basin experiences two major climatic (wet and dry) seasons. These seasons also affect the Hadzabe's coexistence with their neighbors. Based on discussions with the Hadzabe and their neighbors and personal observations, I tentatively identify four Hadzabe land-use and resource utilization systems.

Wet Season Inland Land Use

During wet seasons from late November through late May, Hadzabe move inland to hilly and rocky areas of Masiedha-Siponga, which are richest in water, plant foods, and game during this time. Berries (*Cordia gharaf, C. sinensis*, and *Salvadora persica*) ripen in the inland area during late November and are intensively utilized by the Hadzabe. Hunting and scavenging of large game are intensified during this time. Edible tubers, roots, leaves, and shoots also become abundant during the rainy season. The //ekwaa species, apanjuku, matukwaiyaku, and //xamu tubers are all ready during and after the rainy season, when all other plant foods (e.g., berries) are nearly exhausted. According to Hadzabe informants, //xamu is the most desirable plant food. Honey also becomes available during this period. A large majority of plant foods are found at the bottoms of hills and valley fringes.

During this season, the Hadzabe live in simply constructed shelters near Masiedha-Siponga hills and their rocky outcrops. In 1993 we found one abandoned base camp that had been occupied during the 1992 rainy season. This abandoned base camp was composed of ten shelters. It was located near rock shelters of the hills in an area rich in wild plant foods, particularly //xamu and //ekwaa tubers. Baobab trees surrounded this abandoned base camp. The shelters consisted of poles supporting a roof made of grass with no walls. The sleeping areas of the shelter floors were covered with soft grasses to provide comfort while sleeping. Generally the shelters were small, holding up to three persons. About 30 Hadzabe foragers occupied this camp in 1992 (Madulu Mahiya, pers. comm.).

In addition, the Hadzabe occupy rock shelters found in the nearby hills and rocky outcrops. Remains of Hadzabe material culture such as broken tobacco pipes, calabash fragments, food debris, fire sticks, hearths, meat-hanging pegs in rock crevices, beads, a hide ring, etc., were found at abandoned base camps and on rock shelter floors. Rock shelters with evidence of recent occupation by the Hadzabe were recorded at various locations within the study area.

Late Wet Season

During the late wet season from May to late July, hunting and scavenging of large game continue inland, though to a lesser extent due to animal out migration. Tuber and root foods such as //ekwaa, shumuko, and matuk-waiyaku are still available, though in small quantities. Hadzabe eat fewer tubers and roots, because they are harder to locate with digging sticks and are bitter and fibrous. During this time the Hadzabe depend more on baobab (*Andansonia digitata*) fruits, which have a pleasant flavor and are rich in vitamin C. The white pith covering the seeds is extracted by the Hadzabe to form flour that is used to make a thick porridge. The baobab seeds are eaten as nuts and are rich in fat. Baobab trees dominate the Hadzabe landscape, with dense patches in the Kidero horst and inland areas that fringe the Yaeda-Endanyawishi valley.

This period coincides with harvesting among inland agriculturists and agro-pastoralists. Some Hadzabe families or individuals move close to the agriculturalists and assist in harvesting in return for food and other commodities. They construct simple shelters near corn farms and wet streams where water wells are easily dug. Others move to temporary camps fringing the Yaeda-Endanyawishi valley and in the Kidero horst, where they forage for wild food resources during the rest of the season.

Dry Season

Water and food resources become scarce during the dry season from early August to early November. Some Hadzabe groups move from the inland areas and live in residential base camps in the Lake Eyasi Basin. Others stay inland in large base camps southeast of the Masiedha-Siponga hills along the southern bank of the Udahya River. In 1993, large groups of semi-settled Hadzabe moved from Mungo-wa-Mono to the southeast of the Masiedha-Siponga Hills. These dry season base camps are located near either year-round stream drainages or water holes. As Bunn, Bartram, and Kroll (1988) point out, these dry season water sources have been used by generations of Hadzabe and provide a focal point for nocturnal hunting. During this time, hunting and carcass scavenging activities are primarily restricted to small- and medium-sized animals and birds. Hunting and scavenging of big game are drastically reduced.

Some Hadzabe groups live in base camps in Mang'ola, particularly in Mikocheni village, exploiting sweet potatoes that become available in large quantities during this time. Others utilize the palm fruits (*Hyphaene*) that are available along the northern lake shore from Gisimangedha to Mikocheni. In the Mang'ola area, berry gathering intensifies during late October and early November, and the Hadzabe who live in the government settlements at Endamaghy and those who worked for agriculturalists in return for sweet potatoes return to foraging. During this time, *Cordia gharaf*, *C. sinensis*, and *Salvadora persica* ripen in the Mang'ola area, with dense patches in the Mbarai riverine system, especially at Kambi ya Simba or Kambi ya Mkaa. For six to eight weeks, groups or families of Hadzabe move across the landscape in the Mang'ola area in search of ripening berries. Tubers and root foods found on the bottoms of Lemagrut and Oldeani volcanic mountains and along the Mbarai riverine system are also utilized by the Hadzabe forager during this time. Isolated hunting of baboons (*Papio anubis*) occurs in the *Acacia xanthoploea* woodland surrounding the natural springs (e.g., Gorfani). Baboon meat is highly valued by Hadzabe foragers for its protein and medicinal uses. It is believed that baboon meat, when eaten and the fat applied on the body, protects the Hadzabe from diseases and evil spirits (Manjano Mahiya, pers. comm.). The occurrence of baboon bones at Mumba Rock Shelter (Mehlman 1989) shows the persistence of baboon exploitation in the Eyasi Basin.

Overnight Camps

Hadzabe traverse the landscape for ecological, cultural, or economic reasons, either as individuals, in special task groups, or in families. The land-use markers resulting from such activities are overnight camps. I observed several recently abandoned overnight camps in the Eyasi landscape during my research. The Hadzabe material culture found at these overnight camps was scanty: primarily food debris, a fireplace, fire sticks, and a simply constructed shelter.

Archaeological Implications

Mobility and Site Use

Hadzabe foragers interact with resources at different temporal and spatial scales. It is possible that prehistoric foragers used their landscape in broadly similar ways. The plant foods, water, and game resources in the Eyasi Basin fluctuate in seasonal availability, yield, and quality. During the wet seasons there are dense patches of tubers and roots, and abundant wild game and honey. During the early dry seasons baobab fruits and nuts are plentiful. During the late dry seasons berries are plentiful. Such a pattern of resource availability, quality, and distribution must have permitted flexible foraging economies and land-use strategies by MSA and LSA foragers.

Similarly, the Hadzabe data show that ecological and economic factors are not the sole influences on Hadzabe land use. Less tangible cultural variables play equally important roles. Direct archaeological evidence for the cultural influences on mobility (mate search and conflict avoidance) is, however, meager. It is nonetheless hypothesized that prehistoric forager land use in the Eyasi Basin was also linked to similar cultural factors.

The Hadzabe pattern shows the continuous use of the entire Eyasi landscape. Hadzabe rarely reoccupy abandoned base and temporary camps. Even though certain locations of the landscape are particularly favored for habitation during certain seasons, the Hadzabe usually choose a fresh area nearby when they return, unless the abandoned habitation is a rock shelter or has some other cultural attraction (see also Woodburn 1972). Therefore, one would expect prehistoric rock shelter use to produce deeply stratified archaeological sites at such locales, while open air sites would tend to be occupied only once and are therefore less likely to be preserved archaeologically.

Traditionally, Hadzabe do not move outside the Eyasi Basin, possibly because all the resources they require are found within its bounds. Judging by modern movement of Hadzabe foragers, the lifetime space of prehistoric foragers could also have been primarily confined to the Eyasi Basin. In the archaeological record, this behavior will be reflected by an emphasis on regionally and locally available raw material for making lithic artifacts, despite possible knowledge of good quality chert from Olduvai Gorge and the Lake Natron Basin, and of obsidian from the Kenyan Central Rift Valley, about 300 km north of Eyasi.

Hadzabe continue to use rock shelters used by MSA and LSA foragers. These rock shelters were undoubtedly important during prehistoric times as they provided warmth and offered shelter from rain, sun, wind, and predators. The continuous use of these shelters suggests that (1) the desirable qualities of a shelter have remained stable through time, and/or (2) the cultural preferences of rock shelter inhabitants have remained stable. Ultimately, this suggests that forager perception or cognition of the Eyasi landscape has been relatively stable, so that one finds contemporary forager use of shelters with prehistoric paintings and artifacts. Does this continuity suggest, perhaps, a similar continuity in forager demography, land-use and resource utilization systems, and social organization from MSA times to the present? For example, if a rock shelter with a floor of 47.4 m^2 is occupied by a Hadzabe family of six individuals, is it possible that families of approximately six individuals occupied similar-sized rock shelters in prehistoric times? These possibilities have important implications for understanding not only the anthropogenic behaviors of prehistoric foragers of the Eyasi Basin, but also their population density. Prehistoric population estimates provide the necessary data needed to formulate and test hypotheses about the relationships between demography and past socioeconomic conditions, land-use patterns, burial patterns, and other aspects of past cultural systems (Hassan 1987; Jochim 1976). Unfortunately, many of the attempts to consider group size according to camp space are based on open occupation spaces (Yellen 1977). The results of such studies cannot be directly applied to shelters, because space is unrestricted on open sites, whereas rock shelters impose constraints on group size and access (J. Walker 1995). Thus, this study of Hadzabe rock shelter use points to interesting avenues of research on the relationships between demography and past forager systems.

A recent demographic study of the Hadzabe shows that forager population density is about 0.24 person per km^2 (Blurton-Jones et al. 1992). On the basis of demographic census data recorded in 1966 and 1985, Blurton-Jones et al. identified a Hadzabe population growth rate of 1.3–1.4 percent per annum, culminating in a total of 750 Hadzabe individuals during the 1985 census. As previously noted, Hadzabe population is estimated to be between 600 and 800 individuals. There have been no major changes in Hadzabe demography since the 1970s (Blurton-Jones et al. 1992). In spite of the historical context of Hadzabe demography since the turn of the last century (raids by Maasai, Isanzu, and Sukuma, epidemics, and other hazards [Blurton-Jones et al. 1992 and references therein]), on a diachronic scale the Hadzabe population seems to be stable and below the carrying capacity of the Eyasi landscape. On this basis, I envisage a low population density of MSA and LSA foragers who also lived below the carrying capacity of the Eyasi landscape.

At most Eyasi rock shelters, land surfaces outside the drip line tend to be steep. Consequently, the exterior talus slopes are frequently scattered with discarded food debris and other material culture. Archaeological excavations located primarily in the center of shelter floors are likely to uncover materials that are unrepresentative of prehistoric activities. Unfortunately, cave and rock shelter deposits are often assumed to be sealed deposits representing most if not all the prehistoric activities that took place. This study shows that spatial usage of rock shelters and discard patterns can be influenced by (1) behaviors of the occupants, (2) amount of space available, (3) amount of discard material, (4) anticipated time of occupation, or (5) a combination of these factors. In turn, these factors can also limit the number of rock shelter occupants as well as the amount of discarded materials on the shelter's floor.

Rock Art

Although the Hadzabe do not paint on rock faces, they claim authorship of the prehistoric art in the Eyasi Basin. This claim has significant archaeological implications insofar as the Hadzabe seem to be untapped sources of possible "historical" connections to rock art production and other archaeological phenomena. One obvious problem that faces rock art archaeology is the interpretation of the meaning of the images and the people who produced them. One reason for this is that few archaeologists have asked questions regarding the economic, political, symbolic, social, religious, territorial, or ecological contexts of rock art production (Lim 1992).

Archaeologists need to learn and understand the structures of the systems of human organization that were associated with the prehistoric images. This makes it necessary to collect other kinds of data such as information on the paleoecology and archaeology of the time when rock art was made, as well as present-day ethnographic data. Ethnographic rock art data and the usage of rock shelters by contemporary Hadzabe foragers can provide sources for hypothesis generation and testing concerning the meaning of prehistoric rock art and the motives behind its production. A systematic study of why, when, and how the Hadzabe use the rock shelters and specific paintings will help in understanding the meaning and contexts of prehistoric rock art production in the Eyasi Basin.

Hadzabe rock shelter use is limited to short-term, wet season, or overnight camps. In the Eyasi Basin, rock shelters have yielded diverse archaeological materials including MSA, LSA, and Pastoral Neolithic stone artifacts, human skeletal remains, rock art, animal bone remains, pottery, ostrich eggshell beads, and Iron Age materials (Mabulla 1996a; Mehlman 1989). If we are to understand these sites' occupational histories and activities and the meaning of their rock art, we must examine prehistoric forager land use through ecological, cultural, and economic contexts. Based on Hadzabe data on rock shelter usage, I hypothesize that MSA and LSA foragers in the Eyasi Basin occupied the rock shelters and painted them during the wet seasons and occasionally during hunting and gathering missions when they were used as overnight camps. I also argue that the habitation use of rock shelters was the primary reason that attracted prehistoric foragers to them in the first place and that painting was secondary (Lim 1993).

Hadzabe Foragers Today: An Endangered Cultural Species?

The Hadzabe way of life is dying out. If present conditions continue, they will soon no longer be hunter-gatherers. The key to ensuring their way of life is nowhere in sight. Both Hadzabe foragers and their observers share this grim outlook. How then can a nonviable way of life provide a model for prehistoric forager lifeways? Unfortunately, many researchers do not address this paradox (Bunn, Bartram, and Kroll 1988; O'Connell and Hawkes 1988). Before addressing this issue, let us summarize the events that have contributed to the Hadzabe's present condition.

In talking with Hadzabe about their survival as a cultural group, comments were frequently made on two major issues: (1) encroachment onto their land by non-forager groups, and (2) government interventions into their way of life.

Encroachment by Non-Forager Groups

Faced with major encroachment by non-forager groups upon their land, the Hadzabe are finding it difficult to make a living using their traditional foraging system. Ethnographic information shows that at the time of European contact, the Eyasi Basin was occupied exclusively by Hadzabe foragers (Woodburn 1964). This assertion is supported by Hadzabe oral traditions (Ndagala and Zengu 1989). In fact, local incursions by Datog pastoralists, Iraqwi agropastoralists, and other agriculturalist groups have been recorded beginning in the 1900s (McDowell 1981; Obst 1912; Woodburn 1964, 1988). Today, the Eyasi Basin is populated by different non-forager groups, including Europeans. Some of these non-forager groups practice commercial farming in the lower Mbarai River in Mang'ola area. Others are pastoralists, agropastoralists, peasants, miners, fuel collectors (charcoal and firewood), missionaries, teachers, health service personnel, and traders. As the density of non-forager groups and their needs have increased, however, there has been a marked diminution of food resources for the foragers. Large tracts of land have been cleared either for farming or as a result of tree cutting for building and fuel. The increasing herds are degrading the environment and the water sources. Legal and illegal hunting have significantly reduced the amount of game in the area.

The solution to the encroachment problem is complex and political, because it involves rights, land, and ideology. Perhaps the most problematic issue is land ownership. As perfectly described by Woodburn (1980), the Hadzabe are mobile, egalitarian, immediate-return foragers for whom land is used and owned communally. Indigenous Eyasi Basin inhabitants claim ownership to foraging land. In contrast, non-forager groups in the Eyasi Basin, and the Tanzanian government in general, view land as a multiple-use resource, of significance to the entire nation. Accordingly, the land can be used and owned either privately or communally. This is one of the major institutional differences between Hadzabe forager and non-forager groups in the Eyasi Basin. Through government land tenure system and the increasing influence of non-forager customs concerning land ownership and inheritance, Eyasi Basin lands are increasingly being parceled out to private ownership. Since the Eyasi Basin has passed and continues to pass into non-foraging uses, Hadzabe foragers are experiencing increasing difficulties continuing their traditional lifestyle.

Government Interventions

Attempts to induce the Hadzabe foragers to settle down and produce food have been made repeatedly since the turn of the last century. After Tanganyika (now Tanzania) achieved independence from colonial domination, the government required citizens to live in one place, to receive social services, and to produce agricultural products to contribute to the national economy. Thus the fate of Hadzabe foragers became tied to the emerging national political, social, and cultural system. Throughout the years following independence up to the present, Tanzania and multinational organizations such as the World Bank have endeavored to convert Hadzabe foragers into sedentary peasants (PMFPO 1990, 1992). The dominant goal has been either to force the Hadzabe to become sedentary or at least to put an end to their foraging way of life. In essence, this view is based on a flawed 19th-century theory of evolution: that by sedentarizing the foragers, the state integrates them into the nation's socioeconomic and political system as farmers, government employees, or townspeople.

Recent efforts are essentially the continuation of colonial experiments. To ensure the future survival of the Hadzabe, the Tanzanian government (PMFPO 1990, 1992) has established a comprehensive development program that includes free education and health services, free beekeeping, animal husbandry, and agricultural inputs. The major goals have been to alleviate poverty and further the Hadzabe's "basic human need" to become sedentary. Unlike previous development programs, the recent ones claim to have involved the beneficiaries (Hadzabe) in the identification, planning, and implementation of the programs (PMFPO 1992). This claim is supported by several workshops and lists of names of Hadzabe forager participants provided in the 1990 and 1992 reports to the Prime Minister and First President's Office. Coincidentally, seven of the Hadzabe participants in the government workshops reported in 1990 and 1992 were also my field crew members and consultants. At the beginning, in 1992, my Hadzabe field crew and consultants thought that the hidden goal of my research was to spy on them for the government. After several weeks of assurance that I was not working for the government, they started to talk about government settlement programs. The same people who, as reported in 1990 and 1992, participated in the government workshops did not approve the government programs two years later. This is because basic questions concerning the relationship between the aspirations of Hadzabe themselves and what is expected of and for them by government and development planners were not fully explored. Further, individual Hadzabe cannot speak for this strongly egalitarian community. Finally, individual Hadzabe involvement in mainstream decision-making processes leads them either to rely upon or to accept the opinions of government officials. Unfortunately, such opinions are colored by the values, prejudices, and rationalizations of the government.

Since the Hadzabe lack a political voice in Tanzania, many of them, even the most educated Hadzabe, resist government settlement schemes by withdrawing their children from free schools, abandoning the established farming villages and returning to the bush, boycotting the government hospitals when they are sick, and rejecting government employment in towns. As Kaare (1989, 1993) notes, the Hadzabe have neither adopted sedentary life nor been "modernized" by formal education, as anticipated by the state. Rather, they maintain strong links with the Eyasi Basin landscape and a foraging lifestyle. For the Hadzabe, hunting and gathering activities and a highly mobile lifestyle still have important social, cultural, and economic benefits. The Hadzabe foraging lifestyle is organized and meaningful; the landscape provides, to them, adequate food.

Clearly, ecological factors influence Hadzabe land use, but Hadzabe themselves have adapted socially, technologically, and economically to the Eyasi Basin's marginal landscape, encroachment by non-foragers, and government interventions. The social system involves exchange relationships within and outside the forager group; the technological system involves simple technology; and the economic system includes barter trade, monetary trade, and labor for non-forager groups. Planned mobility defines the land-use system. At any rate, any attempt to make the Hadzabe settle in permanent settlements would go against their own worldview about good health, lifeways, and food abundance. Hadzabe foraging is intertwined with the ecological, cultural, and economic constructions of their lifeways and the landscape and its resources. Overwhelmingly, these are the pressing concerns of Hadzabe daily life. It is time to take Hadzabe insights and knowledge seriously, since government plans that do not coincide with their desires and aspirations are bound to fail.

The Hadzabe perceive their landscape as a provider of all their needed resources including food, material culture, and shelter. In recent years, however, Hadzabe land has increasingly been shared with Mang'ati pastoralists, Iraqwi agropastoralists, and settled agricultural groups. The Hadzabe observe that the economic, social, and cultural activities of non-foragers are destroying the productivity of their land. They are concerned that they have been encroached upon and are increasingly being pushed further into non-productive lands. An important first step toward this direction is to acknowledge the viability of forager land tenure systems.

As a counter to the old orthodoxy and as a means of averting what is happening to the Hadzabe, I suggest that the aspirations and desires of the Hadzabe themselves be our starting point. Scientific, economic, medical, social, and other advice and assistance should support these aspirations and desires. The foraging system of the Hadzabe still offers an opportunity to support a coherent traditional and sustainable foraging culture and population. I believe that we can ensure Hadzabe existence and integrity without significantly changing their way of life. In doing this, I am not inspired by a sentimental preoccupation with the preservation of a supposedly pristine society. Rather, I suggest Hadzabe can survive best as hunter-gatherers. Hadzabe's survival is a political issue that needs political mobilization.

My major task now is to return to the question posed above—how can foraging behavioral models and hypotheses generated from Hadzabe foragers be applied to the archaeological record of the Stone Age? The extent to which one may extrapolate from extant foragers to prehistoric ones remains an open question (Lee 1992; Wilmsen and Denbow 1990; Woodburn 1980). It is clear in this chapter that the contact, political, and economic relationships with non-forager groups and government interventions have contributed to the present situation of the Hadzabe foragers. Today, approximately one-fourth of the total population continues to practice a full-time traditional foraging lifestyle (Bunn, Bartram, and Kroll 1988; O'Connell and Hawkes 1988). The rest practice a combination of part-time traditional foraging and other production activities. Whether the latter economic system is a product of recent developments or not is unclear at present. Nonetheless, the archaeological record suggests that prehistoric foragers and farmers coexisted in the Eyasi Basin from about 3,000 years ago (Mehlman 1989).

The eastern Hadzabe continue to be mobile foragers who eschew accumulation of private property, use portable, utilitarian, easily acquired and replaceable artifacts, and lack a political organization. They continually use the same rock shelters as wet season and short-term occupations. Whether Hadzabe foraging is representative of prehistoric foraging is not the issue here. As Burch argues: "[T]he critical issue is not the basis on which a model is developed, but the extent to which it increases our understanding of the relevant phenomena in an empirically supportable way...[I]f a measurably distinct class of societies (e.g., foraging societies) can be delineated, and if an empirically testable model of that class can be developed, then the model should apply to all members of that class, regardless of when they existed in time" (Burch 1994:446).

Likewise, Bettinger notes: "[I]t is the processes and principles that govern dynamic systems, both past and present, that are important. Firsthand observation of contemporary systems may help us to think about principles and processes, but the principles and processes necessarily transcend individual cases, however instructive these cases might be" (Bettinger 1991:79).

One must accept that empirical generalizations about the forager archaeological record are difficult to come by and that meaningful generalizations about the record must be informed by the behavior of foragers in real life. It would be a mistake to write off our best data about foragers in real life just because of contact with neighbor societies and government interventions (Woodburn 1988). "If anything, the historical changes that have impacted foragers in this century have served to reduce rather than artificially increase the distinctiveness of these societies" (Knauft 1991:392). In terms of behavioral evolutionary ecology, the distinctive features of extant egalitarian foragers are unlikely to have been a function of modern developments (Woodburn 1988). Therefore, ethnographic observations and reasoning can help us imagine what an archaeological record of such foragers might look like, given some understanding of their dynamic systems.

Conclusion

While Hadzabe land use has not received sufficient attention, it can provide important insights into an understanding of prehistoric Eyasi Basin mobility. Three of the four Hadzabe land-use patterns are seasonal and largely structured by resource availability, quality, and predictability. This chapter shows that cultural and political factors also influence mobility and that group mobility and individual mobility have different motivations. While individuals initiate lone moves according to their own desires, group movements are a collective decision. Although prehistoric land use can be studied at the group level, it is necessary to understand land use as a product of both individual and group behaviors.

Hadzabe land-use strategies are repeated at different times and places as selective forces in the regional ecology, human economy, and culture recur. The overall Hadzabe use of the landscape is continuous, and the resulting land-use system seems to be stable through time. On the basis of Hadzabe inferences drawn from interactions with the Eyasi landscape, this chapter has provided much of the ecological, economic, and cultural contexts for prehistoric Eyasi forager mobility that the archaeological record alone cannot reveal.

Acknowledgments

I would like to thank the Ford Foundation and National Science Foundation for supporting my graduate training and fieldwork; the Archaeology Unit of the University of Dar es Salaam and the Tanzania Antiquities Office for permitting me to work in the Eyasi Basin and for their help in granting a permit to ship artifacts to Florida; and the Vice Chancellor of the University of Dar es Salaam for study leave.

4

Ceramic Ethnoarchaeology: Some Examples from Kenya

Simiyu Wandibba

This chapter focuses on production, distribution, exchange, and pottery style among modern Kenyan potters, as well as inter-group interaction and stylistic variability. The factors that create homogeneity or heterogeneity in ceramic styles are examined by looking at who makes the pots, the learning processes involved, organization of potting activities, stylistics of wares produced, and postmarital residential patterns. It also examines vessel life expectancy, recycling, spatial distribution, and disposal. It concludes that some aspects of pottery style are consistent within modern Kenyan ethnic groupings, although variability exists within communities in many aspects of pottery style.

Pottery has attracted considerable attention from archaeologists. One important reason for this is that pottery is durable and at the same time ubiquitous in the later archaeological record. Pottery has been used to define the basic chronological and distributional parameters of prehistoric sociocultural systems in attempts to discover evidence of local and long-distance exchange, to reconstruct the development of craft specialization, to identify ethnic and other social groups, and to reconstruct learning frameworks and elements of social organization (Kramer 1994).

As can be seen in the work of Kramer (1994), the archaeological utility of pottery has almost no limits. All these interests, however, can be grouped according to four broad themes—production, production and social organization, use and disposal, and change (Kramer 1985). Ethnoarchaeological studies of pottery attempt to throw light on these issues, although some topics have tended to attract more attention than others. The issues that have been investigated most extensively are production and the organization of production. Some of the studies have not been systematic enough to yield the kind of information required for cross-cultural generalizations. Let us look at how the four issues have been tackled in Kenya. Most of the work done so far has been of an ethnographic rather than an ethnoarchaeological nature.

Production

Since the mid-1960s, ethnoarchaeological studies of pottery production have shifted from simple descriptions of manufacturing processes to detailed accounts of how production relates to the natural and the socioeconomic environment. Studies now focus on acquisition and preparation of the clay, manufacturing processes (including their location), and distribution. A number of studies in Kenya have addressed these issues, with varying degrees of success (Barbour and Wandibba 1989; Blackburn 1973; Gill 1981; Herbich 1981; Omollo 1988). These studies show that potters are aware that some potting clays require additives (tempering materials) before they can be used, while others do not. If additives are required, they are in the form of sand, grog (crushed pot), or rock. Generally, tempering materials are locally available, but sometimes they may be obtained from afar. The Gikuyu potters of Kiria, for example, use disintegrated granitic rock, which has to be transported over a distance that can be at times more than 40 km. On the other hand, Luo potters at Ng'iya use grog as their tempering material.

Kenyan potters generally obtain clay from river and stream banks, lakesides, and marshy swamps but on occasion potters obtain their clay from *termitaria* (Wandibba 1995). For most potters, both the clay and the tempering materials are found near their homes. In the case of Kiria potters, however, not only is the source of their granitic temper quite distant, the clay also is from a source about 10 km away. Traditionally, Kiria potters relied on donkeys for the transportation of both materials, but they now use motor transport for the temper. In both cases, the potters do not acquire the materials directly from the source but through third parties who exchange the materials for cash. To ensure regular availability, the potters stockpile both materials.

To improve the quality of the raw material, some potters mix together different colored clays instead of using temper. For example, Brown (1972) states that Kamba potters collect clays of three different colors—black, red, and white. The clays are mixed in varying proportions, depending largely on the individual potter's preference (Gill 1981). The Adavida also mix three different clays—gray, red, and blue (Soper 1989)—while some Luo potters mix a red and a black clay (Herbich 1981; Omollo 1988). Logoli potters also mix red and black clays (Barbour 1989).

Most potters use the traditional coiling technique to form their vessels, but some employ slab modeling. Whereas some potters make their pots in one piece, others do so in two pieces. Luyia and Luo potters, for example, build their vessels in one piece, starting with the base and working upward until the pot is completed. Gikuyu, Kamba, Okiek, and Adavida potters manufacture their pots in two pieces, starting with the upper half. Examination of the forms produced suggests that size variation within form classes is related to differential function, such differences often being distinguished by the potter's terminological distinctions. The Bukusu potters of western Kenya, for example, make necked vessels both for carrying and storing water and for cooking vegetables. Cooking pots are much smaller in size, and the two different kinds of pots are referred to by different names.

Sometimes the names may not be different, but the forms will nevertheless be distinct. The Okiek traditionally made three different forms of the honey pot, depending on whether the honey was to be stored in the forest or at home. Although the three forms were ingrained in the potter's mental template, she had no separate names for them and simply referred to all three as "honey pots." Although all three forms had necks, the pots varied in size and body form. The vessel for storing the honey in the forest was elongated in form and had a narrow mouth to accommodate a stopper to facilitate sealing before the pot was buried in the ground for safekeeping. The shape designed for storage in a cave was much bigger and had a rounded body to enable it to stand unsupported on a shelf or the floor. Finally, the house honey pot (the only one of the honey pots still being made today) has a rounded body and a short cylindrical neck, with a tight-fitting leather cover and leather carrying handle (see Blackburn 1973 for more details). It would thus appear that unique functions produce subtle differences in vessel forms.

Function can also precipitate functional elaborations. The Okiek, for example, traditionally had handles on some of their vessels to facilitate their being strung to be carried around. In the same way, many of their small pots had a pair of holes in the sides for securing carrying handles of leather.

In Kenya potting is predominantly a woman's job, but among the Babukusu some men make pots. Traditionally, men only made those pots associated with male-dominated activities such as beer drinking and purification rituals. The men made pots for brewing and serving beer as well as those used in ceremonies associated with twinship. Men never engaged in the manufacture of water or cooking pots, which were used in the domain of activities traditionally reserved for women. In those societies where potting is exclusively a woman's job, women make the whole repertoire of the vessels required by their community.

Kenyan potters generally make pots in their homes. There are no workshops as such, and the potter or group of potters decides on the locale for the work. Once a spot has been chosen it becomes the usual potting area. Some potters do their work away from home. For example, the Adavida have potteries located in rock shelters away from human habitation (Soper 1989). Pokot potters generally use huge overhanging rock shelters as their potteries. Jean Brown (1989a:54) observes that part of the rock shelter may be screened off with poles and brushwood to form an enclosure in which the potter works and where unfired pots can be left to dry unobserved. Like other traditional potters in Kenya, both the Adavida and the Pokot believe that pots in the process of manufacture must be protected from any ritual impurity that could bring about cracking and breakages during the firing process. Siting potteries away from home is one way of guaranteeing such protection.

Potters decorate their wares with obvious regional variations. Abaluyia and the Luo potters in the Lake Victoria basin produce the most elaborate designs, in combinations of knotted or plaited roulette impressions and bands of red ocher or carved roulette impressions. The Kalenjin potters in the Rift Valley decorate their wares using either a twisted or knotted roulette to produce decorative motifs that are quite different from those of the Abaluyia and the Luo. The Gikuyu potters of central Kenya generally decorate their pots with just one or two rows of stab impressions on the shoulder of the vessel. Down on the coast, potters use straws, sticks, and their thumbnails to decorate pots with either incisions or impressions (Wilding 1989). The decoration is not particularly elaborate and occurs either on the neck (incisions) or on the carination (impressions). Finally, the Dorobo potters of Samburu District choose simple decoration in the form of vertical and horizontal ridges (Brown 1989b; Clarfield 1989). Potters occasionally use acacia thorns to superimpose impressions on the ridges.

Some potters do not decorate their pots. Instead, they imprint their wares with individual markings which also serve as a form of trademark. The best examples of these markings are found among the Akamba, executed in the form of incisions, impressions, or both (Brown 1972; Gill 1981). A few potters among the Adavida also use trademarks consisting of dots or lines on a pottery assemblage that is otherwise devoid of any decoration (Soper 1989).

Pots are usually dried away from direct sunlight—indoors or within rock shelters, if such places are used as potteries—to ensure even drying and thereby prevent cracking. In cases of indoor drying in a habitation, part of the house is set aside especially for that purpose. Pots can also be dried under house eaves, as among Gikuyu potters. Some Gikuyu potters now have special shelters where they dry their wares. In either case, Gikuyu potters pile their pots one on top of the other, upside down. In some communities, when the pots are in a leather-hard state they are polished with a water-worn pebble. Polishing is practiced especially by Luyia and Luo potters. Traditionally, the drying took much longer than is the case now when pots are made with the next market day in mind.

All potters fire their pots in bonfires, which are generally located close to the potteries. The firing spot normally consists of a shallow depression made for that purpose. The identification marks of such a spot usually include hardened and discolored earth surrounded by ash. Among the Agikuyu, this space is demarcated by potsherds, which also serve as vessel props. In the past, when forested and woodland areas were plentiful, wood was the usual fuel. Today, with very few trees around, potters have had to resort to whatever firing material is available to them, including grass, cow dung, coconut fronds, wood, shrubs, bark, grain stalks, and leaves.

After firing, the pots are sometimes subjected to some form of post-firing treatment. Among the Luo pots not decorated with ocher are splashed with an infusion of tree bark which sizzles on the pots and turns them a mottled dark brown or black (Herbich 1981). Endo potters immediately cover their pots with cow dung (Welbourn 1989), an activity sometimes also practiced by Okiek potters (Kratz 1989). Pokot potters burn leafy twigs of a particular tree inside the pots before removing them from the fire. This material, which burns with a loud crackling noise and produces dense smoke, is used to blacken the inside of the pots and help seal the pores (Brown 1989a:58).

Distribution

Once the pots have been fired and have undergone any required post-firing treatment, they are ready for distribution. Most of the pottery produced in Kenya is consumed locally through periodic markets held regularly in the areas of production. The wares are generally sold to customers who are from within a 5-km radius of the production centers. This is especially the case when the potters are at the same time the sellers themselves, since their involvement in other domestic chores makes it almost impossible for them to travel long distances that would keep them away for a long time. But in situations in which pots are distributed through third parties who use modern methods of transportation, the distances covered can be great. For example, pots produced in the Lake Victoria basin by Luyia and Luo potters are found not just in all the major urban centers of western Kenya, but also in far-off places like Nakuru, Nairobi, and even Mombasa, which is about 900 km from the centers of production. In this case the pots are transported by truck, bus, or train. Pots made by the Gikuyu potters are transported by vehicles to locales as distant as Nyahururu and Nairobi, about 80 km and 150 km away, respectively. But even within the local areas, pots can be transported over comparatively long distances to satisfy a particular market need. Thus, the pot-making agricultural Pokot take their wares to markets that are 32 km away, where their kin, the pastoral Pokot, come to buy them.

Apart from marketing, pots are also distributed through sales at home and through gift giving. Pots sold at home are usually bartered for food stuffs, especially grain. Such pots may have been bought from the market in the first instance. For example, Herbich (1989) observed that there were some traders who bought quantities of pottery for resale in regions outside the normal catchment areas of the markets, where they would sometimes be sold from homestead to homestead. In the homesteads, the pots were often bartered for grain rather than being exchanged for cash. Among the Endo, pots are partially paid for either by fetching clay or firewood or by giving the potter an equivalent volume of finger millet for each pot (Welbourn 1989).

Traditionally, gift giving was the main avenue by which pottery was distributed among the Okiek themselves. Kratz (1989) records that a woman would simply ask a friend or relative to make her a particular pot, and the potter would not refuse because she would expect a return favor in the future. Today, Okiek pots are also exchanged through secondary distribution in which even non-potting women may give their spare pots to daughters, daughters-in-law, sisters, or friends (Kratz 1989). This gift giving is also practiced by other potting communities. Among Babukusu pots are given freely to relatives, friends, and neighbors.

Production and Social Organization

Archaeologists interested in this aspect of ceramic production have focused their attention on interaction, learning, and stylistic variability. What factors bring about homogeneity or heterogeneity in ceramic styles? To find answers to this question, one would need to investigate who makes the pots, the learning processes involved, the organization of the actual potting activities, the stylistics of the wares produced, and postmarital residential patterns. What does Kenyan ceramic ethnography tell us about these issues?

First, it is obvious that in Kenya potting is almost exclusively in the female domain. However, not every woman in any one potting community is engaged in the craft; in fact, only a small proportion of the women is involved in the trade. In her study area Herbich (1989) estimated that all pots were made by a group of women who constituted less than 1 percent of the population. Among the Agikuyu, potting is now restricted to two neighboring villages that produce all the pottery used in the expansive Gikuyu country.

No woman engages in potting on a full-time basis. Indeed, potting is usually undertaken in combination or alternating with other domestic chores. No potter lives on earnings derived solely from the sale of her wares and must engage in other income-generating activities to supplement the income she earns from pottery. Although in the past the craft was in some areas sometimes restricted to specific clans, today the craft is open to anyone interested.

The studies done so far seem to suggest that there is a variety of means by which potters acquire their knowledge. In some communities, potting skills are passed from mothers to daughters with the learners acquiring the skills by observation and imitation. Even in such communities, any woman interested in becoming a potter is free to do so (Brown 1989a, 1989b). Among the Luo, daughters who learn potting from their mothers must, upon marriage, learn the skill anew from their mothers-in-law.

In other communities the situation is not clear cut. For example, among the Endo (Welbourn 1989), women who take up potting are sometimes daughters, sometimes daughters-in-law, and sometimes just unrelated women who are interested in learning how to pot. The age at which the learning takes place also varies from community to community. Among the Okiek (Kratz 1989), most potters learn when they are grown girls or young women. Some Endo potters learn when young and then take their skills to their new home, while others wait to pick it up until their children are older and they have more time (Welbourn 1989).

Most traditional potters in Kenya carry out their craft as individuals but group potting is practiced by the Agikuyu and the Luo. In the former community, groups of potters come together to pot for a colleague in exchange for money or as part of the communal effort, ~*ngwatio*, to assist one another. Every potter naturally brings in her own expertise and idiosyncrasies. Among the Luo, potters tend to live in homesteads clustered around clay sources, with each cluster operating as a network of potters, forming a kind of community in which the women carry on their potting activities together. This kind of interaction tends to produce artifacts that appear to be unique to each cluster, what Herbich (1987) has described as micro-styles.

All the traditional communities in Kenya are patrilineal and patrilocal. On marriage a woman leaves her parents' home and moves into her new husband's home. Among the Luo, custom dictates that a son and his new wife live in his father's compound until the children of that union are ready for marriage. In this arrangement, a new wife lives under the close supervision of her mother-in-law, whose duty it is to ensure that she conforms to the ideals and expectations of the family. If she happens to have entered into a polygynous union, the new wife will also have to contend with the co-wives, since these have authority over her by virtue of their seniority. This means that the young woman has to learn things anew. As Ominde (1952:51) has observed, once they get married Luo girls have to undergo a long process of re-socialization, which often involves "unlearning" things learned in their mother's home. Thus, a woman who marries into the home of potters will be expected to take up the craft. She cannot refuse this duty because she has to demonstrate that she does not consider herself too good for the work and also has to show that she is willing to take up responsibilities for her new family (Herbich 1987). She acquires the new skills under the close supervision of her mother-in-law or her senior co-wives. Since women undertake all the potting activities as a group, the young woman eventually comes to know the style of that very localized group or cell of potters.

It is not only at the micro-level, however, that one notices stylistic variability; these also exist at the macro-level. Although micro-styles are characteristic of cell production, macro-styles appear to correspond to community production. I have argued elsewhere (Wandibba 1995) that when one examines the pottery produced by a particular community in Kenya one cannot fail to notice its overall uniformity of shape and decoration. Such pottery tends to have certain stylistic idiosyncracies that would distinguish it from pottery produced by another community. Thus, pots made by the various Luo clusters of potters would exhibit overall similarities that would distinguish the vessels from those produced by the neighboring Luyia potters, for example.

In circumstances of contiguous existence, there is also room for borrowing across ethnic boundaries. Other examples of macro-styles illustrating this situation include those of the Okiek and the Akamba. The Okiek pottery assemblage is distinctive in being the only one with honey pots and a snuff-grinding bowl. Not even the other ethnolinguistically related potting communities produce these vessels. Akamba pottery is not decorated but is instead imprinted with the potter's mark, which serves as both a trademark and a guarantee of the vessel's quality. According to Gill (1981), a young Akamba girl uses her mother's mark while she is learning to pot but designs her own individual trademark as soon as she gets married. Gill (1981:207) asserts, "Not only do the marks record information about the individual woman potter, but they also reflect ownership of property by Kamba women, and make it possible to trace the movement of any potter's vessels from village to village."

Use and Disposal

All the studies done so far have addressed the question of the use of ceramic vessels. There appears to be no doubt that all the pottery made by traditional potters is utilitarian and is used to satisfy the various household needs of carriage, storage, cooking, local brewing, and serving. Many pots also serve both intended and unofficial functions. Thus, for example, a pot made specifically as a beer pot will more often than not be found serving as a grain storage pot. Special-purpose vessels serve only the designated purpose, however, such as various rituals or in specialized functions such as straining native salt from ashes.

Issues concerning vessel life expectancy, recycling, spatial distribution, and disposal are all important to archaeologists. Unfortunately, these have not so far received systematic attention, even from the few ethnoarchaeological studies that have been done. Nonetheless, there is some information on a number of the issues. As regards recycling, we know that both damaged and broken pots are normally not discarded wholesale but are put to some other use. Damaged but unbroken vessels are used by Gikuyu potters for aging clay and for storing shelled maize cobs to be used as fuel by the Bukusu community, where such vessels were also traditionally used for holding ashes used in the fermentation of sorghum and for holding sorghum and finger millet during the fermentation period. Sherds are also reused as dishes for serving pets, as grog, as props for holding pots in place during firing, as troughs from which chickens drink, as lids for other pots, as receptacles for carrying live coals of fire and for grinding snuff and medicines for external use, and as support for cooking pots in use.

The life expectancy of a vessel varies according to its size, where it is stored when not in use, and how frequently it is used. Among Babukusu, the life expectancy of a pot appears to increase with vessel size and to decrease with mobility and use frequency. Traditionally the Babukusu made six main types of vessels: beer pots for brewing and serving beer, water pots for fetching and storing water, cooking pots for *ugali*, cooking pots for vegetables and meat, cooking pots for foods other than *ugali*, and serving bowls. The pots for brewing and serving beer on festive occasions would normally be the largest in size, while beer pots for small parties would be of medium size. All the pots were stored in specific areas of the house: water pots closer to the door, where they could be easily reached by nonresidents, and beer pots farther away, in an area not easily accessible to everybody. Because of their size, the beer pots were the least mobile, while cooking and water pots were constantly being moved. Because of their frequent use (mostly by different people), the latter two types broke quite often and therefore needed to be replaced more frequently than the huge beer pots, which were rarely moved. When I was carrying out my research in 1994, one octogenarian man still had some beer pots dating from the late 1940s.

When a pot breaks inside or outside a Bukusu person's house, reusable pieces are selected and put aside and the rest are swept up and discarded on a nearby midden or in the grass at the edge of the courtyard. On the other hand, if a water pot happens to break when being used to transport water tradition dictates that none of the pieces are collected. Because of this, paths leading to sources of drinking water traditionally tended to be littered with such sherds. In such instances, users discarded sherds away from the pots' original use contexts, where they are unlikely to be found by a future archaeologist. Finally, reusable damaged vessels are normally stored beneath granaries or under eaves, where they are protected from damage by wandering animals and from where they can be taken and used when required.

Change

Archaeologists want to find out the types of ceramic changes that have occurred over time and also the factors that are likely to have brought about those changes. To do full justice to these issues, it would be necessary for an ethnoarchaeologist to carry out a diachronic study of a potting community. This is something that has generally not been addressed in the Kenyan context. Nevertheless, several issues seem to emerge from the studies that have been done. In terms of techniques of production, it would appear that potters still use methods that were used by their forebears. For example, the methods observed at the beginning of the last century by Routledge and Routledge (1910) are basically the same methods employed by present-day Gikuyu potters (Brown 1989c; Wandibba, pers. observations 1983 and 1993). The same can be said of Bukusu potters, whose techniques were first systematically observed in the 1930s (G. Wagner 1970). Finally, after investigating Luo potters for over two and a half years Herbich (1989) concluded that technological changes in the system had been minimal, but some changes have occurred: in the way the wares are decorated, in drying methods, and in firing fuels. Whereas in the past pots were dried only away from direct sunlight, today some potters dry pots in the sun the day before firing. With regard to decoration, potters have incorporated new tools and have varied motifs to meet the changing market desires. With regard to fuels, the depletion of woodlands and forests has meant greater reliance on less effective fuels like grass, grain stalks, tree branches, and leaves.

Ethnoarchaeologists are able to observe major changes in the assemblages produced by each community. As factory-made vessels have become more and more popular, potters have needed to eliminate from their assembly lines those wares most easily replaced by such factory surrogates. Thus the Bukusu pot for cooking *ugali* fell into disuse in the 1950s, as first the metal *karai* and then *sufuria* took over its functions. In the same way, in most Bukusu homes today pots for cooking other meals have been replaced by mass-produced metal vessels, and jerrycans have taken over as water-carrying vessels. Other items that have disappeared from the Bukusu pottery assemblage include eating bowls and salt strainers, while pots are nowadays generally not used for cooking bananas or potatoes. Even beer-brewing pots have decreased in numbers following the adoption of metal drums to serve this purpose. The government's ban on traditional liquors in 1978 has also contributed to this decrease. But potters have brought in new forms to serve new needs. Most potters throughout the country now make vessels specifically for tourists and also produce flower pots, neither of which was produced traditionally.

Noticeable changes can also be seen in the distribution of the wares. Before the introduction of a money economy in the country, pots were exchanged through barter, mostly for foodstuffs. Under these circumstances, except for Gikuyu country where production centers were widely dispersed, vessels did not move long distances and were generally consumed within the neighborhoods. With the introduction of the market economy and the subsequent establishment of market centers, it became possible for pots to be distributed beyond the neighborhoods. Because pottery is bulky, however, there has been a tendency for wares that can be transported on foot to be distributed within a 5-km radius of production centers. On the other hand, those potters with access to vehicular transportation have traded their vessels over great distances and usually through third parties. In this way, Gikuyu pots find their way to Nyahururu, Nairobi, and Mombasa, and Luyia and Luo pots travel to Kitale, Eldoret, Nakuru, Nairobi, and Mombasa. Some Kamba potters use vehicles to transport their wares to far markets within Ukambani.

Conclusion

A number of issues are of interest to archaeologists. First, there is a tendency for potters to live fairly close to the sources of the raw materials for potting, probably because they are bulky. Ceramic petrologists should, therefore, seek clay sources in the neighborhood of settlements before going farther afield. This recommendation would apply only in situations where there is no evidence for the availability of long-distance means of transportation, such as water transport. Where such methods of transport were available in antiquity, very heavy materials were in fact moved over long distances.

Second, people who are related ethnolinguistically tend to share some stylistic uniformity regardless of geographical location. However, local clusters of potters within the larger geographical unit could, through interaction at the local level, bring about micro-styles that are unique to each cluster and recognizable to the consumers as such. These micro-styles could account for much of the analogy archaeologists often ascribe to mother/daughter learning processes. In cases where two or more groups share an ethnic boundary, there will be some two-way borrowing across it. As a result of this process, the wares produced at the ethnic peripheries will tend to exhibit a combination of stylistic traits which makes them unique. In such cases it becomes difficult to distinguish style on the basis of ethnolinguistic criteria.

Third, because of recycling, it is unlikely that the sherds recovered by an archaeologist would constitute the complete account of the past ethnographic record. Also, conjoining should not be restricted to pieces recovered from the same stratigraphic context, but should apply to all sherds, as this is likely to provide information on discard at different time periods. Furthermore, breakage and replacement means that vessels and sherds of different ages can enter the archaeological record at the same time and thereby lead to inappropriate chronological groupings.

Fourth, the form and number of vessels vary according to function and use context as well as by household size and composition. Fifth, because some broken pots may not be removed from where they broke, archaeologists need to be aware that many potsherds may be lying in places far removed from the pots' original use context. Finally, ceramic changes can be initiated by factors having nothing to do with postmarital residence or migration.

5

Fipa Iron Technologies and Their Implied Social History

Bertram B. B. Mapunda

Attribute and chemical analyses conducted on metallurgical materials from archaeological sites in Ufipa, Tanzania, have revealed that at least three ironworking technologies, varying in space or time or both, have been practiced in Ufipa during the last five hundred years. This paper uses the spatial and temporal distribution of the technologies, as well as pottery, to reconstruct the social history of Ufipa. Archaeology and oral tradition evidence show that Katukutu *technology, found on the southeastern shore of Lake Tanganyika, was practiced by pre-Bantu peoples. This research adds to a growing body of studies indicating pre-Bantu communities in the southern part of Africa had knowledge of ironworking, pastoralism, and political organization before the arrival of Bantu speakers, and that previous notions of a Bantu "expansion" that packaged all these traits are oversimplified.*

The history of indigenous iron production in East and Central Africa goes back 2,500 years. Since its establishment, ironworking has remained a vital technological invention among African societies until very recently. The technology began to collapse in most places during the first quarter of the 20th century due in great part to competition from relatively cheap European metalware and scrap iron. The availability of both classes of iron increased tremendously following colonialism. Sometimes the colonial governments deliberately repressed indigenous technology to protect a market for European-made products (Brock and Brock 1963). In a few places, where European influence was minimal (mainly due to remoteness), indigenous iron production continued until very recently.

One such place is Ufipa in southwestern Tanzania, where regular iron production continued until the 1930s (Greig 1937; M. Wright 1982) and, under special request by government officials until the 1950s (Wembah-Rashid 1969; M. Wright 1982). During World War II and immediately after (mid- and late 1940s) there was a serious shortage of farm implements in Ufipa, especially imported hoes. To address this problem, the Sumbawanga District Commissioner lifted the ban on local iron production and requested former smelters to resume work. Many smelters did not turn up because they suspected that the request was a government trap to catch them. A few daring ones responded to the request. Among them was Stephano Malimbo who, apart from working in Ufipa, conducted a demonstration smelting at the Village Museum in Dar es Salaam in 1967 to commemorate the sixth anniversary of independence (Wembah-Rashid 1969).

Other locales where indigenous iron production persisted include central western Malawi, among the Tumbuka, where iron production continued until the 1930s (Killick 1990), and northwestern Tanzania, among the Barongo, where the production continued until the early 1950s (Schmidt 1996, 1997a).

The prolonged practice of indigenous ironworking in Ufipa induced me to conduct archaeological research there aimed at examining the development of this technology through time. The research project, conducted 1992–1993, concentrated in Nkansi District—a district that had been neglected by previous archaeologists. Four localities were chosen for intensive investigation: Kirando and Kala along the Lake Tanganyika shore, King'ombe on the Fipa escarpment, and Kalundi on the Fipa plateau (Fig. 5.1).

The research project yielded 75 archaeological and historical sites. Sixty-six sites had evidence of ironworking such as furnaces, slag, tuyeres, iron ore, and charcoal, and four were sources of iron ore. The remaining sites, together with some of the ironworking sites, had materials ranging from microlithic tools to daub, potsherds, and animal bones (for details, see Mapunda 1995a, 1995b).

Attribute and chemical analyses conducted on metallurgical materials have revealed that at least three ironworking technologies, varying in space or time or both, were practiced in Nkansi District. These include the *Katukutu* technology, dating to the 16th and 18th centuries AD and located along the shore and the Fipa escarpment; the *Malungu* technology, dating to the 19th and 20th centuries and located mainly on the escarpment and the Fipa plateau; and the Barongo-type technology, dating to the 19th century and located along the lakeshore (for spatial distribution of sites see Table 5.1).

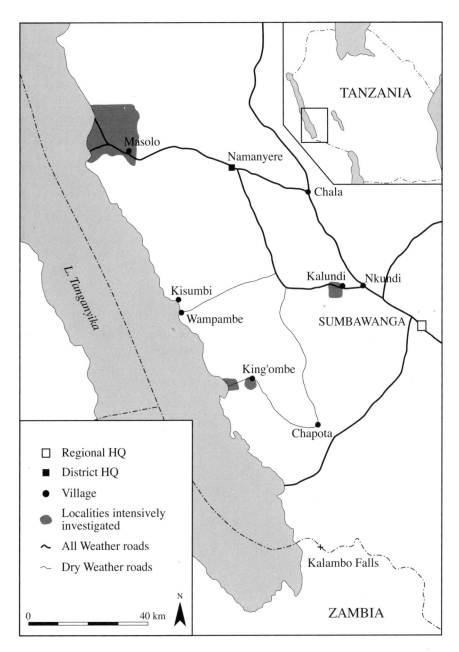

Fig. 5.1 Map of the Fipa area southeast of Lake Tanganyika.

Table 5.1 Distribution of Ironworking Sites by Geographical
Regions

Locality	Malungu	Katukutu	Barongo-type
Kirando (shore)	1	48	3
Kala (shore)	3	1	–
King'ombe (escarpment)	4	2	–
Kalundi (plateau)	4	–	–
Total	12	51	3

Both *Katukutu* and *Malungu* are terms that have been borrowed from
the Fipa language. *Malungu* has its root in *aMalungu* (singular *Icilungu*),
meaning "(tall) iron furnaces." *Katukutu* roots from *Katukutu*, a word for
"short" or "dwarf" (due to the size of such furnaces compared to *Malungu*).
"Barongo-type technology" is similar to that practiced by Barongo smelters
in Mwanza region, described by de Rosemond (1943) and Schmidt (1996,
1997a).

This chapter examines the three Fipa iron technologies with emphasis
on spatial and temporal distribution. In doing so, I attempt to reconstruct
the social history of Ufipa as based on iron technology as well as other cultural traits, especially pottery.

Fipa Technologies Compared

For a long time scholars interested in Fipa technological history
(Willis 1981; M. Wright 1982; Barndon 1992) reported only one type of
ironworking technology, namely the *Malungu* technology. This led to the
belief that this was the only ironworking technology practiced in Ufipa.
There are two reasons for this misinterpretation. First, previous
researchers concentrated only on the plateau, failing to look beyond the
conspicuous *Malungu* furnaces that are still visible on the landscape
there. Second, almost all previous researchers relied mainly on oral
accounts for information. Given the fact that *Malungu* technology continued to be practiced until the mid-20th century, Fipa traditions abound
with information pertaining to this technology. The *Malungu* technology
is therefore better documented than the other two. Important sources
include Wyckaert (1914), Wise (1958), M. Wright (1982, 1985), Killick
(1990), Barndon (1992), and Mapunda (1995a). The Barongo-type technology has been described in detail by only two authors, de Rosemond
(1943) and Schmidt (1997b). The *Katukutu* technology has been studied

exclusively by me (Mapunda 1995a).

A summary of selected variables used to compare and contrast the three technologies (*Katukutu*, *Malungu*, and Barongo-type) is presented in Table 5.2. The *Katukutu* and *Malungu* technologies match in nine variables (nos. 3, 5, 6, 8, 11, 16, 19, 20, and 21) or 41 percent; the *Katukutu* and Barongo-type technologies match in five variables (nos. 13, 15, 16, 20, and 21) or 23 percent; and *Malungu* and Barongo-type technologies match in seven variables (nos. 1, 4, 12, 16, 18, 20, and 22) or 32 percent.

Table 5.2 Selected Variables from the Three Technologies Found in Nkansi District

Variable	*Katukutu*	*Malungu*	Barongo-type
Furnace morphology	globular	truncated cone	truncated cone
Furnace height, cm	70–120	250–350	150–200
Construction materials	termite clay	termite clay	slabs from termite mound
Wall layering	present	absent	absent
Association with termitary	present	present	absent
Furnace reuse	present	present	absent
No. of tuyere ports	8	10	5
Palinyina (Rake hole)	present	present	absent
Tuyere length, cm	40–54	24–30	60–70
Tuyere diameter (external/internal), cm	4/2.5	7/2.5	6/3
No. of tuyeres per port	multiple (3)	multiple (3–4)	single
Tuyere reuse	present	absent	absent
Fuel trees	highly selective	less selective	highly selective
Slag amount	low	high	medium
Slag tapping	absent	present	absent
Slag reuse	present	present	present
Vizimba (charms at the furnace center)	pots and herbs	wood strips	hole
Ore type	magnetite, hematite	limonite, laterite	laterite?
Draft	natural	natural	forced
Distance from residence	away	away	away
Spatial distribution	lake shore and escarpment	plateau and escarpment	lake shore
Chronology	400–300 BP	10–20 BP	100–20 BP

Table 5.3 Refining and Smelting Furnaces by Geographical Region

Locality	*Malungu* Smelting Furnaces	*Malungu* Refining Furnaces	*Katukutu* Smelting Furnaces	Barongo-type Smelting Furnaces	Total
Kirando	1	–	186	3	190
Kala	1	5	2	–	8
King'ombe	12	26	30	–	68
Kalundi	18	3	–	–	21
Total	32	34	218	3	287

Spatial Distribution of Fipa Ironworking Technologies

Katukutu *Technology*

Katukutu technology is located strictly near Lake Tanganyika, along the shore and on the escarpment (Table 5.3). Local informants (hunters and honey collectors) report the occurrence of *Katukutu* furnaces as far north as the Rivers Ifume and Manda around Karema and as far south as northern Zambia. The informants also agree that the furnaces are located within 20 km of Lake Tanganyika.

David Killick reports some relics of ironworking technology in Malawi, over 300 km southeast of Ufipa, which may relate to the *Katukutu* technology. A good example is site LpLc-8, which he excavated (Killick 1990:195-197, 208-209). However, a detailed attribute comparison of the remains of the two places (southeast Lake Tanganyika and Malawi) needs to be established and studied before we can rule out the possibility of coincidence.

Malungu *Technology*

The *Malungu* is mainly a plateau technology, "arching from the Chisinga country on the plateau east of the Luapula river in Zambia, northward to Rukwa and Ukonongo in Tanzania, and then eastward and southward into Malawi and eastern Zambia" (M. Wright 1982:2). The technology is also reported from Unyiha, east of the Fipa plateau (Brock and Brock 1963), and from Utabwa, across Lake Tanganyika in Zaire and Zambia (Roberts 1993).

I also observed some evidence of this technology along the shore of Lake Tanganyika (Mapunda 1995a, 1995b). Two smelting furnaces (one at Kirando and the other at Kala) and five refining furnaces (all at Kala) were found (Table 5.3). According to historical and oral sources, the few *Malungu* furnaces found today along the shore were built by immigrants from the plateau. Shore dwellers in Nkansi District have been migrating up and down the Fipa plateau for years following the fluctuation of the lake. In the 1870s, for example, the lake was about 6 m above the present level (D.D.Y. 1957). But by the end of the 19th century the water level in Lake Tanganyika had decreased significantly, resulting in land reclamation including a large part of the Kirando plain (D.D.Y. 1957; Manyesha 1988). Consequently, a large number of people from the plateau immigrated into the shore area. These people relied largely on the plateau for iron and iron implements. Some of the newcomers, especially those who belonged to the iron smelting clans, tried to manufacture their own iron along the shore using the *Malungu* technology. This, unfortunately, did not work. Accounting for this phenomenon, the Reverend Manyesha says: "[B]efore the lake receded exposing this plain [Kirando] people lived on the plateau.... When they arrived in this land they tried to build 'MALUNGU' [iron smelting furnaces] for forging hoes, axes, and spears as they had been doing at their home, the Fipa plateau. But it seems there was no iron ore [bog ore?] in the ground as in the plateau. This work, therefore, did not live long" (Manyesha 1988:2).

My own research (Mapunda 1995a, 1995b) has shown that the technology was short lived not only because of lack of bog ore, as Manyesha argues, but also because of the influx of European metalware brought by missionaries. The *lilungu* (singular of *Malungu*) found at Kirando, is, therefore, from one of the trial smelts conducted by the immigrants.

A different account is given for the smelting furnace and its single associated *kintengwe* (a miniature refining furnace) found at Kala. Oral traditions hold that these were constructed around the end of the 19th century by smelters from Kitanda (west of King'ombe), a site 10 km to the east, following a request by the early missionaries who wanted to know how Fipa iron production was operated. The remaining *vintengwe* [plural of *kintengwe*] at Kala were constructed and used during the beginning of the 20th century by some immigrants from the Fipa plateau. Informants testify that these people used to go back to the plateau (to acquire resources, especially iron ore and wood) to smelt iron seasonally and then return bringing with them pre-refined blooms (iron smelted from ore in a solid state) to refine at Kala.

Barongo-type Technology

As Schmidt (1997a) observes, the Barongo ironworkers are not a tribe but are a functional group who share the same language or a work association with a common lexicon, *Kirongo*. The lexicon was shared by a variety of ethnic groups living west and southwest of Lake Victoria (mainly in Mwanza Region). So far, no site with Barongo-type technology has been reported south of Kirando. We can, therefore, tentatively say that the technology extended between Nkansi District (Rukwa Region) on the south and southern Lake Victoria (Mwanza Region) on the north.

Social History of Ufipa and the Neighboring Region

First Millennium AD

The linguistic evidence suggests that by the beginning of the first millennium AD the southeastern shore of Lake Tanganyika was already occupied by Mashariki Bantu speakers of the Mwika subgroup, makers of iron and pottery of the Chifumbaze complex (Ehret 1998). It should be noted that this linguistic date is not supported by archaeological findings from Kalambo Falls, a site with a long culture history spanning over 200,000 years to the present (Clark 1974). Clark (1974) observes that the cultural remains of the Early Iron Age population in the Kalambo basin are distinct from those of the present-day inhabitants, the Lungu, in both pottery types and other cultural materials. The Lungu culture is represented only in the uppermost level of the excavations. The lower levels, dating from about AD 400 to about AD 1000, contain the Kalambo tradition—a type of pottery related to both the Urewe Ware (dimple-based) from the interlacustrine region and the Mwabulambo and Gokomere traditions from Malawi and Zambia to the south.

The Early Iron Age components (AD 400–1000) at the Kalambo Falls sites have also yielded some metallurgical materials, including slag, tuyere fragments, hammerstones, an anvil, and iron tools and ornaments such as spears and arrowheads, tangs, arm or leg rings, and finger and toe rings. Furnaces have not been identified. It is clear from the slag and tuyere descriptions, however, that the ironworking technology practiced at Kalambo Falls during the Early Iron Age was different from the three technologies (*Katukutu*, *Malungu*, and Barongo-type) found north of Kalambo Falls.

Kalambo pottery has also been found at six sites at Kirando (Mapunda 1995a, 1995b). Stratigraphic examination at one of the sites (HvLk-58) reveals the Kalambo pottery at the lower levels (30–45 cm below datum). However, no contemporaneous furnaces or substantive slag or tuyere pieces have been found there. Does this mean that the makers of the Kalambo-type pottery in the first millenium AD at Kirando did not make iron? It is very likely they did make iron. The absence or dearth of metallurgical remains there is possibly due to continuous disturbance caused by repeated settlement, as well as the difficulties involved in identifying iron technologies based on pieces of slag and tuyeres found in secondary locations. In other words, it is much easier to identify a potsherd as to its general type or tradition (e.g., Kalambo) than to associate a small piece of tuyere or slag to a particular technology. This is because potsherds, especially rims, bear more diagnostic attributes such as decoration, rim form, temper, paste, burnishing, slip, and many others than do tuyeres or slag. For this reason I am tempted to believe that the slag and tuyere pieces found at site HvLk-58, where Kalambo pottery is also represented, relate to technology practiced by the makers of the Kalambo pottery. Unfortunately, they are too few and too fragmentary to warrant a definitive conclusion.

Other Early Iron Age activities revealed at the Kalambo sites include settlement evidence indicated by daub, grindstone fragments, burnishing stones, and pestle stones; trade is suggested by copper objects (a bracelet and a small, hollow, conical object made from thin copper sheet); and cattle (*Bos taurus*) domestication is indicated by bone (Clark 1974). My investigation at Kirando also revealed some daub, cattle bones, and a copper bead.

In sum, the ethnohistory of southeast Lake Tanganyika during the Classical Age is quite complex. This partly has to do with the lack of archaeological data to support linguistic postulations seemingly suggesting Bantu settlement in the area during the first millennium BC (Ehret 1998). Archaeological evidence points to the post–Classical Age as the beginning of settlement by the first animal herders and ironworkers—be they Bantu speakers or of other linguistic family—in the area. The complexity is exacerbated by the fact that the south Lake Tanganika region, encompassing the borderlands of Tanzania, Zambia, and the Democratic Republic of Congo seems to have been a divide between what Ehret calls the Kaskazi and Kusi Mashariki Bantu speakers. "Interestingly," Ehret remarks, "the societies that first carried the culture of the Later Classical Age into those lands [of predominantly Kusi Bantu] seem most probably to have been of Kaskazi rather than Kusi affiliation," as evidenced by the Muteteshi and Salumano cultures from central and southwestern Zambia, respectively (1998:234–35). Linguistically, the classical Kaskazi are represented by the modern-day Botatwe languages.

Archaeological and ethnographic evidence from Kalambo Falls, Kirando, and Ivuna suggests that the southwestern Tanzania region witnessed continuous population influxes throughout the last 1,600 years. The chronometric date from the Kalambo Falls sites for Early Iron Working and domestication is AD 400 (Clark 1974). The people, probably Bantu speakers, shared a similar culture up and down the southeastern shoreline. They made Kalambo pottery and also produced iron by a technology about which we know virtually nothing. They were also keeping cattle, as well as making or trading copper materials as early as AD 1000. They preferred to settle along the shore or perennial rivers. There is no doubt that this vast and variably resourceful land was occupied prior to the coming of the Bantu speakers. Detailed history of the previous occupants is not known, except the generalization of linguists that prior to the coming of Bantu-speaking people the larger part of subequatorial Africa was inhabited by southern Cushites (Ambrose 1982; Ehret 1998).

Second Millennium AD

Kalambo pottery (and perhaps metallurgical skills) continued to change through time. By AD 1000 a new pottery type became prevalent. The stratigraphic evidence shows that the transition was slow and probably an organic one. Subsequent pottery is referred to here as TIW (Triangular Incised Ware) because of its affinity to the TIW commonly found along the Indian Ocean littoral dating between the 7th and the 12th centuries AD (Chami 1994a). Kirando is the most distant site from the coast (about 900 km) so far recorded with TIW pottery (Mapunda 1995a). Some other interior sites (over 200 km from the coast) with authentic and probable TIW include Dakawa, east-central Tanzania (Håland 1993; Håland and Msuya 2000), Usambara, northeastern Tanzania (Soper 1967), Kilosa, northeastern Tanzania, Kandaga, north of Dodoma, central Tanzania (Chami 1994a), and Ruhuhu basin, southern Tanzania (Mapunda 1991).

Since TIW pottery is traditionally said to be a coastal (Indian Ocean) material culture (Horton 1984; Fawcett and LaViolette 1990), its discovery in the interior often raises questions, particularly with regard to cultural links with the coast. At present, two hypotheses can be used to account for this occurrence. First, as Chami (1994a) would argue, TIW developed organically from the Early Iron Age pottery (e.g., Kwale ware) along the coast (east-central Tanzania) around the middle of the 1st millennium AD and this knowledge, rather than the pots, spread to the other parts of eastern Africa. This pattern of spread is in line with the gradual transition observed at Kirando (site HvLk-58). The second hypothesis is similar to the first one in mode of spread, but differs in place of origin: it postulates that instead of originating along the coast the TIW originated in the interior (probably east of the great lakes region) and spread to the east. To test these hypotheses we need further research, especially in the interior.

The cultural stratigraphy both at Kirando and along the Indian Ocean littoral shows that the transition from Early Iron Age pottery to the TIW was gradual rather than abrupt. This seems to oppose the view that the spatial distribution of TIW pottery in eastern Africa was caused by population migration (Soper 1971b, 1982; Horton 1984). It is very likely that trade, both short distance and long distance, as well as inter-ethnic relations such as marriage, was the principal medium of transfer of TIW pottery in eastern Africa. This does not necessarily mean that pots per se were physically transported from place to place (e.g., as long-distance trade items). Rather, trade facilitated the spread of the knowledge of pot making. In other words, trade brought about inter-ethnic interaction resulting in the spatial transfer of the knowledge of pot making. Physical transportation of TIW pots over long distances was perhaps hindered by the large size of some of the pots and the fragility of clay pots in general.

The cultural stratigraphy at Kirando shows a sparse distribution of materials (Ivuna pottery) that date between the 12th and the 15th centuries, suggesting a low population density. Since the hydrologic history of the lake indicates that the 11th century was a period of high water level (Livingstone 1965; Haberyan and Hecky 1987; Scholz and Rosendahl 1988), we can hypothesize that at this time period the lakeshore dwellers migrated to the interior following the lake floods. As the lake receded in subsequent centuries, emigrants—including the present-day inhabitants, the Fipa in the north and the Lungu in the south—slowly reoccupied the shore, only to abandon it again, however briefly, in the 19th century for the same reason, lake floods (D.D.Y. 1957).

However, it is interesting to note that farther east, along the Lake Rukwa valley (Ivuna salt-working site), Fagan and Yellen (1968) report an abrupt appearance of a pottery component (Alpha) in the early 13th century. They note that "Component Alpha does not...belong to the channel-decorated pottery tradition, which is associated with the earliest Iron Age settlement of the northern parts of Zambia," and "the carbon dates from Ivuna indicate that the salt-working villages are slightly later than the closing stages of the Kalambo sequence" (1968:32). Since this pottery type (Component Alpha) occurs at Kirando above the TIW pottery, and if it is true (as hypothesized above) that some lakeshore dwellers migrated to the interior following the lake encroachment after the 11th century, it is very likely that Component Alpha was introduced to the interior (including the Lake Rukwa basin) by migrants from the southeastern shore of Lake Tanganyika. The pottery found above Component Alpha at Ivuna, called Component Beta, has some affinity with the pottery of the present-day inhabitants of the area, the Nyamwanga, Wanda, and Nyiha, who are believed to be the direct descendants of the makers of Component Beta (Fagan and Yellen 1968).

The period between 1550 and 1750 witnessed significant sociocultural changes in Nkansi District. The changes are associated with the introduction of the *Katukutu* ironworking technology and the related pottery (*Katukutu* tradition) along the shore of Lake Tanganyika. The abrupt appearance of full-fledged iron technology and a new pottery type indicates that a large-scale population influx took place during this time (16th–18th centuries) and that these newcomers brought with them *Katukutu* iron and pottery skills.

Who were these people and where did they come from? Oral traditions indicate that these people were the present inhabitants of this area: the Lungu south of Kala (including Kalambo Falls) and the Fipa north of Kala (including Kirando). According to Clark (1974), the genealogy of the Tafuna chiefdom on the lakeshore suggests that the Lungu oral traditions hold that Kalambo was initially inhabited by the Fipa. "If so," Clark argues, "it would seem that the Fipa must have entered the valley sometime after the eleventh century, perhaps in the sixteenth century, since up to the earlier date, if not later, it was occupied by the makers the Kalambo Falls Industry who, though most probably of Bantu Negroid stock, made a very different kind of pottery" (Clark 1974:1), namely, Kalambo tradition.

The genealogy of the Milansi kingdom of the Fipa indicates that the Fipa arrived in their present-day home (north of Kala and the Fipa plateau) around the mid-17th century (Willis 1968, 1976, 1981). Although so far no archaeological research has been conducted at the royal villages, evidence from the excavated sites along the shore (Mapunda 1995a) support Willis's genealogical reconstruction.

While the Lungu traditions claim that their present land was occupied by the Fipa prior to the 17th century (Clark 1974), the Fipa have two different accounts as to who was in Ufipa before their arrival. The first claims that the land was empty, while the second, which is more popular among them, claims that the land was inhabited by people of a small stature, called Mbonelakuti, "who often took to hiding when they came into contact with the Fipa." They also believe that the *Katukutu* technology was made by Mbonelakuti (or Batwa).

According to Vincent Kayanda (aged 79 or 80), interviewed at Kala on November 28, 1982, the Mbonelakuti legend is not unique to Nkansi District but is, instead, common among Bantu speakers in East and Central Africa (Clark 1950; Procter 1960; Rangeley 1963). These people are referred to differently in Bantu folklore. Their names include Mwandionerakuti (or some variation of that name such as Mwandionerapati, Amambonela, or Mbonelakudene), Akafula, Batwa, Mbolela pano, Utunuta mafumo, Utunkula mafesa, etc. (Clark 1950; Rangely 1963). Although different names are used, all Bantu traditions agree that these "were little people, hardly reaching to the waist of a man [Bantu person?], and they were very touchy about their small stature" (Rangeley 1963:37).

The name derives from their stature. As Rangeley further reports:

> If a person met one of them, the little man would come close and ask "mwandionerapati?" or "mwandionerakuti?"—"where did you see me?" If the answer was given "I saw you a long, long way off" the little man was satisfied, because it showed that he was a big person capable of being seen a long way off, but if the reply was given "I saw you close by," woe betide the man, for the little Mwandionerakuti would shoot him in the stomach with their poisoned arrows. (1963:37)

In regard to ironworking there are two opposing views. Some scholars (e.g., van der Merwe 1980; Juwayeyi, pers. comm.) hold that the Mbonelakuti were Stone Age people and had no knowledge of ironworking. Van der Merwe, for example, writes:

> Before the advent of Iron Age, eastern and southern Africa was populated by sparsely distributed bands of Stone Age hunter-gatherers. Modern surviving remnants of these peoples can be found among the Bushmen [San?] of Botswana and the Kalahari desert....During the second half of the 1st millennium A.D. and during the Later Iron Age which follows, Iron Age populations increased progressively in the southern subcontinent. The area involved is vast and there was little competition against these metal-equipped farmers and pastoralists. The Stone Age inhabitants were absorbed through client relationships and marriage, or compressed toward the southwestern tip of Africa. (1980:480, 482)

Other scholars, including Clark (1950) and Rangeley (1963), hold that some Mbonelakuti knew how to make iron. Insisting on their knowledge of ironworking, Rangeley writes: "What clearly and sharply distinguished them [Mbonelakuti] from the Bushmen [San] was their knowledge and use of iron, and the entire lack of stone implements. Their arrows were made either of wood with no more than a fire-hardened point or were tipped with iron. They had a characteristic long heavily barbed iron head without the usual flattening and broadening, which were either arrow heads or spear heads" (1963:38).

I believe that some of the Mbonelakuti communities had the knowledge of ironworking. In addition to the claims by some Bantu speakers, such as Fipa, Lungu, Bemba, Cewa, and others, that the Mbonelakuti made iron, linguistic and archaeological studies in southern and southwestern Africa support this line of thought. New studies (Ehret 1982; Denbow 1990; Kiyaga-Mulindwa 1993) challenge the traditional claim that iron technology in southern Africa was recent.

It is now evident that iron technology, pastoralism, and political organization date to the 4th century AD or probably earlier in that area (Kiyaga-Mulindwa 1993). This offers two possible alternatives: First, Bantu-speaking people migrated into southern Africa much earlier than initially thought. This alternative, Kiyaga-Mulindwa notes, does not tally with the prevalent explanation of the spread of Bantu-speaking people in the region. This new evidence replaces the two-streams theory in favor of multiple streams over a broad front (Kiyaga-Mulindwa 1993:389).

The second alternative is that the pre-Bantu communities (including Mbonelakuti) had the knowledge of ironworking, pastoralism, and political organization before the arrival of Bantu speakers (Ehret 1982; Denbow 1990).

Does this therefore suggest that the *Katukutu* technology found on the southeastern shore of Lake Tanganyika is a product of the Mbonelakuti? It is difficult to make a definitive statement at this time. Although oral traditions attribute the *Katukutu* technology to the Mbonelakuti, the archaeological evidence seems to contradict that claim. For example, the chronometric dates of the *Katukutu* technology (16th–18th centuries) comply with the genealogical dates which point to the arrival of the Fipa and Lungu from Uluba. Additionally, a comparative analysis of some important technological attributes (Table 5.2) between *Katukutu* and *Malungu* technologies indicates that the two technologies are historically related: the *Malungu* technology very likely evolved from *Katukutu* technology. This also suggests that the smelters of the two technologies may have been ethnically related. Since we know that the *Malungu* technology was practiced by Fipa people, it is highly probable that the *Katukutu* technology was also practiced by them.

Who practiced the Barongo-type technology in Ufipa? The oral traditions are not specific on this matter. There are accounts, however, of individual smelters who immigrated from the north around the beginning of the 20th century. For example, one informant (Elias Mwami), who lives in Kirando, claims that his grandfather, Mzee Makangila, was an iron smelter who had migrated from Ugogo (Dodoma Region). When he arrived in Ufipa, Makangila settled at Ntunchi, on the plateau, where he conducted one smelting experiment with a low-shaft, Gogo furnace. When asked why Makangila did not continue with his work, Mwami answered readily, "his 'dawa' [medicine] was not as powerful as those of the Fipa."

Although Makangila did not come from Mwanza Region (the center of the Barongo technology), his case shows the possibility of individual Barongo smelters immigrating into Kirando from the north and experimenting with their home technology there. This would not be unusual, because immigrants (Sukuma herders and farmers) from Mwanza and Shinyanga Regions to the north continue to immigrate into Nkansi District to the present day.

Conclusion

This chapter has presented a technological and social history of Nkansi District, in particular, and southwestern Tanzania, in general, from the Early Iron Age to the present, along with noting several gaps that call for further work. For example, researchers have not been able to establish with certainty the ethnic identity of those who occupied Fipaland prior to today's inhabitants. Although circumstantial evidence seems to suggest that the predecessors were ancient Fipa, the Mbonelakuti hypothesis cannot be ruled out unless direct evidence, such as skeletal remains or DNA traces, is found. Meanwhile, collecting more materials (other than technological) can help to tell more about the people with whom we are dealing.

Second, we also know that the period between the 16th and 18th centuries witnessed major population movements in the corridor. The source and causes of these movements are only known through oral traditions. We need, for example, to trace the alleged routes back to Lubaland, Tabwaland, and Bembaland to verify these oral accounts.

Third, excavations need to be conducted at the royal villages of the Fipa and Lungu chiefdoms aimed at directly verifying the oral traditions on the arrival of the two peoples in this area. And fourth, although local people claim to have seen the *Katukutu* furnaces as far south as northern Zambia, we are not sure of their chronology. We need archaeological research that will yield materials to confirm that the technology is the same. We also need to obtain datable materials that will provide a chronological sequence for the two regions.

Acknowledgments

The research in Ufipa (Fipaland) was conducted in partial fulfillment of my doctoral degree. My Ph.D. studies were supported by a scholarship from the Ford Foundation, and this research was made possible by grants from the Ford Foundation, NORAD, Sigma Xi, and the University of Dar es Salaam.

6

Early Ironworking Communities on the East African Coast: Excavations at Kivinja, Tanzania

Felix Chami

This chapter discusses excavations at Kivinja on the central Tanzanian coast and their implications for understanding Early Iron Age inhabitants of the East African coast. This site is the first Early Iron Working (EIW) site to be found on the East African coast and one of the earliest to document extra-African trade relationships. Evidence of trade at this site strongly challenges long-held assumptions that non-African colonists founded complex cities of the Late Iron Age. Rather, these cities developed from indigenous origins.

The excavations at the site of Kivinja on the Tanzanian coast are significant for East African Iron Age archaeology since this site, along with two others—the Limbo site (Chami 1992) and the Kwale Island site (Chami and Msemwa 1997a, 1997b)—provides the first evidence of the Early Iron Age cultures that existed from AD 1 to 500 on the East African coast. Prior to the discovery and excavation of these sites, only Late Iron Working (LIW) sites with standing ruins were known. All three of these sites contain beveled and fluted pottery, which is associated with farming peoples.

Until 1999, Kivinja and other sites contained the earliest-known remains of foreign trade goods, including glass, beads, pottery, and Roman beads dated between the last century BC and the 5th century AD (Chami 1999).

Since then several Late Stone Age/Neolithic sites have been found on the island of Zanzibar and Mafia, which have trade goods dating back to the 8th century BC (see Chami 2002b). These numerous EIW sites on the islands, littoral, and hinterland of the central Tanzanian coast paint a picture of a culture that shared its pottery style with inland groups but was also in trade contact with the Roman and the Near Eastern worlds. These sites confirm the coastal city of Rhapta, mentioned by the Romans as a trading partner (Casson 1989). The evidence of very early trade contacts on the part of indigenous Africans with hinterland origins, or at least connections, has profound implications. To understand them, we must place the finds in the context of the history of East African coastal archaeology.

Archaeological Background

The archaeology of the East African coast began with the work of Kirkman (1964) at Gedi and of Chittick (1962) at Mafia and Kilwa. Their interpretations of these sites vindicated long-held speculations that a Persian and Arabian empire had existed on the east coast of Africa from the 9th to the 15th centuries AD, when Islamic groups were historically known visitors to the East African coast. Chittick (1975b) argues that 9th-century Arab immigrants founded the coastal towns and established an Islamic culture there. Chittick was the doyen of East African coastal archaeology until his death in the early 1980s. In his many archaeological works, especially that on Manda (Chittick 1984), he argued firmly that Africans played no part in coastal civilization. Arab immigrants, whose cultural and economic relationships were with the Middle East rather than with Africa, built the Swahili towns. Black Africans were hinterland peoples who arrived on the coast from the Congo forest much later in time (Oliver 1965).

Soon, however, this theory became difficult to reconcile with accumulating data, in particular with EIW coastal sites, such as Usambara (Soper 1967) and Upper Tana (Phillipson 1979), that contained pottery styles similar to those of the interior. These sites yielded EIW and Triangular Incised Ware (TIW) pottery, which is associated with interior early farming villages of East Africa. Because these sites did not fit with the non-African origin of the coastal town builders, they were interpreted as belonging to a cultural group distinct from the coastal town inhabitants.

Challenges to this interpretation arose when, in the early 1980s, archaeologists consistently observed, in the lowest levels of excavations at the sites like Unguja Ukuu, EIW pottery similar to that of the hinterland (Chami 1994a). Linguists in particular (Nurse and Spear 1985) corroborated these challenges, pointing out that Swahili speakers of the coastal littoral were related to Early Bantu speakers of the coast. In contradiction, archaeologists suggested that Cushitic pastoralists, not Arabs, had migrated from southern Somalia to found early Swahili coastal sites (see Horton 1987; Abungu 1989). Cushites were also thought to have established trade contact with Greco-Romans (Horton 1990; Sutton 1990).

In the early 1990s, Chami (1994a) and others at the University of Dar-es-Salaam (Schmidt et al. 1992) found numerous EIW and TIW sites on the littoral and hinterland of the central coast of Tanzania. The study of these sites, which were dated to the pre-Islamic period (before the 9th century AD), suggested their occupants had cultural affinities with EIW Bantu speakers (Chami 1994a). In all cases, an EIW Bantu tradition, including Kwale and related pottery wares, was followed by occupations including TIW pottery. Numerous features, including a gradual transition between the two wares and continuity in associated finds, argue for cultural continuity from one tradition to the next. Remains of imported goods in both EIW and TIW horizons indicate early trade contact. Below, I present a detailed report from one such site, Kivinja.

Site Survey

The Kivinja site (Fig. 6.1) was found by Paul Msemwa of the National Museum, Meno Welling, a Dutch student at the University of Dar-es-Salaam, and myself, as part of a major coastal archaeological survey sponsored by the Swedish Agency for Research and Cooperation (SAREC) through Uppsala University. Paul Msemwa and I intended to find ancient sites near the Rufiji Delta that could illuminate ancient cultural dynamics on the coast and relate them to cultural environment, human adaptation to deltaic resources, and cultural change.

The Kivinja site extends about 3 km along the coast and inland for 1 km. EIW cultural materials were seen across the surface in several levels of occupation (Fig. 6.2). The site was excavated in September 1995 and November 1996. The major aim of the excavations was to understand the cultural sequence of the site, its chronology, and its history of cultural contacts. Excavating this first of the sites in the Rufiji Delta area was expected to contribute to understanding ancient human exploitation and environmental impacts in the region.

The First Excavation Season

During the first excavation season, five trenches were dug. Trowels and hoes were used for the first four spits where the sediments were compact sands and clays. For most spits, arbitrary levels of 10 cm were used. Trench

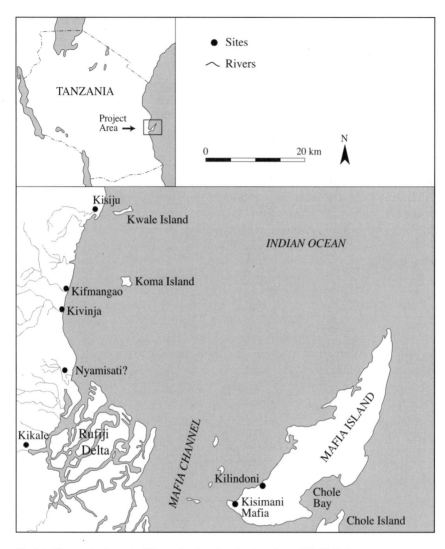

Fig. 6.1 The central coast of Tanzania, showing the location of Rufiji Delta.

1 (Table 6.1) was 2 × 2 m in size and was located near the old shore close to the northern limit of the pottery surface scatter, where it was particularly dense (Fig. 6.2). The first two levels of trench 1 had 3 glass beads and 61 potsherds in the post-16th-century AD occupation. The first 10 EIW Kwale Ware sherds were found at about 30 cm. This level included only EIW cultural materials and two fragments of a pilled-off glaze of early green and blue ware, slag, 4 marine shells (*Terabralia palustria*), and fragments of gum ara-

bic. The major layer of Kwale Ware cultural occupation was at 40 to 50 cm. This level and that below it are dated to AD 431–598 (see Chami and Msemwa 1997b). The level below these (60–70 cm) was sterile. The soils of this trench were mostly sandy clays. They changed color from the humus of the first 20 cm to grayish-brown in the next 20 cm to pale brown between 40 and 70 cm.

Trench 2, about 100 m west of trench 1 and 1 × 2 m in size, yielded a similar sequence to trench 1 (Fig. 6.2). In the main EIW layers, green and blue glass fragments were found, some with many spaces of bubble (indicating great antiquity), and green-blue glazed fragments of ware with white-millinary paste. In the third pit, 100 m west of trench 2, the cultural sequence was different. The first level (0–20 cm) also yielded post-16th-century AD materials, but from 20 to 40 cm the pottery was completely plain (termed "Plain Ware" [PW]; see Chami 1998). The pottery from 40 to 60 cm was in the TIW tradition, and associated with a hearth, green-blue glazed pottery, slag, and an unshaped piece of lead. Trenches 4 and 5 (1 × 1 m in size and at the far western and far southwestern areas of the site) and trench 6 also had a sequence of PW above TIW potsherds, but their cultural materials were only found above 40 cm.

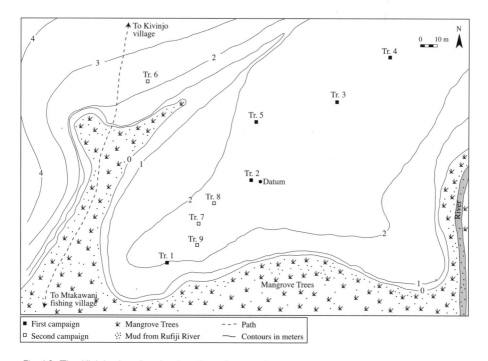

Fig. 6.2 The Kivinja site, showing location of excavations.

Table 6.1 Artifacts Excavated from Kivinja (First Season of Excavation in Trenches 1–5; Second Season of Excavation in Trenches 6–9)

Trench	Depth	EIW	TIW	PW	17th c. ware	Glass	Beads	Slag	Lead	Shell	Imported pottery
1	0–20	10									
	20–30	774									
	30–40	1429			61			3		4	2
	40–50	378		3	126			1		34	
	50–60							1		13	
2	0–10				12						
	10–20				16						
	20–30				3						
	30–40	42									
	40–50	66			1	5					
	50–60	53				2					
	60–70	15									
3	0–20		125	90						14	
	20–40		33							7	
	40–60									1	
4	0–20		84	41						4	
	20–40						1		1		
	40–60										
5	0–20		55	10							
	20–40		8								
	40–60										
6	0–20	121									
	20–50			63							
	50–70			348							
7	40–50	94	61				1				
	50–60	241	174			2	2			1	
	60–70	22				1	2				
	70–80										
8	40–50	1	87			1					
	50–60	19	23					1			
	60–70										
9	40–50		15								
	50–60		29								
	60–70	36						1			
	70–80	6									
Total		3327	695	562	308	9	11	6	1	2	43

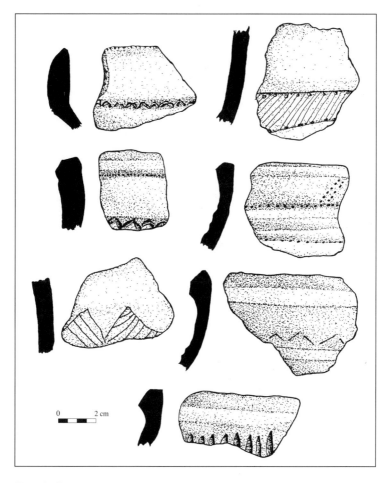

Fig. 6.3 Early Iron Working Kwale pottery from Kivinjia.

The Second Excavation Season

Surprisingly, trenches 6 through 9 yielded a different cultural sequence. At trench 6, for example, in the southern part of the site, a thick occupation of PW was found at 0 to 50 cm.

From 50 to 70 cm, an EIW Kwale Ware occupation was found. Trenches 7, 8, and 9 were located near trenches 1 and 2, and like them they included EIW sherds in association with other artifacts, including bead grinders, a lead object with a hole in it, glass fragments, and milky paste sherds, with easily flaking glazes. Some EIW pottery is illustrated in Figs. 6.3 and 6.4.

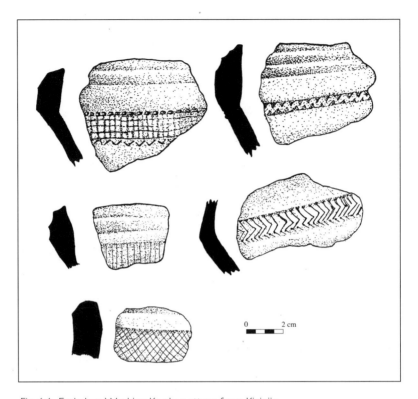

Fig. 6.4 Early Iron Working Kwale pottery from Kivinjia.

A History of Occupation at Kivinja

The Kivinja site was on the seashore during most of the period it was occupied. Over the period of human settlement here, silt from the Rufiji River aggraded in the site area. By AD 1000, at the end of PW tradition occupation, the site was completely inaccessible from the ocean. Makers of four cultural traditions occupied the site. The earliest occupants made Kwale Ware pottery, which appears at 60 to 70 cm in trenches 2, 6, 7, and 9 and at 40 to 60 cm in trenches 1 and 3. Two charcoal samples from the EIW occupation in trench 1 yielded radiocarbon dates of between the 4th and 6th centuries AD, similar to other Kwale Ware dates in East Africa (Table 6.2). The next ceramic tradition at the site is the TIW tradition, found between 40 and 60 cm in trenches 3, 4, 5, 7, 8, and 9. The PW tradition and post-16th-century AD traditions follow in most of the trenches.

Different patterns of sediment aggradation across the site area, or different occupation patterns, may explain the differences in cultural sequences

Table 6.2 Radiocarbon Dates from the Kivinjia Site

Trench	Depth	Lab Number	Radiocarbon Years BP	Calibrated Age AD
1	50–60	Ua–10931	1395 ± 70	598 ± 70
1	40–50	Ua–10932	1515 ± 65	431 ± 65
2	50–60	Ua–10933	1110 ± 65	783 ± 65
3	30–40	Ua–10934	99.8 ± .8	Modern

in the excavated trenches. The EIW culture was the tradition that was most widely distributed over the site; our test trenches indicate that almost all of the 3 × 1 km extent of the site includes an EIW component hinterland. The other traditions occur over smaller areas of the site; these may have been smaller settlements. Also, some areas of the site may have been disturbed by post-depositional processes, especially the area around trenches 2, 3, and 8. For instance, charcoal from trench 2 associated with an EIW occupation was radiocarbon-dated to AD 783, a date more commonly associated with TIW (see Table 6.2). Charcoal from trench 3's TIW hearth feature yielded a modern date of 99.8 years (Table 6.2). In trench 8, EIW sherds were found in the same levels with TIW sherds, which is highly unusual.

When excavated, Kivinja was the first EIW Kwale Ware site to include imported ceramics. The EIW and TIW cultural horizons have remains of imported glazed ceramics and glass wares. Although the thin green/blue glass is similar to that found in other TIW sites (Chami 1994a), another type of thicker, more greenish glass is found with EIW levels at Kivinja. Trenches 1, 2, and 7 contain blue-green pottery, which Chittick (1984) identified as Sassanid Islamic. Another sherd with a milk paste has a thinner, glassy glaze easily pilling from the paste. The glaze is also milky white but with a bluish splash.

Discussion

By 1996, the Kivinja site was the first-known near-shore Kwale Ware occurrence, and is one of the first evidences of EIW occupation of the littoral of the East African coast. Other EIW sites are Ziweziwe near Kisiju (Chami and Kessy 1995), Kwale Island (Chami and Msemwa 1997a), Koma, and Mafia Island (Chami and Msemwa 1997b). EIW potsherds are also found in the lowest levels of Unguja Ukuu, the LIW site on Zanzibar Island (Chami 1994a). The TIW pottery at Kivinja is also the first found near the shore between Dar-es-Salaam and Kilwa; it shows cultural links between the Rufiji

Delta on the coast and hinterland TIW sites like Misasa (Chami 1994a) and other TIW sites in the hinterland of the Rufiji (Chami and Mapunda 1997).

The Rufiji site and other early Tanzanian coast sites clarify the culture-historical sequence on the East African coast. They show that TIW follows EIW and that the former was derived from the latter, contra Horton (1990) and Sutton (1994/95), who reverse the temporal relationship of these two wares. EIW Limbo tradition pottery is earlier: on the coast it dates from the 1st century BC to the 3rd century AD. Succeeding Kwale sites date to between the 3rd and 5th centuries AD and are followed by another EIW Mwangia tradition of the 6th century AD (see Chami 1998). At Nkukutu-Kibiti, the EIW-TIW sequence is preceded by Later Stone Age microlithic stone tools (Chami and Mapunda 1997).

The presence of an 11th-century PW culture on the coast is document-ed at several sites (Chami and Msemwa 1997a). The mainland communities of this period, as opposed to the island communities, were poverty stricken, being small village sites without imported goods. By contrast, coastal sites of this period were embarking on a period of increasing wealth through partic-ipation in trade, documented at sites like Kilwa, Kisimani, Mafia, and Kwale Island (Chittick 1974; Chami and Msemwa 1997a). This tradition is firmly dated to the 11th to the 13th centuries AD (Chami 1994a; Chami and Msemwa 1997a). This critical period of state formation deserves more atten-tion than it has received to date (see Chami 2002a).

Perhaps most importantly, Kivinja and Nkukutu-Kibiti are the first sites to yield imports associated with EIW cultural materials, dating from the 1st through 6th centuries AD. One of the Roman beads is of gold/silver-in-glass made at Rhodes in the Mediterranean (Chami 1999). Some of the glass from Kivinja is of Syrian origin in the 6th century AD. A Roman pottery was also found in the same context. Other early imports are known on the coast of East Africa, but they are found in later, 6th- to 7th-century contexts and asso-ciated with TIW cultural materials at Kiwangwa, Misasa, and Unguja Ukuu (Chami 1994a; Juma 1996). We now know that the trade good remains from the EIW sites are not the earliest-known evidence of trade goods reaching the Azanian coast (see Chami 2002b).

EIW ancient trade objects on the East African coast corroborate the *Periplus of the Erythrean Sea* and other Greco-Roman documents by Ptolemy (Freeman-Grenville 1975) and Pliny (J. Miller 1969). The documents show a trade connection between the coast of East Africa and the Greek and Roman worlds. Pliny indicates that the connection extended to southeast Asia. The emporium of Rhapta was a central trade entrepot in East Africa. A debate has been simmering on where the emporium of Rhapta was located (Kirwan 1986; Casson 1989; Horton 1990; Chami 1994a). Its exact location would enable scholars to assess the southern limit of Greco-Roman trade contacts. The Kivinja site finds show that trade contact reached the Rufiji

Delta, where EIW Bantu speakers lived. Evidence of trade at this site strongly challenges long-held assumptions that non-African colonists founded the complex cities of the Late Iron Age (Chittick 1984). These sites provide evidence that these cities developed from indigenous origins; Indian Ocean trade has a more than thousand-year history on the coast.

Kivinja has provided the earliest-known EIW cultural material on the littoral of East Africa. Most of it remains unexcavated, and much of the excavated material has yet to be analyzed. After clarifying the culture history of the Tanzanian coast, I hope to conduct more work with this and other similar sites, to delve more deeply into the lifeways of inhabitants of these poorly understood settlements.

7

Ironworking on the Swahili Coast of Kenya

Chapurukha M. Kusimba and David Killick

Few archaeologists have considered the possibility that control of local craft production and distribution may have been important in the development of sociopolitical complexity on the Iron Age Swahili Coast. Metallographic analysis of iron artifacts from Swahili sites reveals important information regarding the variety of ironworking techniques practiced. Swahili ironworkers were capable of producing high-carbon steel and even cast iron in their bloomeries. Artifacts of crucible steel from Galu, an iron forging site on the Kenya coast, are the first crucible steel samples known from sub-Saharan Africa and may have been locally produced. If iron formed a major commodity of Indian Ocean trade it may have crossed the ocean in many directions at different manufacturing stages—as bloom or finished artifacts. Coastal iron technology and its trade may have played a key role in Indian Ocean trade and social complexity among the Swahili.

This chapter considers the role of ironworking technology in Iron Age communities of the East African coast, where standing stone ruins attest to the development of city-states during the 12th–16th centuries AD. The city-states are attributed to Swahili-speaking peoples and were found along the coasts of Somalia, Kenya, Tanzania, Mozambique, Madagascar, and the Comoros (Sinclair 1991, 1993). The region has many exploitable resources that have attracted settlement by different peoples and subsistence economies throughout time.

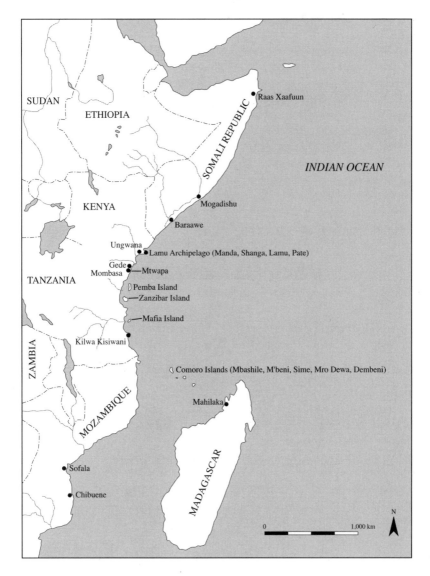

Fig. 7.1 Archaeological sites along the Swahili Coast.

A large number of archaeological sites along the Swahili Coast possess standing ruins of coral and coral rag (Fig. 7.1). Many sites also contain mosques, the earliest of which has been dated to the 9th century AD (Horton 1996, 1997; C. Kusimba 1997). Written sources have documented contact between East Africa, the Mediterranean, the Near East, and South Asia from the 1st century AD (Casson 1989; Chami, Chapter 6 this volume; Chami and Msemwa 1997b). Contact between coast peoples and Near Easterners and Indians was largely commercial in nature, yet such interactions stimulated cultural and technical communication between these societies. Trade resulted in the accumulation of wealth and the development of hierarchy (Ehrenreich 1995) among previously egalitarian communities. Friendships, alliances, and other relationships necessary to foster peaceful trade and exchange networks may also have provided opportunities for biocultural and technological transfers (e.g., Gibbons 1997:535-536).

Even before the coast's entry in the international maritime trade network in the Red Sea, Persian Gulf, and Indian Ocean, the Swahili peoples had developed trading partnerships with each other and traded up river and overland with hinterland peoples. For example, 10th-century Malindi north of Mombasa had large-scale iron smelting and forging industries and was the main supplier of most iron needed by hinterland societies. Kilwa and Sofala, south of Mombasa, supplied most of the textiles, beads, and iron tools to interior societies, which provided the coastal towns with ivory, gold, copper, and cereals (C. Kusimba 1993, 1999a, 1999b).

The relationships between the coastal settlements and the interior may have been relatively egalitarian, including clientship, trade partnerships, debt patronage, fictive or real kinship, friendships, and gift exchange (Nicholls 1971:42, 56). The coastal towns offered finished manufactured goods in exchange for hinterland products, inducing the hinterland to enter into the regional economy voluntarily. Coastal settlements had large, stable populations drawn from different communities including hinterland traders and foreign merchants, and a lucrative economy that attracted and supported settlement of a skilled clientele. In order to get the maximum profit from trade, these settlements sought to produce as many goods as possible themselves, through techniques which hinterland peoples could not duplicate.

Excavated sites have yielded evidence of manufacturing activities, possibly in excess of local needs (Abungu 1990; Chittick 1974, 1984; Horton 1996; C. Kusimba 1996a; Mutoro 1979; T. Wilson 1982). Thus some Swahili towns had specialized craftspeople to make finished items (Bakari 1981:159). Coastal-produced items, including marine shells and shell beads recovered in Central and West Africa as far away as Shumlaka in Cameroon, attest to the nature of exchange networks in Africa which included both direct trade and "down the line exchange" (Mapunda 1995a; Pikirayi 1993; Maret, pers. comm. 1997).

Interregional interactions made possible the development of systems of networking, exchanging, processing, and sharing of resources that made East Africa a viable trading partner with Near Eastern and South Asian polities. Involvement in international maritime trade AD 800-1500 created possibilities for accumulation of wealth by the coastal elites, possibly those already involved in trade and craft production (Horton 1997; C. Kusimba 1997). This trade intensified both interregional exchange and interpolity rivalry and encouraged local production of food surplus as well as craft specialization (C. Kusimba 1996a). Ivory, rhinoceros horns, iron, timber, furniture, ambergris, leopard skins, turtle shell, gold, and slaves were the main exports from East Africa to the Persian Gulf, India, and China (Lewicki 1969; Verin 1986:57; Ylvisaker 1982). Textiles, ceramics, and beads were primary trade imports to East Africa (Chittick 1977a).

Although it is now widely recognized that coastal Swahili culture is largely an indigenous phenomenon, few studies have focused specifically on types and quality of trade items that were made and exchanged in this trade. Precious little is known about the role local craft production played in the early development of Swahili settlements (Chami 1988; C. Kusimba 1996b; Kusimba, Killick, and Creswell 1994; Prins 1961). We report in this chapter results of an archaeometallurgical study carried out on a group of iron artifacts from Swahili sites (Table 7.1).

The Chronological Context of Ironworking

Pioneer archaeologists traditionally relied on imported ceramics and numismatics for determining the chronology of Swahili sites (Kirkman 1974:87). Archaeologists currently working on the East African coast are showing greater faith in chronology determined by radiocarbon dating (Chami 1994b; Sinclair 1991). The data in Table 7.2 alert us to the possibility that some of the settlement on the Kenyan and Tanzanian coast may predate the Late Ironworking Period (Chami 1994b; Chami and Msemwa 1997b; Fawcett and LaViolette 1990; C. Kusimba 1993) and thus may span the time of the *Periplus of the Erythrean Sea* (Casson 1989). The implication of this

Table 7.1 Analyzed Metallurgical Samples from Swahili Archaeological Sites
Note: From Kusimba, Killick, and Creswell 1994.

	Galu	Mtwapa	Mwana	Shanga	Ungwana	Total
Sample Type						
Iron	54	11	4	21	78	168
Copper	0	0	1	0	5	6
Lead	0	0	0	0	1	1
Brass	0	0	0	0	5	5
Total	54	11	5	21	89	180

Table 7.2 Radiocarbon Dates Reported at Swahili Archaeological Sites

Site	Sample No.	Radiocarbon Years BP	Calibrated	Reference
Kilwa	SR-76	1060±110		Chittick 1974:29
Kilwa	SR-77	1370±110	AD 630	Chittick 1974:29
Kilwa	SR-78	1020±100	AD 930	Chittick 1967:49
Kilwa	GX-0398	1825±110	AD 125	Chittick 1974:29
Manda	N-338	1170±110	AD 780	Chittick 1967:49
Manda	N-339	1480±110	AD 470	Chittick 1984:49
Manda	N-1066	730–760±100		Chittick 1984:67
Shanga	SA-0590		AD 965±35	Sinclair 1991:214
Shanga	SA-0616		AD 890±45	Sinclair 1991:214
Shanga	SA-0659		AD 850±50	Sinclair 1991:214
Shanga	SA-1512		AD 780±45	Sinclair 1991:214
Shanga	SA-1647		AD 770±40	Sinclair 1991:215
Shanga	SA-1892		AD 715±35	Sinclair 1991:215
Ungwana	TO-3889	870±100	AD 990–1300	C. Kusimba 1993:180
Ungwana	TO-3890	530±90	AD 990–1300	C. Kusimba 1993:180
Ungwana	TO-3891	1210±140	AD 595–1030	C. Kusimba 1993:180
Ungwana	TO-3892	1360±650	AD 785–1785	C. Kusimba 1993:180
Galu	TO-3893	1400±240	AD 125–1050	C. Kusimba 1993:180
Galu	TO-3894	740±70	AD 1170–1400	C. Kusimba 1993:180
Galu	TO-3895	1300±70	AD 630–890	C. Kusimba 1993:180
Misasa	UA-2593	1975±50	98 BC–AD 68	Chami 1994:91
Misasa	UA-2594	1725±45	AD 239–395	Chami 1994:91
Misasa	UA-2595	1295±55	AD 659–775	Chami 1994:91
Misasa	UA-2597	1485±50	AD 536–639	Chami 1994:91
Mpiji	UA-2592	1340±60	AD 642–765	Chami 1994:91
Mpiji	UA-2087	1420±60	AD 576–658	Chami 1994:91
Mpiji	UA-2088	1390±80	AD 582–678	Chami 1994:91
Kiwangwa	UA-2598	1405±55	AD 599–662	Chami 1994:91
Kiwangwa	UA-2599	1275±45	AD 671–797	Chami 1994:91
Kiwangwa	UA-2097	1440±60	AD 556–650	Chami 1994:91
Kiwangwa	UA-2098	1250±60	AD 676–863	Chami 1994:91
Masuguru	UA-2095	1290±60	AD 660–797	Chami 1994:91
Masuguru	UA-2096	1430±60	AD 562–654	Chami 1994:91
Kaole	UA-2092	1270±60	AD 667–801	Chami 1994:91
Kaole	UA-2093	1130±60	AD 781–984	Chami 1994:91
Kaole	UA-2094	720±60	AD 1258–1285	Chami 1994:91
Changwehela	UA-2089	870±50	AD 1042–1221	Chami 1994:91
Changwehela	UA-2090	650±60	AD 1279–1391	Chami 1994:91
KI/MA 1	24619	2470±70	AD 600±100	Schmidt et al. 1992:57
KI/MA 1	24620	2910±70	AD 1115±126	Schmidt et al. 1992:57
KI/MA 1	24621	1940±60	AD 35±95	Schmidt et al. 1992:57
KI/MA 6	24622	1030±50	AD 1020±70	Schmidt et al. 1992:57
KI/NY 9	24623	1700±60	AD 265±95	Schmidt et al. 1992:57
KI/NY 9	24624	1980±90	AD 20±105	Schmidt et al. 1992:58
KI/NY 9	24625	1610±60	AD 415±85	Schmidt et al. 1992:58
KI/NY 9	24626	1970±60	AD 25±95	Schmidt et al. 1992:58
KI/NY	26264		AD 20±60	Sinclair 1991:215

dating is that before the rise of urbanism, coastal peoples traded with the ancient merchants mentioned in the *Periplus* (Casson 1989). According to the author of the *Periplus*, East Africans imported metal goods like spears, axes, knives, and awls manufactured in Muza (near present-day Aden). We consider technological innovation and transfer to be an important variable in the development of iron and other metallurgical traditions on the Coast.

Ironworking Techniques

According to our present knowledge, all indigenous African techniques of reducing iron ores to metal belong to the family of techniques known as the bloomery process, now extinct. In bloomery iron smelting the metal is not tapped from the furnace as a liquid but is removed in solid form. Bloomery iron smelting furnaces are batch processors, meaning that smelting must be periodically interrupted to remove the product. The bloomery process was a versatile method of iron smelting; it was adaptable to a very wide range of ores and could be adjusted to produce wrought (pure) iron, steel, and even cast iron (Rostoker and Bronson 1990:211; Tylecote 1986:239; van der Merwe 1969:113).

The indirect process, in which iron is actually melted, produces cast iron; wrought iron and steel are produced from cast iron by decarburization, or the removal of carbon from the product, through oxidation (van der Merwe 1969:113). The invention of the indirect process has been credited to the Chinese in the 4th century BC (Needham 1980; Raymond 1984:72; D. Wagner 1994). Cast iron contains between 2 percent and 4.5 percent of alloyed carbon (Rostoker and Bronson 1990:212). Cast irons are brittle (Tylecote 1986:239) and difficult to hammer-forge without elaborate heat treatment, so for production of edge weapons, axes, and other tools, cast iron was first decarburized to wrought iron or steel (Maddin, Muhly, and Wheeler 1977:124; van der Merwe 1969:113)

Examining the microstructure of the highly polished surface of an iron artifact with the aid of high-power magnification provides a window into the history of the manufacturing techniques used. Different techniques, for example rates of heating and cooling iron, determine the microstructure of iron and steel, which in turn determines properties such as hardness, ductility, and resistance to wear (Maddin, Muhly, and Wheeler 1977; van der Merwe 1969; Rostoker and Bronson 1990; Tylecote 1986). The microstructure of bloomery iron, examined at high magnification, tends to show silicate slag inclusions trapped in the bloom during smelting. The distribution of carbon is usually heterogeneous and irregular, a consequence of variation in carbon content during reduction in the furnace. The quality of carburized iron may be enhanced at the forge through several techniques, including repeated hammering and folding, quenching, and tempering. Quenching is the technique of quickly cooling a hot piece of metal by plunging it into water. Quenching results in a microstructure called martensite, a hard yet brittle structure (Maddin, Muhly, and Wheeler 1977:129; Tylecote 1986:239240).

Repeated hammering and folding breaks up slag and evenly distributes the carbon. When an artifact is hot-forged and slowly air-cooled it develops a coarse pearlite microstructure comprised of alternating plates of cementite (iron carbide, Fe_3C) and ferrite (pure iron). Rapid air-cooling of an iron artifact causes it to develop a fine pearlite microstructure. Steels which have been fairly rapidly air-cooled from high temperatures (ca. 1000°C) develop a mesh-like structure called "Widmanstatten" as a result of the ferrite or cementite being ejected along certain places of the structure (Tylecote 1986:241).

To reduce the brittleness of quenched metal, the steel piece is heated up to, but not above, the "A1 temperature," i.e., 727°C. This technique is known as tempering, in which carbide precipitates and coalesces by diffusion. This reduces the hardness of the martensite phase but increases toughness. The temperature attained at the forge and the time the article is held at that temperature determine the amount of iron carbide that coalesces and hence the final hardness and ductility of the metal (Maddin, Muhly, and Wheeler 1977:130). Other techniques of forging include hammer welding which involved the hot hammering of two pieces of iron together. The following analysis of iron artifacts relies on examination of their microstructures to reconstruct their manufacturing techniques.

Preindustrial Swahili Ironworking Technology

We carried out a metallographic analysis on 180 specimens of metal artifacts from five Kenya coast sites (Table 7.1; Kusimba, Killick, and Creswell 1994). Metallographic analysis of the metal artifacts was primarily undertaken using reflected light microscopy of polished sections. Select samples were further examined using scanning electron microscopy and energy dispersive X-ray fluorescence (EDXRF or EDAX) for elemental composition.

Sample Selection and Preparation

Samples were selected for analysis based on size, shape, and magnetism. Only samples considered unimportant for exhibition purposes by Kenyan museum curators were selected for metallographic analysis and sent outside the country. Samples were cut with a diamond-impregnated wafering blade wheel, mounted in thermosetting plastic or epoxy resin, and ground and polished by conventional techniques (e.g., Bachmann

1982; Rostoker and Dvorak 1990; Samuels 1982; Scott 1987). The slag samples were prepared as polished 24 × 48 mm thin sections. All mounted metal samples were studied and photographed with a metallographic microscope both unetched and etched. The etchant was 3 percent nital (v/v nitric acid in ethanol) which makes the grain boundaries and distribution of carbides in the specimen visible (Killick 1990:211; C. Kusimba 1993:253; Kusimba, Killick, and Creswell 1994; Notis et al. 1986:273). Opaque minerals in these samples were identified by polarized light techniques, both in air and under oil immersion, which was essential for the correct optical identification of the opaque oxides. Sample constituents were identified with the aid of standard reference works (Rostoker and Dvorak 1990; Samuels 1982).

Out of a total of 180 microsections of metal examined in reflected light microscopy, 146 were completely mineralized. Twenty-four iron samples and ten other metal samples still had non-corroded areas where metal was preserved. All samples from Shanga, Mwana, and Mtwapa were completely mineralized. This was a serious setback to the goals of the study. The high proportion of corrosion is attributed to: (1) salt spray from the sea settling on the site and permeating the soils; (2) poor conditions for storing artifacts; and (3) the age of these sites.

Salt contamination is ubiquitous in coastal sites and is a serious problem for the archaeometallurgy of Swahili sites. Immediate treatment and laboratory analysis of samples as soon as they are excavated may partially solve the problem. Excavation of sites during the dry season is the best solution for the protection of finds in the field. The results of our analysis are fully reported in Tables 7.3–7.7.

Results

The analysis of 24 iron artifacts from Galu and Ungwana reveals important information regarding (1) the variety of ironworking techniques on the coast; (2) site use patterns in ironworking; and (3) the presence of crucible steel on the coast.

Ironworking Techniques on the Coast

Although there is extensive archaeological evidence on the Kenya coast for ironworking (C. Kusimba 1993, 1999a; Kusimba, Killick, and Creswell 1994) there is as yet little information on the ironworking technology itself, and few iron smelting sites are known. Black sands found at Mtangawanda on Pate Island were long thought to have been exploited for iron. A recent analysis by one of us (DJK, Table 7.8) shows that these sands have an unusu-

Table 7.3 Analyzed Bloom Samples from Ungwana and Galu

Note: For explanations of technical notes in Constituents column, please see Fig. 7.2.

Sample No.	Trench	Artifact	Constituents	% Carbon
32/007a	2C/L2	bloom	pearlite, graphite, slag	2.5
35/052a	2C/LI	flattened ball	equiaxed ferrite, slag	0.1

Figure 7.2 Technical terms appearing in Tables 7.3 through 7.7.

Austenite: Iron and iron alloys exist in two atomic arrangements or crystal forms. The high-temperature form, called austenite, transforms to ferrite on cooling.

Cementite: The iron carbide in the microstructure of steel and cast iron. It has the nominal formula Fe3C. The hardness of a steel or cast iron is proportional to the number and close spacing of cementite crystals.

Ferrite: See *austenite.*

Hammerscale: A surface deposit of oxide, primarily magnetite and wustite, formed while a piece of iron is heated for forging, that scales off during hammering.

Hypereutectoid: A steel that is high in carbon. Such steels tend to be hard and brittle.

Pearlite: One of the transformation products of slowly cooled austenite (see above) with a structure of interleaving crystals of cementite and ferrite. Most steels are forged in this condition.

Widmanstatten structure: Steels which have been fairly rapidly air cooled from high temperatures of around 1000°C develop a mesh-like structure as a result of the ferrite or cementite being ejected along certain planes of the structure.

ally high titanium content which makes them highly unfavorable for iron smelting. It should be easy to tell if they were used, as both the smelting slags and the slag inclusions in the metal should be full of titanium-rich phases like ilmenite and titaniferous magnetite.

Table 7.4 Bloomery Iron Samples from Ungwana and Galu

Note: For explanations of technical notes in Constituents column, please see Fig. 7.2.

Sample No.	Trench	Artifact	Constituents	% Carbon
28/004	1C/L3	knife blade	grain boundary cementite, large ferrite grains, elongated slag stringers	<0.05
31/005a	2B/L2		ferrite, spheroidized pearlite, cementite, slag, hammerscale	0.10
31/005b	2B/L2	nail	ferrite, some cementite, much slag	0.05
32/007b	2C/L2	nail	slag, hammerscale, silicate grains, equiaxed ferrite	<0.10
37/011a	3B/L1	flat iron plate	little slag, copper plating, ferrite, Widmanstatten structure	0.20
34/013a	3B/L1	spherical lump	Widmanstatten structure, ferrite, pearlite distortion by cold-working, little slag	0.15
33/052b	2C/L1	fish hook	equiaxed ferrite grains, some slag stringers with 10–15:1 aspect ratio	0.00

However, a survey of modern-day smiths provided some clues about the organization of recent iron production on the coast (C. Kusimba 1996b). Iron was smelted from magnetite sand, bog ore, and hematite ore locally available in the area. According to one smith, Omar Ahmed of Witu, the Swahili used three techniques to work iron: smelting, melting, and forging. Smelting was carried out in bowl furnaces 50 × 30 × 30 cm in size. Melting to refine and consolidate the bloom was carried out in small *vyungu* (crucibles). The bloom from the first smelt was placed in a closed crucible and heated until the slag drained from it. When the fire had cooled down the refined bloom was retrieved from the crucible by breaking it. The third process was forging, in which the bloom was fabricated into objects.

Analysis of iron and slag samples from the sites of Galu and Ungwana documents a variety of smelting and forging techniques. Swahili iron-workers were capable of producing high-carbon steel and even cast iron in their bloomeries (Kusimba, Killick, and Creswell 1994). Sample 32/007a (Table 7.3), for example, is a cast iron bloom with over 2.5 percent carbon,

Table 7.5 Bloomery Steel Samples from Ungwana and Galu

Note: For explanations of technical notes in Constituents column, please see Fig. 7.2.

Sample No.	Trench	Artifact	Constituents	% Carbon
26/001	1B/L1	?	small cementite and ferrite laths; large cementite blocks, no pearlite, some slag	1.5
29/002b	1B/L3	knife or hoe blade	Widmanstatten grains around austenite grains, fine pearlite structure, slag with aspect ratio 6–9:1	0.7
36/009	2B/L3	knife?	slag with aspect ratio 5:1, Widmanstatten structure, proeutectoid ferrite and pearlite	0.5
15/3061a	4/L13	nail head	stringers, equiaxed ferrite grains, spheroidized pearlite	0.2

Table 7.6 Welded Bloomery Iron and Steel Samples from Ungwana and Galu

Note: For explanations of technical notes in Constituents column, please see Fig. 7.2.

Sample No.	Trench	Artifact	Constituents	% Carbon
2408	4/L7	pike	well dispersed homogenous eutectoid steel, abundant slag inclusions, pearlite	0.8/0.2
11/2660b	4/L11	rod	2 pieces welded together: (1) spheroidized carbides, cementite spheres; (2) Widmanstatten ferrite and pearlite,	1.3/0.5
17/2692b	3/L9	?	much slag with 15:1 aspect ratio 2 strips welded together, fine pearlite, slag inclusions	0.1/0.8

directly dated by Accelerate Mass Spectrometry (AMS) radiocarbon dating to 740±70 BP (sample no. TO 3894). Since the gray cast iron was too brittle to be forged into artifacts, the only way to make it workable would have been to remove carbon from it before forging it into desired objects or selling it to smiths for forging (Childs 1991:36). We are not sure whether the ironworkers of Galu and Ungwana were able to decarburize cast iron. One method would have entailed heating the iron in the hearth and making the desired object in an oxidizing atmosphere (Killick 1990; D. Miller 1996; Todd 1985). The second method probably would have involved consolidating a

Table 7.7 Crucible Steel Samples from Ungwana and Galu

Note: For explanations of technical notes in Constituents column, please see Fig. 7.2.

Sample No.	Trench	Artifact	Constituents	% Carbon
29/002a	IB/L2	rod	homogeneous high-carbon steel, no slag inclusions, partially spheroidized proeutectoid cementite, fine pearlite	>1.5
33/006b	2B/L2	rod	proeutectoid cementite formed around austenite grains, Widmanstatten morphology, no slag	>1.1
193	IC/L3	nail or point	clean metal, no slag, small polygonal ferrite and pearlite grains, spheroidized cementite, slightly austenized hypereutectoid steel	1.0–1.2
194	IC/L3	nail	hypereutectoid steel, thick rims of spheroidized proeutectoid cementite outlining austenite grains, spheroidized pearlite, no slag	1.0
2/2966a	4/L12	knife	Homogeneous hypereutectoid steel austenized and normalized, pseudo-morphs of cementite in Widmanstatten morphology, fine austenite grains, very coarse pearlite	ca. 1.0
12/3061c	4/L13	rod	2 types of hypereutectoid steel: (1) remnants of proeutectoid cementite; (2) remnants of cementite laths in the pearlite, homogeneous throughout, absolutely no slag	1.0
15/3061d	4/L13	nail or point	subrectangular and subrounded cementite grains, 5–10 μm, spheres of cementite in ferrite with residual pearlite, partially spheroidized proeutectoid cementite, thoroughly clean and homogeneous with very few stringers of tiny brownish glass	1.4

Table 7.8 Analysis of Pate Black Sands

Note: Analysis no. 17970 by Saskatchewan Research Council.

Major Compounds		Trace Elements	
	%		ppm
SiO2	12.40	B	7
Al2O3	1.89	Ag	<0.5
TiO2	42.70	Ba	15
FeO	39.22	Be	<0.5
MnO	2.32	Ca	2.8
MgO	0.76	Co	600
CaO	0.62	Cr	400
K2O	0.02	Mo	<0.5
Na2O	0.50	Ni	2.2
P2O5	0.04	Pb	28
SO2	0.04	Sr	35
Loss on ignition	0.17	Zn	300
		V	800
		Zr	850
Total	100.68		

bloom in an open crucible at the hearth (David et al. 1989; C. Kusimba 1996b). Analysis of refractories, ceramics, and crucibles excavated at Swahili sites will be necessary to test this hypothesis.

The majority of samples from Galu are scrap—cut off and discarded—an expected pattern at a forge (C. Kusimba 1993, 1996b). Most of the iron recovered from the forge area is encased in a jacket of corrosion within which are embedded tabular flakes of hammerscale and tiny spherical pellets of air-cooled slag—the signatures of a forge. That the quality of iron produced and used at Galu was quite uneven is confirmed by the variability in the carbon content of the samples. Both hot and cold forging were undertaken at Galu and Ungwana. There is no evidence of quenching or tempering of objects. Cold hammering is evidenced by broken slag inclusions in sample 31/005b and by the distortion of its microstructure. At these sites, cold forging was probably used in the fine finishing of smaller objects such as nails and knives, since cold hammering increases the hardness of metal. The tool kit was probably simple, including stone hammers, and the artifact may have been held with tongs or even by hand. With such utensils cold hammering would have been the easiest way to finish small tools.

Pressure welding was systematically employed by Swahili blacksmiths to fabricate desired objects. Pressure welding was achieved by heating individual metal pieces at high temperatures in the forge and then quickly hammering the pieces together to join them. Samples 2408, 11/2660b, and 17/2692b were welded from pieces of varying carbon content (Table 7.6). The indications that low-carbon steel was hot welded to high-carbon steel reasonably suggest that the technique of hot hammering or welding probably had the aim of improving the quality of the object forged. The fact that two of the welded pieces are nails supports this hypothesis, because soft, low-carbon steel is a better material for cushioning shocks from a hammer while the high-carbon steel's brittleness gives nails a sharp edge for penetrating wood.

Site-Use Patterns in Ironworking

Several factors influenced the location of industrial sites. They included availability of ore and fuel as well as water and labor. Iron smelting industries posed a great risk to settlements and were thus located outside built-up areas. Ironsmithing was undertaken in most Swahili settlement sites but seems to have been confined to certain quarters of a settlement, especially the periphery of towns. Both ritual and practical reasons may have influenced the choice of industrial sites for industries (C. Kusimba 1993, 1996a).

In recent times, smelting and melting were shrouded with mystery and were limited to few families or clans. Such secrecy was common in much of sub-Saharan Africa (Herbert 1993; Schmidt 1997b). Although no archaeological evidence exists to reconstruct the social space of coastal ironworkers, they may have formed their own communities close to the larger settlements which they supplied with their products. The community of ironworkers may have been organized into guilds that maintained a patron-client relationship with larger settlements. The elites of the larger settlements may have controlled access to critical ore and fuel resources as well as to farmland. At the same time, the elites controlled the distribution of finished products (C. Kusimba 1999b). This relationship ensured that ironworkers maintained a subservient relationship with the larger settlements by supplying them with all the basic needs for assault, defense, and domestic needs in exchange for subsistence and protection.

That no large-scale ironworking sites have been located at Mtwapa, Ungwana, Mwana, Pate, Manda, and Shanga, even after intensive survey, supports the hypothesis that iron smelting industries were often located far from settlement sites. On the other hand, the discovery of a fairly large smelting site with a pit/bowl-type furnace at Galu (Fig. 7.3) supports the idea that

Fig. 7.3 Pit/bowl-type furnace found at Galu.

some settlements may have been founded specifically for iron production. More work is needed to confirm this hypothesis.

Hammerscale, charcoal, broken slag, and other forging debris found on the edges of several samples from Galu, along with the unfinished artifacts that still contain charcoal and hammerscale, suggest that Galu was a smithing site as well as a smelting site. There is definite evidence of forging at Galu and of iron smelting at Galu and Ungwana. It is not possible to make estimates of the quantity of bloomery iron production at these or other Swahili sites, though estimates can be made by using the weight or volume of slag as a proxy measure (Killick 1990:164–167).

Crucible Steel on the Coast

Seven samples of crucible steel were found (Table 7.7), the first reported from sub-Saharan Africa (C. Kusimba 1993; Kusimba, Killick, and Creswell 1994). Could these crucible steel artifacts from Galu and Ungwana have been imports from India or the Middle East? Both regions had established commercial relations in long-distance maritime trade with East Africa by the 10th century, so it is possible that finished iron artifacts or bloom may have been among imports to East Africa as early as the 2nd century AD (Casson 1989). Indian ironworkers are credited with inventing the crucible or "wootz" process in the 6th century AD (van der Merwe 1969:49). Raymond (1984:80) describes the crucible ironmaking process:

Indians made clay crucibles about the size of a rice bowl, and filled them with short pieces of wrought iron, together with about four to five percent by weight of wood and the leaves from specific plants. The crucibles were sealed with clay and placed in a pit about a meter deep, which was then filled with charcoal. The fuel was lit, and air blast from bellows directed into the pit to raise the temperature. The firing continued for several hours…When the iron in the sealed crucibles melted, the carbon from the plant material became evenly distributed through the molten liquid. Because of the uniform distribution of the carbon through the iron—smelting which had never been possible by forging and hammering, even by the later method of heating bars of iron with charcoal in the furnace—wootz steel was remarkably homogeneous, and superior to anything else known.

By the late 1st millennium AD, Indian ironworkers were making substantial quantities of crucible steel for export to Europe and the Middle East (Chakrabarti 1992). According to Rostoker and Bronson (1990:127): "Crucible steel was made in crucibles and sold in 'cakes' that were shaped like crucibles, and forged—in Iran and elsewhere in Southwest Asia as well as South Asia—into blades, some of which had a characteristic pattern called by Europeans damasked or damascene from its supposed origin at Damascus in Syria."

The crucible steel process was adapted in the Near East in the 7th century and in Toledo, Spain, a little later (Hassan and Hill 1986). Islamic scholars, including al-Biruni in the 11th century and al-Tarsusi in the 12th century, noted the crucible steel process was widely used and understood in the Islamic world (Rostoker and Bronson 1990; Hassan and Hill 1986). The only known centers for the production of crucible steel before the 18th century were in Arabia, South India, Sri Lanka, China, Turkmenistan, and Spain (Bronson 1986; Buchanan 1807; Hassan and Hill 1986; Kusimba, Killick, and Creswell 1994; Raymond 1984; Taylor and Shell 1988:208).

The Swahili were exporting iron in quantity to India, as stated by al Masudi and al Idrisi (Freeman-Grenville 1962; M. Shinnie 1965). Arab and Indian merchants may have imported African bloom and melted it in their crucibles, a process which would save fuel, which was in short supply in Arabia. It is also possible that the Swahili were importing Indian or Arab items made of crucible steel, including swords and daggers. But Indian crucible steel is known to have been an expensive commodity (Bronson 1986), so why did the Swahili use it for as mundane a purpose as the making of nails? Considering the high quality of crucible products, why would Indian merchants who visited East Africa claim East African iron was of better quality than their own (Freeman-Grenville 1962; M. Shinnie 1965)? Indian importation of African bloom can be attributed to its cheapness and high quality.

Conversely, most Indian consumers may have found crucible steel too expensive to buy for utilitarian items and opted to import African steel, which was cheaper.

Iron formed a major commodity of Indian Ocean trade and was transshipped in many directions at different manufacturing stages, for example as bloom or finished artifacts. The relative importance of different iron smelting and working techniques, their origins and development, the relationship of ironworkers to the general society, and the changing role of iron in this trade should be understood in the development of coast polities in this context. As an important technological innovation and wealth-creating industry, iron production attracted the local elites who attempted to control its sourcing, processing, and distribution through the creation of specialized ironworking communes such as those at Galu. It is these elites who later monopolized international maritime trade by capitalizing on the economic boom of 12th–15th-century Indian Ocean trade (C. Kusimba 1999b).

This study not only underscores the important role of iron in the development of sociopolitical complexity on the East African coast but also demonstrates the richness of applying scientific analytical techniques in the study of archaeological data. We must now undertake detailed metallurgical analyses of more iron artifacts from Swahili sites to test these hypotheses.

Acknowledgments

CMK would like to thank Bryn Mawr College for the Marguerite N. Farley Fellowship which funded his graduate education, the National Science Foundation, Wenner-Gren Foundation, the Royal Anthropological Institute, the Swedish Institute for International Cooperation, and the National Museums of Kenya for supporting this research. We thank G. Abungu, Mark Horton, and A. Lali Omar for granting access to their excavated materials.

8

Iron Age Settlement Patterns and Economic Change on Zanzibar and Pemba Islands

Emanuel T. Kessy

This chapter examines settlement patterns and economy in several Iron Age settlements on the islands of Pemba and Zanzibar, Tanzania. The first section looks at social, political, and economic influences on site location. Historical documents provide one source of information about site location strategies, but other evidence indicates that the relative importance of different determinants of site location varied over time. The second section analyzes settlement pattern changes from the 8th through the 19th centuries AD. The final section looks at trading systems that linked the islands and the resources that might have been exchanged within the islands and beyond.

The distribution of known archaeological sites on Pemba and Zanzibar Islands can tell us much about factors that influenced site location. Present site distribution, of course, may be a construct of the present state of research and the research designs of previous studies. First, most research projects have concentrated on coastal sites. The few known inland sites contain standing monuments and are consequently quite easy to find. Second, research to date has been conducted on sites known historically from either Arabic texts or oral traditions. As only sites with visible surface remains—especially stone monuments—have been studied, many sites probably remain to be found.

In spite of the incomplete nature of previous research and the biased nature of the site sample, this chapter seeks to shed light on how site distri-

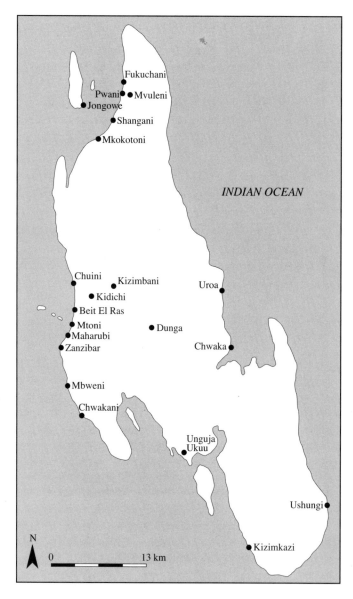

Fig. 8.1 The archaeological sites of Zanzibar.

bution patterns can verify the accuracy of known historical information on social, political, and economic changes in the ancient towns of the East African coast.

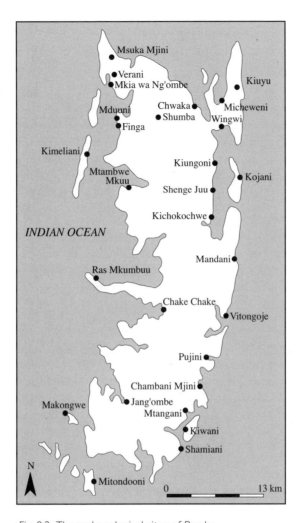

Fig. 8.2 The archaeological sites of Pemba.

Site Locations

The locations of the early harbors and sites along the coasts of Zanzibar and Pemba are of great interest (Figs. 8.1 and 8.2). Through the use of occupation dates of the sites and the examination of site locations, one can determine some of the factors that influenced site selection. The accessibility of the harbors to sailing activities in different seasons of the year is one factor. Some sites can be used for sailing throughout the year, while others cannot.

Soil fertility and climate also act as significant factors in the question of site location.

Physical attributes, such as good beaches and other natural features, surely did affect site location as much as economic and political factors. Water, stones, and salt were doubtless important commodities. However, knowledge of geological resources such as iron ores on the islands is poor, even though iron artifacts are found there in archaeological contexts.

Climatic factors, especially soil development and fertility and rainfall, affect resources and, in turn, site location. With the exception of Tumbatu Islet, most of the areas along the coasts of Zanzibar and Pemba have adequate water supplies, either from small streams or ground water, accessed from shallow pits or wells (Al Maamiry 1980:64). The western sides of Zanzibar and Pemba Islands are better watered and more fertile (Gray 1977:136). On the eastern sides of the islands, soils are poorly developed and infertile, and in some areas the land consists of coral up to the surface. In general, however, Pemba is more fertile than Zanzibar.

On Zanzibar's main island, the relationship between land and sea resources and archaeological site location is clear. Of the 18 coastal archaeological sites on Zanzibar Island, only 3 sites are on the eastern side (Fig. 8.1). Although fishing probably played a major role in the subsistence economy, these sites are all near fertile pockets of land, implying that early inhabitants probably practiced cultivation as well as fishing.

The presence of Tana Ware at Unguja Ukuu, Fukuchani, and Mkokotoni in Zanzibar, which date to the 8th century AD (Horton and Clark 1985), and at Mtambwe Mkuu in Pemba links these societies to farming practices. Along the mainland coast, Tana Ware is associated with Iron Age farming societies; it is also found along the East African coast from southern Somalia to Mozambique, extending inland over 100 km (Håland and Msuya 2000; Mapunda 1995a; Chami 1994a; see also Chami, Chapter 6, Mapunda, Chapter 5, and Kusimba and Killick, Chapter 7, all in this volume). Allen (1984:226) has indicated that agriculture could have played a more important role in Swahili settlements than trade.

The pattern of settlement in Pemba is different from that of Zanzibar. Although most Zanzibar sites are located on the more fertile, western side of the island, the Pemba sites are equally distributed on the western and eastern sides. Although Pemba's eastern side has more rainfall and more fertile land, sea-related economic activities, such as fishing and trading, would be more easily practiced from this side as well.

The islands' coastlines and site orientation also affected settlement location. The islands lack natural physical barriers against the strong sea waves that originate from the depths of the Indian Ocean and pound their eastern shores. Strong currents on these eastern shores restrict sailing from May to August. These ocean currents disturb the ecology of many species of fish adapted to low currents. The subsequent decline or absence of fish disrupts fishing and trading.

Pemba and Zanzibar have adapted to this problem in different ways. Bays and inlets break the strong sea currents in certain areas and enable some fishing year round. Chwaka Bay in eastern Zanzibar is an example. The eastern part of Pemba Island also has bays and inlets (Fig. 8.2). However, the intensity of the currents from mid-May to August limits the use of water in the bays, and fishing and sailing in these areas is very difficult.

These restricting conditions could have led the earliest inhabitants to settle on the western parts of the islands first. Archaeological evidence supports this hypothesis. With the exception of the 12th-century Shungi site on the eastern part of Zanzibar, nearly all archaeological sites on the eastern sides of the islands of Pemba and Zanzibar were occupied after the 14th century (see Tables 8.1–8.5). Recent surveys have found an additional two early sites on the eastern coast of Pemba. Adria LaViolette (pers. comm.) found Tana Ware and early Islamic ware approximately 500 m inland at Chwaka, which may push the dating of the site back to the 9th century. The second site is the 15th-century site of Pujini; the discovery of Tana Ware near the site provisionally dates it earlier than the 14th century (LaViolette 1995).

Sites which predate the 9th century include Fukuchani, Jongowe, Kizimkazi, Mkokotoni, Shungi, Shangani, Unguja Ukuu, Zanzibar Gereza, Mkia wa Ng'ombe, Mtambwe Mkuu, and Ras Mkumbuu. Most of these sites yielded Tana Ware in their earliest occupation levels. Some have early trade artifacts from the Near East, India, and China. Mtambwe Mkuu, for example, has early Sgraffiato pottery and sherds of Islamic white glaze, dating to around the 10th century (Horton 1991:14). Ras Mkumbuu has Tana Ware, and a sherd of Sgraffiato pottery dating to approximately AD 1000 to 1100 was recovered (Horton 1991:18–19). Abbasid Gold dinars have been recovered from Mtambwe Mkuu and Unguja Ukuu, dating to AD 810 and 798, respectively (Chittick 1966:163; Horton 1991:21).

Being the first to be settled, these sites were probably the first to develop urban centers. Most of the sites, like Unguja Ukuu, Tumbatu Islet, Mtambwe Mkuu, and Ras Mkumbuu are mentioned by early travelers to the East African coast. By AD 956, Masud mentions a place called Kanbalu in the land of Zanj (Ingrams 1967:81), possibly Mkumbuu on Pemba (Chittick 1982b:57). Masud also mentioned the presence of Muslims and non-Muslim Arabs and Zanj, and he recorded the exportation of ivory, tortoise shells, and other items (Shepherd 1982:136). Tumbatu Islet is described by Yakut Bin Abdulla, another early traveler, as being populated by Muslims in the 12th–13th centuries. According to Yakut Bin Abdulla, ships traveled to this islet (Horton 1991:10). Yakut Bin Abdulla also mentioned Lanjuya, possibly the site of Unguja Ukuu in Zanzibar.

Table 8.1 Archaeological Sites of Pemba and Zanzibar (P = Feature Present)

Note: Source for chronology: Horton and Clark 1985; date for Uroa site: Gray 1975.

Site Name	Date Occupied (AD)	Site Area (ha)	Mosques	Stone Bldgs.	Tombs
Fukuchani	700–1000	1400–1600	–	–	P
Mtambwe Mkuu	800–1300, 1600	125	P	P	–
Shangani	700–2000	–	–	–	
Mkokotoni	700–2000	–	–	P	
Zanzibar	1100–2000	–	–	P	–
Ras Mkumbuu	800–1500	12	P	P	P
Mkia wa Ng'ombe	1100–1400	–	P	P	P
Jongowe	1100–1300	25	P	P	–
Kizimkazi	1100–1300	–	P	P	–
Shamiani	1300–1500	–	P	–	–
Uroa	1400–1600	15	–	P	–
Pujini	1400–1600	–	P	P	–
Unguja Ukuu	700–900	15	P	–	–
Pwani Deburi	1200–1300	–	–	P	–
Mtangani	1130–1400	–	P	–	–
Mvuleni	1400–1500	–	–	P	–
Chwaka	1400–1500	P	P	P	–
Chake Chake	1500–1600	–	P	–	–
Chambani Mjini	1500–1600	–	P	–	P
Chwaka	1600–1700	–	P	P	–
Kichokochwe	1600–1700	–	P	–	P
Kimeliani	1600–1700	–	P	–	–
Kiungoni	1600–1700	–	P	–	–
Shungi	1200	–	–	P	–
Kiwani	00	–	–	–	–
Makongwe	1300	–	–	–	–
Mandani	1300	–	P	–	–
Mduuni	1300	–	–	P	–
Mitondooni	1300	–	P	–	–
Msuka Mjini	1400	–	P	–	–
Kiweni Island	1400	–	P	–	–
Shengejuu	1400	–	P	–	–
Verani	1400	–	P	–	–
Vitongoje	1400	–	P	–	P
Kiuyu	1700	–	P	–	–
Kojani	1700	–	P	–	–
Micheweni	1700	–	P	–	–
Shumba	1700	–	P	–	–
Wingwi	1700	–	P	–	–
Beit el Ras	1800	–	–	P	–
Chuini	1800	–	–	–	–
Chwakani	1800	–	–	–	–
Dunga	1800	–	–	P	–
Kidichi	1800	–	–	P	–
Kizimbani	1800	–	–	P	–
Maharubi	1800	–	–	P	–
Mbweni	1800	–	–	P	–
Mtoni	1800	–	–	P	–
Finga	1800	–	–	–	–
Jambangombe	1800	–	P	P	–

A need for security may also have affected site locations. This need would have been especially apparent during and after the arrival of the Portuguese in the 14th century. Sites situated near good harbors would have facilitated escape by sea during times of danger, but only if attack came from inland. Coastal sites with good harbors might even be especially vulnerable. Sea attacks would have targeted these sites and used convenient access to block escape while advancing the attack. Therefore, sites with bad harbors may have limited the access of invaders and minimized the risk of sea attack. Even when faced with sea attack, however, coastal sites maintained an advantage. On the eastern side of Pemba, the sea currents are so strong that even today ocean vessels with sophisticated technology face problems, especially from mid-May to August.

The 14th century saw a growth in trading activities and wealth along the East African coast; most of the complex stone ruins associated with Swahili archaeology date to this period and later. The increasing concentration of sites on the eastern half of Pemba during and after the 14th century reflects a greater concern with secure access to sea trade.

The coming of the Portuguese in the 15th-17th centuries created considerable political instability and disrupted East African coast settlements. Most large cities were abandoned at this time. Small Muslim settlements sprang up along the coast of Mozambique as the Portuguese captured and took control of the larger towns (Newitt 1978:117). Although many sites were occupied at the time of the Portuguese arrival, and were abandoned immediately afterwards, none of the ancient buildings in Pemba show Portuguese influence (Horton 1985:170). The number of old sites abandoned and new sites occupied at Pemba increased significantly during the

Table 8.2 The Occupation and Abandonment of Sites on Eastern Pemba Island

Chronology (AD)	Abandoned Sites	New Sites	Total Sites Present
800	–	–	–
900	–	–	–
1000	–	–	–
1100	–	–	–
1200	–	–	–
1300	–	4	4
1400	2	3	5
1500	3	1	3
1600	1	2	4
1700	2	4	6
1800	5	–	1

Table 8.3 The Occupation and Abandonment of Sites on Western Pemba Island

Chronology (AD)	Abandoned Sites	New Sites	Total Sites Present
800	–	2	2
900	–	–	2
1000	–	–	2
1100	–	1	3
1200	–	–	3
1300	–	3	6
1400	4	2	4
1500	3	–	1
1600	1	2	2
1700	1	1	2
1800	1	2	3

Table 8.4 The Occupation and Abandonment of Sites on Pemba Island

Chronology (AD)	Total Sites Present	Abandoned Sites	Newly Established Sites	Total Sites (Eastern Side)	Total Sites (Western Side)
800	2	–	2	–	2
900	2	–	–	–	2
1000	2	–	–	–	2
1100	3	–	1	–	3
1200	3	–	–	–	3
1300	10	–	7	4	6
1400	9+	6	6	5	4
1500	4+	6	1	3	1
1600	6	3	4	4	2
1700	8+	3	6	6	2
1800	4	7	2	1	3

Note: Additional sites as stated below:
  In the 15th century one site was established in the northern tip
  In the 16th century one site was established in the northern tip
  In the 18th century one site was established in the northern inland

Portuguese period (Tables 8.2, 8.3, and 8.4).

Rapid population growth or resource exhaustion may also have contributed to site abandonment during this period, as did the apparent move-

Table 8.5 The Occupation and Abandonment of Sites on Zanzibar Island

Chronology (AD)	Total Sites Present	Abandoned Sites	New Sites	Total Sites Eastern Zanzibar	Total Sites Western Zanzibar
700	4	–	4	–	4
800	4	–	–	–	4
900	4	–	–	–	4
1000	3	1	–	–	3
1100	5	1	3	–	5
1200	7	–	2	1	6
1300	6	1	–	–	6
1400	6	3	3	1	5
1500	5	1	–	–	5
1600	6	–	1	1	5
1700	4	2	–	1	3
1800	12	1	9	–	12

ment of people into smaller, scattered settlements on land that was previously considered marginal. Determining changes in population during this period is difficult. Although the number of sites increased during this period, this does not necessarily imply population growth. For example, a society based on slash and burn farming requires more land (due to the rotation of cultivated and fallow lands) than a farming society that uses manure to replenish the same land for annual use. The organization and use of space is also affected by societal beliefs and cultural aspects, and these qualities may be very difficult to support with archaeological evidence.

In conclusion, site location on Zanzibar and Pemba before the 17th century seems to have been affected by access to marine resources and high-quality land. Political instability and population growth, especially during the 14th century, may have led to the abandonment of old sites and the establishment of new sites in more varied and diverse strategic locations. The establishment of sites without access to both maritime trade and fertile land may have necessitated a shift to dependence upon only one of these resources.

Settlement Pattern Changes

We shall now look at the settlement changes from the 8th to the 19th centuries, in particular the cause of these changes and what these changes may imply in the history of the settlement.

Historically, the period between the 8th and 11th centuries marks the initial stages of the islands' involvement with the outside world (Sutton 1990:65; Martin 1978:25). (However, it is worth noting that new discoveries from a cave at Unguja Ukuu [Machaga cave] suggest contacts of the island of Zanzibar to the external world might be earlier than thought [Chami 2001].) Therefore, it is quite possible that the effects of international contacts on the structures of the island societies may have been very limited. Although international contacts are thought to have caused some changes in site location, natural resources were probably the prime determinant of site location.

Between the 12th and 15th centuries, there was an increase in numbers of sites on the islands as well as a high rate of site abandonment (Tables 8.2-8.5). An increase in exotic materials indicates that trade networks had expanded. The growth of external ties would have increased social stratification, competition among social groups, and the need for security. Demographic pressure may also have led to an expansion of population, although the focus of further research should be the question of population growth.

Site numbers decline sharply in the 16th century, when Portuguese colonial domination began (Tables 8.2-8.5). Both the Portuguese and indigenous East Africans built fortresses during this period of strife.

Both Zanzibar and Pemba show an increase in the number of occupied sites in the 18th century (Tables 8.2-8.5). This may be associated with an Omani takeover of the coast which, although it did not end a period of foreign domination, did return political stability to the islands.

On both Pemba and Zanzibar site numbers increase slowly from the 8th to the 17th century. In the 18th and 19th centuries, clove plantations were established on both islands. The differences in soil fertility should have affected the islands: Pemba encompasses more fertile land than Zanzibar, and therefore should have received greater benefits from the new economy.

At the time when the Omanis assumed control of the East African coast in the beginning of the 18th century, a form of centralized leadership began to develop within the islands. This was later strengthened when Sultan Seyyid Said shifted his capital from Oman to Zanzibar. The island of Zanzibar then became an administrative center, not only for the islands but also for a large part of the East African coast. The increased power and responsibility accorded to Zanzibar caused the rapid development of the island, and Zanzibar town is reported to have expanded dramatically after the Omani conquest in the early 18th century (Martin 1978:27).

An Explanation of Settlement Patterns

Before the 19th century, sites on Pemba and Zanzibar were always located along the coast, although the timing of their establishment and abandonment varied. Inland sites are seen for the first time during the 18th and 19th centuries.

Historical records, such as the *Periplus* (Casson 1989) and Portuguese records, indicate that the East African coastal towns existed as independent political units. Each town maintained independent control of its trade systems. This lack of integration created problems from the early periods up to the arrival of the Omanis in the closing years of the 17th century. The lack of unity and support between the towns enabled the Portuguese to employ single-target attack-and-conquer strategies.

The Portuguese could have created a powerful empire by unifying the towns along the East African coast, but the significant opposition of both Arabs and local people weakened their rule. Omani rule led to the unification of the East African coastal towns into large states. This unification allowed the establishment of centralized control over formerly independent economic structures, and systems of taxation and trade organization were implemented. Under Omani rule, the slave market along the East African coast grew rapidly, and the trade system expanded to include more foreign members. By the beginning of the 19th century, Zanzibar and Pemba had already established trade contacts with several European countries and with America.

Centralized control of trade reduced the size and prosperity of formerly autonomous towns; the populations of these towns had to employ alternative economic strategies. The production of cloves and sugar, crops with an expanding international market, initiated an agricultural revolution in Zanzibar and Pemba at the end of the 18th and the beginning of the 19th century (Swai 1984:27; Sheriff 1987). The cultivation of these cash crops allowed the towns to alternate their involvement in Omani-controlled trade with cultivation.

In the beginning of the 19th century, Britain became the first country to ban the slave trade (Swai 1984:27; Sheriff 1987). Zanzibar, a major trading center, suffered economically as a result. (Swai 1984:26). The merchants soon realized, however, that they could export the products of slave labor (Sheriff 1987:48). The establishment of clove and sugar plantations turned slave labor into a commodity (Curtin et al. 1978:402–403). These changes, including the monopolization of trade, the establishment of a unified state out of free, independent polities, and the beginning of the plantation economy, led to changes in the settlements of Zanzibar and Pemba. The majority of the people shifted from the maritime trade economy, which was subject to the restrictions of the monopoly system, to land-based subsistence systems.

New infrastructure, such as the establishment of small towns and roads, had to be implemented to support this new type of economy, though sea transport remained important.

The Shumba site in Pemba was established in the interior during the 18th century, and the sites of Kizimbani, Kidichi, and Dunga (Fig. 8.2) were established in the interior of Zanzibar during the 19th century. Sherrif (1987:50) reports that Kizimbani had 4,000 clove trees at the first half of the 19th century. As a result of Zanzibar's successful plantation economy, Zanzibar became the center for all commercial activities on the East African coast. Seyyid Said, recognizing the economic and administrative potential of Zanzibar, shifted his capital from Oman to Zanzibar.

In conclusion, what do the historical changes of the 18th and 19th centuries tell us about the archaeology of Pemba and Zanzibar? A centralized government may have been established by the 17th century and was certainly operating in the 19th century. This was accompanied by the centralization of international economic affairs, including trade. Trading contacts also increased. Another change was an increase in production for exchange, for instance, change from a slave export economy to a plantation economy based on slave production of sugar and cloves.

By contrast, the 17th-century towns were economically independent polities based on fishing and sea trade. Reliance upon these would have required access to both land and sea resources, and sites established prior to the 18th and 19th centuries were almost always located along the coast. The towns competed for major resources; competition within a town led to the fissioning of communities and explains the archaeological pattern of regular abandonment and reestablishment of sites and their comparatively small size. According to the *Periplus of the Erythrean Sea*, a 1st-century AD document, each town's political leader controlled its trade system within a defined territory (Casson 1989; Chittick 1984).

According to Freeman-Grenville (1988:4, 132), Pemba had at least five kings, and more than one sultanate sought its dominion during the 15th and 16th centuries. Jao dos Santos, a 17th-century Portuguese, reports large settlements of Moors working and living as merchants in cities governed by kings (Newitt 1978:113). The king of each city probably collected taxes to increase his wealth and, with it, his power. These historical accounts suggest that the towns existed as self-supporting units. The arrival of the Omanis destroyed this independence and led to the decline of the free economy–based towns. The population within those towns retreated inland and adopted land-based economic strategies. These strategies proved advantageous as the new international trade provided a large market for agricultural products.

Trading Systems

Historical sources inform us that Pemba and Zanzibar were trade destinations of both the African mainland and Asia (Curtin et al. 1978:315-401). Archaologists have recovered a number of imported objects, including pottery and glass, from the Gulf, Asia, China, and Europe—evidence of extensive trading contacts. Seven coins, for example, have been found at the earliest sites, such as Mtambwe Mkuu (AD 800 [AH 184] and AD 810 [AH 195]) (Horton 1991; Horton, Brown and Oddy 1986:117).

The diversity of local and imported materials invites examination of the initiation, control, and growth of trade systems. The *Periplus* informs us that the materials that were traded along the East African coast included ivory, tortoise shell, rhinoceros horn, palm oil, cinnamon, frankincense, and slaves (Ingrams 1967:67-68; Connah 1987:156; Shepherd 1982; Phillipson 1985:197-198). In return for these export items, the island and coastal traders received awls, glass, wheat, wine, daggers, and hatchets.

Some of the earliest-known sites on the islands, such as Mkokotoni, Unguja Ukuu, and Fukuchani, have shown evidence of craft production, much of it destined for trade. Crafts included pottery, perfume and mat making, textiles, ivory and bone carvings (Newitt 1978:122; Connah 1987:173; C. Kusimba 1993), production of salt (Chittick 1975a:151), boat making, bead making, and house construction (Horton 1991; C. Kusimba 1993). Many sites on the islands have yielded iron slag in association with craft production, but substantial amounts of iron slag have only been recovered from the site of Unguja Ukuu. Basketry, cloth, and wooden artifacts are not well represented in the archaeological record due to their perishable nature or poor preservation. Spindle whorls, however, have been found in several areas of the island.

Specialized activities would have necessitated exchange of the different commodities. To establish a working exchange system, the people must have been capable of initiating and accepting a trade economy and must have developed structures to accommodate the trade system. In this sense, it means that some sort of reciprocity must have existed. In addition, one important principle of exchange is the existence of customs or law structures to ensure fair transactions, which the early towns displayed in their trade contacts and activities. The settling of foreign traders at sites occupied by indigenous peoples is an indication of the symbiotic relationship that might have developed at the time.

Two controversial questions regarding the trading activities on the islands are: (1) How did the islands manage to maintain the trading system? (2) Where were the sources of raw materials or commodities during ancient times? The strongest agent for stability in the growth of the cities may have been an adequate food supply. The sites of Tumbatu and Fukuchani provide evidence that the sea acted as a rich environmental source for the supply of protein (Horton 1991:4); and other sites provide evidence for the domestication of cattle, goats, and fowl (Horton, pers. comm.). No serious research has been done to quantify the potential of the agricultural products. Archaeological and linguistic speculation, however, suggests that if the early inhabitants of the island migrated from mainland agricultural societies (perhaps the Bantu societies that grew sorghum and millet) they would have cultivated the same crops on the islands. Connah (1987:171) has mentioned that such southeast Asian crops as rice, coconuts, bananas, and sugar cane were already introduced to the East African coast by the beginning of the Christian era. These plants flourish very well along the East African coast, and there is no doubt that the islanders grew them. These crops would have produced enough food to support the populations in the towns as well as surplus food for export (Martin 1978:27).

Masud, who visited Kanbalu (Pemba?) in AD 916, reports the presence of a small population of Arabs on the islands by the 9th and 10th centuries. The Arabs may have come to pursue trading, as refugees from wars in their home, or for missionary purposes; the adoption of Islam by the islanders may have been the result of social contacts. The arrival of these groups would have stimulated and created new social situations in trade and activities such as the production of materials for exchange. At this time, there was an increase in trading activities as revealed by an increase in exotic materials in the archaeological record as well as by rapid expansion of the towns. The range of artifacts, which include glass bottles, glass beads, and copper and gold objects, indicates that raw materials were imported from the African mainland as well as from the Asian continent.

We do not know how the islands obtained materials for international exchange. Archaeologists focus on goods that were produced from local materials. In addition to surplus food, other exports from the islands to the Near East included mangrove poles, at a time when there was a shortage of forest products (Sheriff 1987:12; Connah 1987:156). Other materials that could have been available from the islands include honey, animal skins, and salt extracted from the sea. Even slaves could have been sold during the early period of contact. Other products of exchange were secondary to the islands—for example, copper and gold, which are available on the mainland of Africa but not on the islands. Secondary exchange items were imported to the islands for direct exchange with other areas or they were manufactured as secondary products for resale.

The islands assumed the positions of trade accumulation centers, that is, the islands functioned as distribution centers for the East African coast and the Near East (Curtin et al. 1978:395–401). As almost all natural resources available on Pemba and Zanzibar are also available on the African mainland, the islands did not possess exotic, raw trade materials. How, then, did the islands obtain materials for exchange with their African mainland partners? The island populations may have employed one or more strategies to establish and maintain trade relationships with the mainland.

Trading relationships result from value, quality, and content differences in the items of exchange, so materials of different values, qualities, and content must have existed on the islands in order for the reciprocity system to work. The islands also may have relied on the modification of such secondary exchange items as copper, ivory, and gold imported from the mainland into finished secondary products that could be traded to the mainland. Island populations may also have traded import items from the Asian continent to the African mainland. The islands might have acted as an industrial base of some kind; the people may have processed materials to make finished goods and acted as middlemen in their exchange. A certain phase at Mkokotoni, for example, has yielded thousands of beads of glass and other materials and many bead grinders. The amount of beads at the site, as well as the bead grinders, leaves no doubt that this site was a large production center for these items. Another site of comparable production potential is Fukuchani; archaeologists have found a substantial number of bead grinders, although they have not established the amount and type of beads that were produced.

Iron production is another noteworthy industry on the islands. Iron slag has been found at the early sites: Kizimkazi, Unguja Ukuu, Mtambwe Mkuu, Pujini, and Fukuchani. Since no significant structures connected with iron production have been found (but see C. Kusimba 1993, 1996a; Kusimba, Killick, and Creswell 1994; Kusimba and Killick, Chapter 7 this volume), the production of iron is a matter of further research. A certain red-burnt feature with a substantial amount of iron slag and blow pipes were found at Pujini by LaViolette in 1993 (pers. comm.), but the material recovered has not yet been analyzed.

The history of the islands' resource potential becomes complicated at the point of the late-15th-century arrival of the Portuguese, which triggered a decline in the prosperity of towns along the East African coast. After the arrival of the Omanis late in the 17th century, trade systems are better documented, and these records indicate that cloves (primarily products of the islands), ivory, and slaves (products for which the islands acted as middlemen) dominated the international market.

In conclusion, our understanding of the ancient trading systems of the islands demands further research, which may involve analysis of the local economic potential of the islands (as opposed to the external economic potential) and the islands' contributions to international trading systems. There is also a need to study the sites to see if site location can help in understanding the economic strategies of the islands in relation to both local and international trade systems. A detailed inventory of the perishable and nonperishable materials that may have played a role in the exchange systems could provide a more extensive conclusion about local and international exchange systems of the islands.

9

Politics, Cattle, and Conservation: Ngorongoro Crater at a Crossroads

Charles Musiba and Audax Mabulla

Mass tourism in Tanzania's national parks, game reserves, and conservation areas threatens the very ecosystems and communities these areas seek to protect. Until the mid-1980s, management of these areas stressed wildlife management and long-term mass tourism development. Tourist vehicles, hotels, and camping facilities are causing many stresses on the environment in the Ngorongoro Conservation Area (NCA). Maasai relocation from the crater floor and prohibition of their seasonal burning practices has disrupted the ecological balance and led to rampant poaching. The world-famous sites of Olduvai Gorge and Laetoli have suffered from vandalism and insufficient maintenance. Sustainable tourism would include Maasai habitation of the NCA, Maasai employment and participation in the tourism industry, establishment of appropriate facilities at the archaeological sites, control of tourist flow by NCA officials, and use of donkey safaris. In the long term, sustainable eco- and archaeo-tourism will be more beneficial economically, ecologically, socially, and culturally to Tanzania.

East African tourism primarily features wildlife, local customs, historical sites, and spectacular landscapes. Like many other developing nations, Tanzania has created national parks and other forms of protected areas (reserves and conservation areas) to boost the country's economy and protect these areas for future generations. In Tanzania, most national parks, game

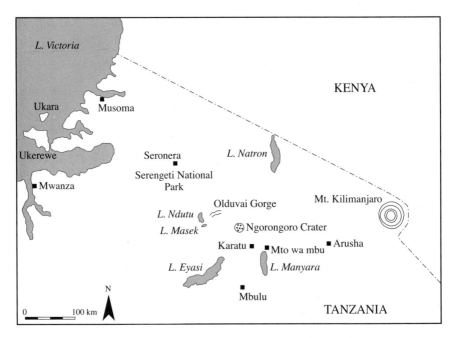

Fig. 9.1   Northern Tanzania, showing Ngorongoro Crater and Olduvai Gorge.

reserves, and conservation areas are located within the savanna ecosystem, which supports a wide range of wildlife. In principle, national parks and game reserves in Tanzania are part of the nation's heritage and should therefore provide Tanzanians with sustainable and improvable subsistence and revenue (Nyerere 1968, 1974). However, some researchers have concluded that adverse environmental effects caused by mass tourism exceed the benefits generated to communities surrounding the parks, game reserves, and conservation areas (Århem 1985b; Bell 1986; Homewood and Rodgers 1991). Ironically, mass tourism in Tanzania's national parks, game reserves, and conservation areas threatens the very ecosystems and communities these areas seek to protect.

Mass tourism in one of Tanzania's most valued and well-protected parks, the Ngorongoro Conservation Area (NCA) in the Serengeti Plains of northern Tanzania, has been socially, economically, and ecologically disruptive in spite of its potential benefit. In particular, mass tourism threatens fragile natural lands and wildlife, pastoralist grazing lands, and archaeological sites including Olduvai Gorge. This chapter is based on long-term observations and interactions between the authors and the Ngorongoro's Maasai communities, conservation officers, and representative members of the National Parliament.

National Parks in Tanzania

Before colonialism, village community councils in Tanzania had their own ways of managing the environment. They set aside lands for different activities: agriculture, pasturage, ranging, hunting, and sacred areas. The livelihood of all communities in Tanzania, regardless of their subsistence strategies, depended heavily on appropriate land use. The connection of humans to the land was always very strong. The land was sacred.

When the Germans conquered Tanganyika (now known as Tanzania) and established direct rule in the mid-1890s, traditional land rights and land use changed dramatically. The objectives of the colonial policies were clearly based on serving the interests of the German empire. German rules controlled all major population centers and trading routes between the coast and the hinterland. Taxation, plantations, and forced labor created a peasantry. At the same time, areas were reserved for special interests, much as hunting grounds and game reserves for the kaiser of Germany.

Great Britain and its allies defeated Germany at the close of World War I, and Tanganyika was mandated a British territory under the authority of the League of Nations. In theory this gave Great Britain transitional powers to administrate Tanganyika, powers that were to expire within ten years when the people of Tanganyika were to be granted autonomy. In fact, it was 1960 before the promise of independence was fulfilled.

In 1922, the British accepted what the League of Nations referred to as their "moral obligation to govern Tanganyika." They created a system of indirect rule that incorporated indigenous political systems into the colonial framework. They established native authorities to ease colonial control. Although hailed as progressive by the British aristocracy, this approach led to the invention of ethnic boundaries, which in a real sense did not exist, but effectively eased colonial control. The British colonial administration introduced a monetary economy based mainly on agriculture and mining. They also introduced national parks, game reserves, and conservation areas to help rejuvenate the colonial economy. When it became apparent that these areas were not very suitable for any large-scale economic activities (agriculture, ranching, and the like), they were set aside for settler recreation and hunting.

In 1961, Tanganyika's newly formed independent government inherited a designated classification of protected natural areas from the British Protectorate Administration of Tanganyika. Under the National Parks and Land Tenure Acts, as amended, these protected areas were to be secure and sustainably used (Mackinnon et al. 1986). The protected area classification, which was modified in the 1960s and 1970s by guidelines from the Commission on National Parks and Protected Areas (CNPPA) and International Union for Conservation of Nature and Natural Resources

(IUCN), includes three categories of protected environments.

1. *The national parks* are relatively large natural areas not materially altered by human activities. These areas, such as the Serengeti National Park, are of national or international significance for scientific, educational, and recreational use.

2. *The game reserves or wildlife sanctuaries,* areas naturally set aside to maintain biotic processes in an undisturbed state, provide ecologically balanced ecosystems which are true representative examples of the natural environments. These areas are made available for scientific study, environmental monitoring, education, and maintenance of biodiversity, such as Gombe Stream National Park in western Tanzania.

3. *Conservation areas* are strictly designated for multiple land-use management to provide for sustainable utilization of natural resources. Use of resources such as water, timber, wildlife pasture, and tourism, primarily oriented toward nature conservation, can continue while supporting economic activities of the surrounding communities (CNPPA/IUCN 1976; IUCN 1978, 1980, 1984). Ngorongoro Conservation Area (NCA) in northern Tanzania is an example.

The Ngorongoro Conservation Area

The Ngorongoro Conservation Area (NCA), which is situated in the northern part of Tanzania within the Serengeti Plains, covers about 8,288 km^2. The NCA's elevation is between 1,350 and 3,000 m. It was formed after a volcanic eruption some eight million years ago. The cone collapsed leaving a round caldera, 700 m deep, 20-15 km in diameter, and covering more than 300 km^2. The NCA is a complex highland ecosystem bordered to the east by the East African Great Rift Valley which runs from southern Tanzania to the north, through Lake Manyara and Lake Natron. To the west, the NCA is bordered by the vast Serengeti Plains (including Olduvai Gorge and Laetoli areas). The crater is surrounded by six peaks ranging from 2,300 to 3,648 m in height. The NCA includes areas of highland forests, scrubs, swamps, and savanna grasslands that are used by wildlife and human beings. Ngorongoro Crater is the largest known intact crater in the world, and is home to hundreds of thousands of animals and millions of birds. The crater's magic stems from its physical beauty coupled with the abundance of unusually docile game animals such as zebras, wildebeests, giraffe, lions, buffaloes, antelopes, and other wildlife that attract many visitors.

Lying within the NCA, and 45 km northwest of the Ngorongoro Crater, is Olduvai Gorge, a steep-sided river gorge of Pleistocene fossiliferous beds (Fig. 9.1). Olduvai Gorge was among the first archaeological sites to provide stratigraphic paleoanthropological and archaeological evidence of human evolution. The gorge is divided into a main and side gorge. The main gorge runs eastward from Lake Ndutu, cutting through the Pleistocene beds, and joins a side gorge from the south, which drains into the Olbalbal depression at the foot of the Ngorongoro-Olmoti highlands to the east.

Olduvai Gorge today is a ravine 2 km deep and 50 km long cutting into the grassland plateau of the Serengeti Plains. Olduvai Gorge first gained prominence as a paleoanthropological site in 1911 when a German paleontologist from Munich named Kattwinkel collected faunal remains there. Thereafter, the site attracted many scientists, including the well-known Leakeys (Louis and Mary), who in 1959 made the major paleoanthropological discovery of the first-known australopithecines (*Zinjanthropus boisei*). To this day Olduvai Gorge remains an important archaeological site. It was listed as a world cultural heritage site in 1974.

About 36 km south of Olduvai Gorge, and still within the NCA, lies Laetoli, a Pliocene site that was first reported by another German scientist. The name Laetoli (Laitoli) is derived from a Maasai word that means "salty plains"; it has also been interpreted as a "place of red lilies" (M. Leakey 1979; Leakey and Hay 1979). Laetoli was identified as a paleoanthropological site in 1935 after it was brought to the attention of Mary and Louis Leakey by a young Maasai warrior (*morani*). Mary Leakey conducted extensive scientific work at Laetoli in the 1970s and discovered over twenty hominids and several animal footprint trackways, including the famous hominid footprints at site G. The site remains one of the most significant findings in paleoanthropology.

In 1959, just before independence, the British colonial government had designated Ngorongoro Crater as a conservation area. Late in the mid-1960s, the NCA received its own mandate from the Tanzanian ministry of land, natural resources, and tourism and became known as the Ngorongoro Conservation Area Authority (NCAA). In 1980, UNESCO listed the NCA as a world heritage site in recognition of its marvelous natural and cultural legacy. Although the Ngorongoro Crater was established as a conservation area, the Tanzanian government issued guidelines, mainly focused on wildlife conservation, that were not always in harmony with local pastoralist community structure and land use. Since the NCA's establishment, Maasai residents have been imperfectly involved in planning and decision making.

Pastoralist groups in the area, especially the Maasai and Tatog-speaking Barabaig, were unprepared for the long-term effects of wildlife conservation on their lifestyle (Perkin 1995). For example, Maasai pastoralists near the end of the dry season regularly practice burning of grasslands to improve pasture quality during the rainy season, but burning is now prohibited by the NCA authorities. The Ngorongoro Ecological Monitoring Program (NEMP) suggested in 1989 that the lack of regular burning has progressively worsened pastureland quality in the crater.

As in many African countries, Tanzanian land laws fail to recognize land rights and land use of pastoral communities (Berry 1993). From the NCA's beginning until the mid-1980s, it stressed wildlife management and long-term mass tourism development (Campbell and Hofer 1995; NCA 1995). These concerns did not address the material and cultural needs of humans, thus creating a dysfunctional ecosystem. Unfortunately, conservation policies in Tanzania assumed that pastoral land use and resource conservation are incompatible. Nowadays, however, it is widely accepted that the East African savanna ecosystem is a cultural landscape that is the result of interaction between pastoralist humans and savanna herbivores (Campbell and Hofer 1995; Århem 1985a, 1985b).

Problems Facing the NCA

Environmental Stresses due to Tourism

Poorly planned and uncoordinated mass tourism is consuming a disproportionately large share of Ngorongoro's resources and progressively reducing Ngorongoro Crater's carrying capacity at the expense of wildlife and poor pastoral communities struggling to survive. As a crater sanctuary, Ngorongoro is one of the most sensitive ecosystems in eastern Africa. It is especially vulnerable to soil compaction and erosion. Based on studies of the effect of vehicles from other East African parks, it is very likely that the ecological impact of vehicle-related activities on the crater floor are much higher than in other conservation areas (NCA 1995; NEMP 1989). The four-wheel-drive tourist vans cause irreparable scars to the ancient crater ecosystem. In the early 1960s, when the few vehicles visited the crater through the eastern rim road, there was less ecological damage, but with the completion of the Olduvai Gorge/Mbulu and Arusha/Makuyuni roads as well as the Kilimanjaro international airport, the number of vehicles increased from 3,250 in 1985 to 30,000 in 1989, carrying between 140,000 and 160,000 tourists (Forsbrooke 1990; Geo 1989). In 1995, over 180,000 vehicles entered the crater floor carrying over 900,000 tourists (Lazarus Mariki, head conservator of the western zone, which covers Olduvai Gorge and Laetoli, pers. comm.). Only four-wheel-drive vehicles such as Land Rovers, Toyota Land Cruisers, and specially equipped trucks capable of crossing through wetlands, sand, and mud are allowed to enter the crater floor.

Despite a network of interconnected gravel roads in the crater and an off-road driving prohibition, vehicles still exert pressure on soil, causing compaction and soil erosion and inhibiting growth of grasses during the rainy season. Hardening of the soil kills vegetation and destroys plants' ability to withdraw water through capillary mechanisms. Vehicular exhaust pollutes the air and water. Noise disturbs animals; the crater's walls act as noise bumpers producing a nearly continuous and amplified echo that affects animals' hearing sensitivity (NEMP 1989).

Animals suffer heavily from noise disturbance. They are constantly disturbed from their resting or feeding areas, also making it more difficult for tourists to view animals (NEMP 1989; NCA 1995). Vehicles advancing into the crater floor produce both direct and indirect ecological damages to wildlife. When tourist vehicles enter the crater floor, they come into contact with animal breeding and feeding sites. This contact increases species' vulnerability to competitors and natural enemies. According to studies by Edington et al. (1990) and Georgiadis (1995), among wildebeests there is a critical window of opportunity immediately after birth for bonding between offspring and their mothers. This bonding is very crucial for the survival of the newborn animals. For example, female Thompson gazelle are more timid than males and readily leave their territories when disturbed by approaching vehicles. This separation of sexes can last for long periods and reduce breeding success (R. Leakey 1991; von Lawick-Goodall 1970; Lent 1974).

Intense and inadequately controlled competition between tour operators, coupled with frequent demands from tourists to seek out the famous savanna cats for closer observation and spectacular photo opportunities, tempts tour operators to leave the designated routes and follow off-road ways. As a result, they disrupt the wildlife and cause serious behavioral and ecological damage to the animals. Although the present wildlife viewing system has serious negative ecological effects, a better-managed tourist system of fixed viewing posts and tunnels could provide spectacular and safe natural viewing possibilities.

By 1996, five upscale lodges had been built in Ngorongoro Conservation Area. These complexes are built on the crater's rim to provide tourists with a spectacular view of the crater's floor. Our observation of the crater lodges revealed that in order to achieve standardized tourist comforts, most of the lodges on the crater's rim were built with imported materials that do not harmonize aesthetically with the environments. In order to attract more tourists and make them feel at home, facilities like swimming pools have been introduced. The major problems associated with these lodges include: (1) garbage and wastewater produced by a large number of visitors staying overnight; (2) gradual decrease in groundwater levels because of intensive use of water in swimming pools and lawn sprinkling; (3) introduction of polluting chemicals into ground and surface water as a result of frequent use of paints, varnishes, polish, and pesticides; (4) change of the natural landscape by development of roads linking the hotels, which results in disruption of the natural ecosystem and shrinking of the natural pastures; and (5) proliferation of troublesome plant and animal species because of poorly designed organic-waste disposal facilities, resulting in health hazards to animals and humans.

Ngorongoro also has two large camping areas for caravans and tents. Lack of well-outlined and well-enforced camp procedures let tourists harm the ecosystem. For example, in 1993 a tourist operating company known as Tanzania Wildlife Safaris (TAWISA) established a campsite at the rim of Olduvai's main gorge. TAWISA's camp personnel used to litter all kitchen refuse into the main gorge, not far away from the famous site FLK where the remains of *Zinjanthropus boisei* were discovered. This raised concern over the future of Olduvai Gorge among both indigenous and international pale-oanthropologists who visited the site during an international congress in 1993. The uncontrolled campsites accelerate problems: littering at the camp-site causes small animals to die through choking and snaring on garbage, which attracts scavengers who disrupt stratigraphic contexts on exposed areas of the main gorge. Visitor noise at night also frightens nocturnal animals.

Social and Cultural Stresses on the Maasai

Before Tanzania was colonized, the area covering Ngorongoro and most of the eastern part of the Serengeti Plains was used heavily by the Maasai people. They used the area for pastoral and spiritual activities. During the colonial period, both German and British administrations restricted the Maasai from utilizing the northern highland forest area as pasturelands. The German colonial government relocated the Maasai people to areas unfavorable for their cattle in order to create wheat plantations on the eastern part of the Ngorongoro highlands overlooking Lake Manyara.

In 1987–1988 about 25,000 Maasai pastoralists resided within the NCA, together with a herd of some 286,000 livestock (Perkin 1987). In the late 1970s, permanent Maasai settlements on the crater floor were evicted under the Ujamaa policies, which sought to bring together dispersed households into village centers. (The term Ujamaa equates to communal living based on traditional African extended family structures. The basic ideology of Ujamaa is living together, and should not be confused with modern socialism in the northern hemisphere [Nyerere 1968].) Maasai pastoralists were relocated to the NCA's western zone mostly at Endulen, Silal, and Kakesio areas.

Because the relocation of the Maasai pastoralists from the crater's floor caused extreme grazing-land shortages, NCA introduced a scheme of sharing of grazing rights on the crater floor to ease grazing competition among Maasai. At the same time, however, the NCA imposed a total ban on dry sea-son fire-burning. The removal of the Maasai from the crater also allowed increased poaching of rhinos and elephants. This change disrupted the eco-logical balance within the crater floor resulting in a tremendous decrease in the rhino and elephant population.

The eviction of the Maasai from the crater also led to an uncontrolled increase of buffaloes (up to 2,000). According to Forsbrooke (1990), a scientific survey carried out in the 1950s revealed that over 100 rhino lived in or visited the crater floor while more than 60 were to be found in and around Olduvai Gorge. By the mid-1980s the Olduvai rhinos were completely extinct and the crater population was reduced to around twenty individuals. For many years the Maasai presence within the crater floor helped tremendously to control poaching. Maasai morani were effective voluntary guards (Godfrey Ole Moita, pers. comm.).

Although Maasai are pastoralists, occasionally they practice corn farming to substitute for their traditional milk diet. With the exception of a small pocket of land in the western zone around Endulen village, Maasai are not allowed to garden within the conservation area. Under the conservation guidelines, gardening in the conservation area is still prohibited, and can only be done under presidential discretion. The concentration of Maasai pastoralists on the NCA's western zone has resulted in progressive deterioration of the western grassland grazing areas, and compels the pastoralists to move their livestock into the northern highland forest reserve during the dry season. NCA's neighboring agriculturist communities at Karatu and Oldeani also cut down this forest for building material and firewood.

The above-mentioned problems have forced the NCA to reformulate policy in order to establish a comprehensive set of conservation and development objectives. The NCA's newly formulated conservation objectives include: (a) the protection of critical wildlife habitat, namely the short-grass plains, the crater floor, the migration corridors between the crater floor (including the lowlands), and the northern highland forest reserve; (b) the maintenance of species diversity of flora and fauna populations; (c) the maintenance of wildlife populations to ensure the continuation of their survival and genetic viability.

Furthermore, Ngorongoro's development objectives include (a) provision of water supplies to meet human and livestock demands; (b) provision of livestock development assistance, for example, veterinary services, breeding programs, and marketing facilities; (c) provision of economic opportunities for residents mainly through employment; (d) provision of social services including health, education, transport, and food security; (e) community participation in decision-making at a managerial level.

In the 1980s, NCA's management of multiple land use was reviewed. Most reviews revealed that the NCA failed to achieve its development objectives. For example, a water supply study by Aikman and Cobb (1989) indicated that the majority of water systems were non-functional and were shared with livestock, thus making them unfit for humans. Although the NCA's provision of livestock assistance, especially veterinary services, has been appraised by the government and many other institutions, only one veterinarian has been employed by the NCA. To the surprise of many pastoralists in the area, although NCA has trained Maasai livestock managers, none of them have been employed by the authority (Miriam Ole Moita, pers. comm.). Despite its importance to the pastoral economy in the area, livestock management has been neglected (Rigby 1985; Århem 1985b; Field, Moll, and Ole Sonkoi 1988).

Ironically, of the 300 people employed by the NCA since 1989, only 13 have been Maasai residents in the area. Similarly, hotels and lodges at the crater's rim almost exclusively employ staff from other parts of Tanzania. There have been no efforts to create a revenue-sharing system which could provide benefits to the Maasai community from the NCA's sizable and ever-increasing tourist trade (J. Kone, member of parliament for Silal area, pers. comm.). Furthermore, there have been no efforts by the NCA to assist Maasai communities in establishing alternative income-generating activities within the tourist industry (Perkin 1995). One Maasai *boma* (a typical Maasai household complex) has been built by the NCA as a cultural attraction, which assists only one village near the NCA headquarters.

Lack of a buffer zone and clear boundary on the northern highland forest reserve has led to frequent fire outbreaks and illegal over-exploitation of the forest by people living outside the conservation area. Buffer zones are marginal areas at parks and reserves that are specifically created to provide access and utilization of park resources for neighboring communities which border them. A buffer zone could allow part of the conservation area to be utilized by the local people, thus providing incentives to participate in conservation programs (Holland 1991).

Until recently, tourism has not included the participation of local communities in activities such as cultural interpretation and conservation. As a result, young Maasai spend most of their time posing for pictures along the Ngorongoro-Serengeti Road. According to the Maasai Elders' Council at Endulen, young people no longer value a traditional, pastoralist way of life. But with the diminishing number of Maasai livestock, young people have no economic alternatives in villages to prevent their migration to urban centers. Although the conservation area provides health care, education, and veterinary services to Maasai villages, it has failed to help the Maasai morani establish alternative income-generating means such as participation in locally based tour operations. For many generations, the Serengeti landscape was a cultural and spiritual space under the Maasai stewardship, and government-imposed restrictions have greatly altered pastoralist perceptions of the human-environment relationship.

Stresses on Olduvai Gorge and the Laetoli Footprint Sites

The primary responsibility of maintaining, safeguarding and sustainably using paleoanthropological and archaeological resources within the NCA and in Tanzania in general requires full-time commitment of Tanzanians at all levels. The need to manage and to protect these resources has become increasingly important globally in recent years. As physical and cultural forces continue to damage the paleoanthropological and archaeological resources that document the historical events that shaped our existence at Olduvai Gorge and Laetoli, drastic measures to curb these destructive processes should be part of the long-term conservation plans for the NCA. The importance of Tanzania's paleoanthropological and archaeological resources is on par with Tanzania's wildlife resources. Therefore, it is our task to ensure that the future existence of these spectacular resources is well secured.

In 1993 the Department of Antiquities of Tanzania in collaboration with the Getty Conservation Institute (GCI), embarked on a project of preserving the famous hominid footprints at Laetoli within the NCA area. The project, though well intended, missed a wonderful opportunity to include the Maasai community at Enduleni, who could have participated by guiding controlled tours to the site. Tanzanian anthropologists have proposed to the government that a proper, state-of-the-art site museum be erected at Laetoli so that surrounding communities could not only benefit from it economically but also culturally and educationally, by better understanding Tanzania's contribution to the archaeology of human origins (TAAP 1995). Instead the establishment chose to focus exclusively on conserving the 3.5-million-year-old footprints.

It is very unfortunate that the voice and concerns of indigenous anthropologists who better understand the dilemma of the Maasai communities within the NCA were not heard by the Tanzanian government (Mabulla 1996b). Tanzanian paleoanthropologists appealed to the government to reconsider its position on the footprint conservation issue and establish an educational and cultural center at Laetoli which would provide young Maasai (morani) training as cultural interpreters (Mabulla 1996b; TAAP 1995; Musiba 1995). Since its inception, the project dismissed the pastoral community around Laetoli as equal participants. As a result, less cooperation has been offered by the Maasai and indigenous anthropologists, who have been excluded from formulation and implementation of the entire project.

Since 1984 to 1999 there has been no improvement to the existing facilities and important localities at Olduvai Gorge, and no repair of the roads connecting the different localities—the visitor's center, the on-site museum, the laboratory, and staff quarters—which are in sad disrepair. In 1992 the devastating acts of vandalism at Olduvai Gorge made news in the Tanzanian media, and raised concerns over the future of the site. Unfortunately, the main custodian of the site, the Department of Antiquities, took no action to prevent additional vandalism or to correct other destructive processes.

The existing problems that have been identified for Olduvai Gorge and Laetoli include the following.

1. *Repeated vandalism of several on-site museum exhibits at Olduvai Gorge, particularly at sites DK, JK, and MNK.* As a result, these sites have been virtually destroyed (Karoma 1996). We urge that the current custodian of Olduvai Gorge undertake major repair work at sites DK, JK, and MNK. Since most of the required material is readily available locally, the repairs should not be costly and could be funded through revenues generated from the Antiquities Fund from gate fee collections at Olduvai Gorge, and excavation fees paid by scientists conducting paleoanthropological excavations in Tanzania.

2. *Lack of a properly maintained visitors' center at Olduvai Gorge.* The existing visitor's center, also known as the museum center, requires regular maintenance. The center needs massive repair work on walls, floor, roof, and ceiling, as well as new doors and windows. Dividers to protect the display from direct contact from visitors should be erected in the exhibit area.

3. *Lack of water and power supply at Olduvai Gorge.* Although Tanzania's hydro-geological maps indicate that Olduvai Gorge is within waterhole sources (Olduvai Sheet 38/3-6, 1-TSD, Series Y742 Maps), the site suffers heavily from lack of water during the dry season. The existing water cisterns at Olduvai Gorge are not capable of holding enough water to last through the entire dry season. No attempts have been made to bore deep wells that could provide sufficient water for the visitor's center, research center, and personnel quarters.

4. *Lack of proper housing at Olduvai Gorge.* There is no single permanent and proper housing facility for the resident archaeologist and his support staff at Olduvai Gorge. The corrugated makeshifts are unbearably hot and may not be classified as houses. The site needs low-cost, well designed and environmentally friendly houses made of burnt bricks appropriate for the area. Tiles made locally from the rich clay soils of the Serengeti region would be preferable to corrugated iron sheeting.

5. *Lack of visitors' car parking area at Olduvai Gorge.* The center needs a visitor's parking lot rather than the existing system in which tour-operated vehicles park in front of the center, frequently blocking the entrance. A well-designed parking lot will help to control tourist flow and other activities within the center's perimeters.

6. *Lack of office space for staff archaeologist at the visitors' center at Olduvai Gorge.* It is essential that offices be added to the visitors' center to enable the head of the center, guides, and other personnel to function fully.

7. *Lack of proper rest rooms for visitors at Olduvai Gorge.* With an increasing flow of visitors, hygiene is an issue at Olduvai Gorge. The center does not have proper bathrooms; the existing pit latrines are in bad shape and unwelcoming to visitors. There have been many complaints about rest rooms at Olduvai Gorge. This is a necessity.

8. *Poor display facilities and site interpretation information guide at Olduvai Gorge.* Over 70 percent of the interpretive information at Olduvai

Gorge has typos and other mistakes. For example, the Bed I crude Oldowan tools are described as being preceded by the *levallois* tools from the Naisuisui Bed. But Bed I is not overlaid by the Naisuisui Beds. This kind of misinformation leaves a visitor with the impression that *Australopithecus boisei* used *levallois* technology. Both qualified stone tool typologists and geologists should work together to produce easily understandable interpretations, written in English and Swahili, of geochronological and archaeological events at Olduvai Gorge.

The exhibit cases are in very poor condition. The site map that shows the distribution of stone tools and raw material within the gorge needs to be encased in a glass display case. Displayed raw materials for stone tool manufacturing have been removed by tourists from the map (including green quartzite, trachyte, phenolite, gneiss, and the fine-grained purple quartzite). Photos highlighting the Leakey family's active research years at Olduvai Gorge are in poor condition. They need proper restoration work on acid-free paper and glass covers. Some names that were used to define various stratigraphic sequences have been corrected and written in what were thought to be proper vernacular names (in the Maasai language), but unfortunately they do not always conform to the guidelines for the International Association of Geologists.

9. *Lack of road connection between Laetoli and Olduvai Gorge.* These two sites should be connected and a permanent road constructed. The distance between the two sites is about 25 to 30 km and may easily be connected by a road, which need not be paved. Today, it takes about half a day in an overland vehicle to reach Laetoli from Olduvai Gorge.

10. *Lack of supporting infrastructure for Laetoli.* Although Laetoli has made big news in the field of paleoanthropology, no efforts have been made to create an outlying museum on the site. The establishment of an on-site museum at Laetoli will help bring the two sites (Olduvai Gorge and Laetoli) together into a joint educational center of our evolutionary history. Today, Laetoli suffers heavily from neglect because without a trained staff archaeologist and other essential personnel there is no one permanently available to monitor the site.

Toward Sustainable Tourism and Community Participation at NCA

In the 21st century, new trends in traveling and tourism are emerging. The socioeconomic and environmental problems caused by the quest for development will lead to changes in every industrial sector, including tourism. Developing countries need careful, well-planned, and ecologically oriented tourism infrastructures that emphasize appropriate or alternative technological models (May-Landgrebe 1989). The common objection that ecologically and culturally centered tourism hampers economic development is false. Tourism that undermines the stability and viability of its attractions is clearly unsustainable. Carefully planned and sustainably implemented ecotourism could be part of long-term solutions to most of the NCA's tourism-induced environmental problems.

In the long term, sustainable tourism will be beneficial economically, ecologically, socially, and culturally to Tanzania. Sustainable tourism at the national level frequently brings in valuable foreign exchange, and at the local level it stimulates profitable domestic industries such as hotels, restaurants, transport systems, souvenir manufacture, handicrafts, and cultural interpretation centers. Returns on tourism to natural areas could be very considerable. For example, the ongoing experimental projects in Maasai Kenya have yielded promising results. The Maasai within the foothills of the Ngurman Escarpment in southern Kenya have received ownership of an area adjacent to Chyulu National Park, where they have created a Maasai-owned company "Maa O'Leng" in collaboration with "Art of Venture." They manage accommodation facilities and tour operations which bring in money to their communities (Tremaine 2003). Furthermore, in northern Kenya, another sustainable locally owned ecotourism project within an area adjacent to Marsabit National Reserve is underway (Saitoti, pers. comm.). A similar project would be ideal for the NCA, where a true conservation and land management scheme could be put into practice, especially on short-grass areas around the western zone. The entire western zone could be allocated to the Maasai and used sustainably under the NCA's guidance to generate income to compensate for the diminishing pastoral resources, notably cattle.

The NCA's failure to understand the basic requirements and priorities of Maasai pastoralists has led to conservation efforts residents find unacceptable. Many conservationists assumed that pastoralism was detrimental to conservation efforts in the area. Deeper understanding of pastoralist traditions and socioeconomic priorities would help resolve conflicts between conservationists and pastoralists. For example, the NCA's prohibition of traditional Maasai fire management practices resulted in a total ban on fire-burning and has led to conflict between pastoralists and NCA officials. Better understanding of the cultural and ecological role of fire-burning will help the NCA devise a better and more controlled fire-burning program. By understanding ecological, socioeconomic, and pastoral attitudes toward fire, the NCA will be able to provide properly timed fire-burning schedules. Normally, traditional fire-burning as practiced by Maasai pastoralists reduces the spread of unproductive species like ticks, certain species of plants, and so on.

Issuance of daily grazing permits on the crater floor could be replaced by weekly permits. A weekly permit scheme could be implemented together with a block oriented ecological monitoring program. This program would help maintain grass species and provide rich pastures to wildlife and livestock.

Olduvai Gorge and Laetoli have been grossly underutilized for over fifteen years, and they have suffered, in consequence, from vandalism and insufficient maintenance. It is of the utmost importance that these sites be put again into use and a conservation program established. Once this has been accomplished, the establishment of a field school at Olduvai Gorge and Laetoli can best serve the long-term future of these sites. Such a program will provide opportunities for students at all levels ranging from primary schools to graduate schools to learn at first hand about their rich biological and cultural evolution (Musiba et al. 2002). Furthermore, with the establishment of a field school at Olduvai Gorge and Laetoli, permanent facilities will have to be be provided at these two sites. These could attract more tourists to the two sites while serving as public information centers for paleoanthropological and archaeological endeavors in Tanzania. Opportunities must be available for Tanzanian children, students, and citizens to visit the sites to be amazed by the vast and rich paleoanthropological heritage of Olduvai Gorge and Laetoli. The two sites will provide unique opportunities, including serving as a backdrop for documentary filmmakers such that fees and royalties obtained from such projects will accrue to the field school and laboratories. Opportunities must be provided for controlled tourism while appropriate facilities—lavatories, souvenir shops, and field museums—are made available to the general public (see Musiba et al. 2002).

Control of the tourist flow into the NCA, especially the crater floor, should be introduced by the NCA authority. We recommend to the NCA that an effective system that will allow advanced booking with a restricted number of visitors per day be implemented. There should be a system that will allow the NCA's liaison office in Arusha to coordinate all bookings between the tour operators, hotels, and the NCA offices at Ngorongoro. This will reduce the number of vehicles entering the crater. According to the Ngorongoro Ecological Monitoring Program, the suggested number of vehicles on the crater's floor should be reduced to around 400 per day (NCA 1992).

As part of these solutions, ecotourism and/or archaeo-tourism as suggested by Mabulla (1996b) is the best solution available for the Maasai–NCA land-use problems. We strongly believe that a well-established, NCA-supervised Maasai tourism enterprise that offers donkey safaris and cultural interpretation of the Maasai early settlements on the crater floor will attract more visitors while exerting no ecological pressures on the environment. To many visitors, this will not only be an enriching lifetime experience but also an authentic cultural adventure provided to them by the pastoral people of the area. The NCA will directly benefit from such an enterprise in the tremen-

147

dous reduction of the number of vehicles entering the crater floor. Ideally, establishment of environmentally friendly permanent viewing posts in designated areas in the crater should be explored in order to reduce the stress on the crater's wildlife caused by vehicles. From such easy-to-manage viewing centers, visitors will have the opportunity to view the Ngorongoro wildlife in a more culturally authentic and ecologically sound atmosphere.

In conclusion, the NCA is the only conservation area in Africa which combines both wildlife conservation and multiple land-use management to provide for sustainable utilization of natural and cultural resources. So far the NCA is the only area that provides insight on how to manage conservation and development at the same time. Development programs that are deeply rooted in Economic Adjustment Programs are generally incompatible with conservation. We believe that the NCA, if well planned and managed, could provide a model for use by other African countries to promote community-oriented and integrated national parks programs. The NCA could act as a model for other areas of the world where the interests of pastoralist communities have yet to be heard.

Acknowledgments

We thank the following institutions: the Wenner-Gren Foundation for Anthropological Research, the National Science Foundation (NSF), the University of Chicago, the University of Florida Center for African Studies, the University of Dar es Salaam (Archaeology Unit), the Commission for Science and Technology (COSTECH, Tanzania), and the Ministry of Science and Technology (Tanzania).

10

The Origins of the State in East Africa

Peter Robertshaw

This chapter uses a set of models that emphasize power and social agency to understand state formation in the Bunyoro-Kitara region of western Uganda and, by way of contrast, on the Swahili coast of East Africa. Building on Blanton et al.'s (1996) distinction between exclusionary (network) and corporate power strategies—the former founded upon wealth-based finance and prestige-goods systems and the latter upon staple-based finance and public works (monuments)—I contrast state formation processes in these two areas. The Swahili coast elites practiced exclusionary power strategies, while Bunyoro-Kitara social stratification was an outcome of corporate power strategies in which elites were reluctant to differentiate themselves through the use of prestige items. The theories explain the apparent invisibility of Bunyoro-Kitara elites.

Among the major goals of archaeology—one of its "Big Questions" (Binford 1983)—is the explanation of the development of sociopolitical complexity or, in more grandiose terms, the rise of civilization. For archaeologists studying sub-Saharan Africa, this question has often been recast as one of origins: Did states arise as the result of migrations of people from elsewhere or were they indigenous African phenomena? Alternatively, might states have arisen among indigenous African peoples with the knowledge and perhaps the accoutrements of statecraft coming from elsewhere? Answers to these questions have been influenced by the context of research. Colonialism and nationalism have tended to set the agendas for archaeological research, even if the results of research have not always been in accordance with dominant ideology (Robertshaw 1990). Thus, the indigenous identity of the builders of Great Zimbabwe was firmly established, at least in the minds of archaeologists and historians, by Caton Thompson in 1929 (Caton Thompson 1931), if not many years earlier by Randall MacIver (1906), despite the preferences of the Rhodesian colonists (M. Hall 1990). Clearly, identification of the site's builders was considered the major mystery of Great Zimbabwe, whereas explanation of the process of state formation was relegated to a secondary role.

The study of state formation in East Africa mirrors the history of the investigation of Great Zimbabwe, in that the identity of the agents of change has been accorded as much (if not more) attention as the process of change. Was it Muslim traders from the Persian Gulf or indigenous African entrepreneurs who founded the Swahili city-states? Is the rise of the kingdoms of the Great Lakes region most correctly attributed to the spread of ideas of divine kingship up the Nile to its headwaters or to the migration of "Hamitic" pastoralists or to local developments?

At least in recent years, answers to these questions have favored indigenous origins, as indeed might be expected after more than thirty years of independence from colonialism. Muslim colonists at the coast and Egyptian divine kingship in the interior have virtually attained the status of dialectical straw men. Thus, with the problem of identity either solved or subjugated to a dominant ideology, attention has begun to focus on questions of process. Explaining the process of state formation in East Africa, however, has not proved as easy a task as that of identifying the actors. To resolve this issue, I make use of a set of models that emphasize power and social agency. My discussion focuses upon the Bunyoro-Kitara region of western Uganda, where I am conducting field research. By way of contrast, I also briefly consider the Swahili coast.

Bunyoro-Kitara

European explorers in the 19th century entered the Great Lakes region (Fig. 10.1) in their search for the sources of the Nile and encountered state-level societies whose leaders seemed to merit the use of the English term "king" (Speke 1863; Grant 1864; Baker 1866) and whose kingdoms included Buganda, Bunyoro, and Nkore, which were later to be incorporated in modern-day Uganda. Since these states were so far removed geographically from historical international trading networks, their origins posed an immediate puzzle, particularly in the prevailing climate of colonialism.

Oral traditions, recorded in the context of the royal courts (Fisher 1911; K.W. 1935; Nyakatura 1973), indicated that the 19th-century states, especially Bunyoro, represented the rump of a much larger Cwezi "empire," centered

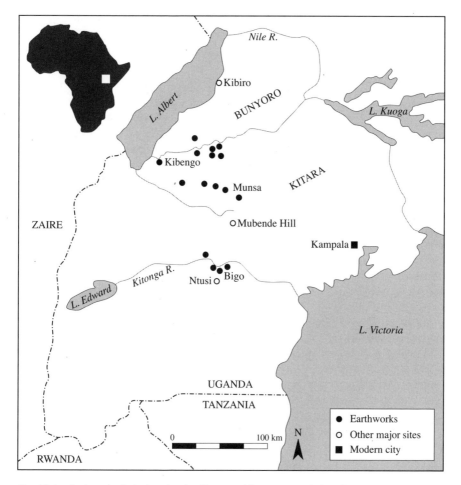

Fig. 10.1 Archaeological sites in the Bunyoro-Kitara area of the Great Lakes region of Uganda.

in Kitara and dating to about the 14th century (Oliver 1953). However, drawing attention to this earlier polity did not, of course, solve the problem of origins. Both oral traditions and ethnography (Roscoe 1923) emphasized the importance of cattle as a source of wealth; cattle were herded by a Huma (Hima) nobility that held sway over an Iru peasantry. Thus, with notions of a diffusion of Egyptian divine kingship or other exotic origins for the state having been dismissed by serious scholars, theories of state formation in Bunyoro-Kitara have emphasized accumulation of wealth in cattle and the control of prime grazing lands (e.g., Posnansky 1966; Sutton 1993). In addition, control of regional trading networks, particularly in salt and perhaps

151

also in iron, has been offered in explanation, as has raiding of surrounding polities for cattle and other booty (e.g., Connah 1987:225–226).

Discussion of cattle and grazing lands as important factors in state formation was not only based on oral traditions and ethnography but also invoked the archaeological evidence. The major monuments in Bunyoro-Kitara are earthworks (Lanning 1953), whose construction implies a ruling elite that possessed the ability to organize, if not coerce, a large labor force. The largest of these earthworks, Bigo, is located in a savanna environment occupied in the recent past primarily by cattle keepers. These observations, together with the limited amount of settlement debris within the earthworks, prompted interpretation of the systems of trenches that comprise the earthworks as large animal enclosures. The earthworks may have been built both to control access to grazing lands and to augment the prestige of elites as well perhaps to serve a defensive function (P. Shinnie 1960; Posnansky 1969; Sutton 1993:50).

The explanation of state formation in Bunyoro-Kitara in terms of cattle, limited grazing lands, and control of internal trading networks begs several questions and requires the acceptance of assumptions that do not jell easily with what is known of African pastoralists. We have no evidence of the size of herds or whether the animals were under any ecological stress. Cattle are the most common animal in the faunal remains recovered from Bigo and other sites (Posnansky 1969), but we have no idea of their relative importance at most other sites lacking earthworks, nor do we know the relative contributions to the subsistence of livestock and agriculture. Although we may in part dismiss some of the criticisms as merely a reflection of the paucity of archaeological data, it is hard to envisage the construction of earthworks as in any way linked to the protection of grazing rights (but see Sutton 1993). Not only are the trenches often poorly sited for defensive purposes but the usual response of pastoralists to pressure upon grazing or to raiding is to move their animals elsewhere or to mount reprisal raids.

There is also little or no archaeological evidence for elite control of intraregional trade networks. There is little evidence for craft specialization linked to the earthworks, if these were indeed the settlements of the elite; nor is there evidence for elite control of the procurement of raw materials or of the distribution of manufactured goods. Indeed, one of the most intriguing aspects of the archaeological record in Bunyoro-Kitara is the paucity of any evidence for wealth accumulation by elites, except, perhaps, in cattle. Indeed, both archaeologists and historians, based upon their separate fields of inquiry, have voiced skepticism about the very existence of a Cwezi state (e.g., Schmidt 1990; Robertshaw 1999; Steinhart 1980; Tantala 1989). Archaeologists are then left to ponder the earthworks, whose construction presumably required considerable labor but not necessarily the organizational and bureaucratic structures of a state-level society.

Various models have also been proposed to account for the rise of the later Nyoro state, though often these models have conflated explanations of the rise of this state with that of the earlier Cwezi state and the earthworks discussed above. The Nyoro state encountered by Europeans in the 19th century and described by ethnographers in the 20th was founded upon a feudal-like system of land tenure in which surplus production was expropriated in the form of tribute (Beattie 1960, 1971). It has been suggested that the differential impact of droughts and consequent famines upon pastoralists and agriculturalists was crucial to the development of the tributary mode of production (Steinhart 1984). Alternatively, the rise of the ruling dynasty was attributed to the ability of its members to act as mediators between pastoralists and farmers in the context of scarce resources (Oliver 1977). Although these ideas represent more or less plausible scenarios, they are speculative constructs. Moreover, they cannot easily be evaluated using archaeological evidence, though this may not, of course, worry historians unduly.

In summary, archaeologists working in the Great Lakes region have either skirted the question of explaining state formation or have proposed rather vague materialist models (e.g., Robertshaw 1997), in which they have often given priority to cattle and intraregional trade (Connah 1987: 225–226). While archaeologists have had very limited data from which to work, research at Kibiro (Connah 1991, 1996; Fig. 10.1) and Ntusi (Reid 1991; Sutton 1993:52ff.; Fig. 10.1), as well as more extensive surveys (Robertshaw 1994), is beginning to rectify this situation. Nevertheless, the models of state formation that have been proposed have mostly invoked ecosystemic processes that ignore factors of social agency and ideology, and overlook the variations in polity scale and complexity that resulted from these processes. Although social agency and ideology have usually been considered difficult to investigate archaeologically, new theoretical perspectives within the discipline now facilitate the integration of these factors into interpretation.

The Swahili Coast

In contrast to the Great Lakes region, the East African coast has been the subject of concerted archaeological and historical research for many years (Fig. 10.2). Thus, it is difficult in this instance to sustain the argument that a lack of relevant data hampers explanation. Historical documents describing the East African coast date to as early as the 1st century AD (Casson 1989). There is abundant historical and archaeological evidence from about AD 800 onward, though recent archaeological research is also beginning to provide information about the missing centuries of the 1st millennium AD (Chami 1994a; Juma 1996). From AD 800, we have evidence of the development of

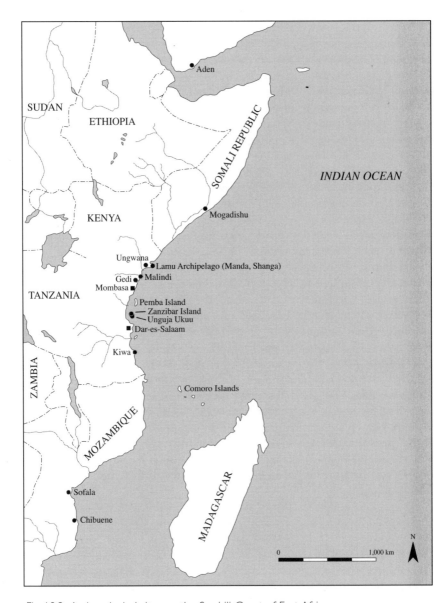

Fig. 10.2 Archaeological sites on the Swahili Coast of East Africa.

urbanism along the coast from southern Somalia to Mozambique, with towns developing at numerous locations where oceangoing vessels could safely breach the coastal reefs. These towns are characterized by an elite quarter, with buildings of coral-rag, surrounded by more extensive areas of mud, timber, and thatch dwellings. Mosques occur in the towns, and Islamic building styles are evident in the stone structures (for a summary of the evidence, see chapter 7 in Connah 1987). On the basis of these building styles, the adherence to Islam, the presence of large quantities of ceramics imported from the Persian Gulf and elsewhere around the Indian Ocean and even China, and the oral traditions of many elite families (which traced their origins to maritime migrations from outside Africa), Swahili towns were often interpreted as trading centers founded by foreign merchants and precariously perched on the shores of Africa (e.g., Kirkman 1964). Thus, international trade, which was dominated by extra-African colonists and facilitated throughout the Indian Ocean by the shared beliefs of Islam, was seen as the major means to the accumulation of wealth and hence, the prime mover in state formation along the East African coast.

This interpretation has been challenged repeatedly in recent decades by both archaeologists and historians who have rejected the model of extra-African colonists and have stressed instead the indigenous African roots of coastal society (e.g., Allen 1993; Masao and Mutoro 1988; Nurse and Spear 1985). Having substituted African origins for exotic ones, some of these researchers have nevertheless remained trapped within the debate over origins, simply transferring the debate to African soil: "which Africans" founded the Swahili towns (e.g., Allen 1993; Horton and Mudida 1993)? Nevertheless, this shift in the debate has prompted new research on coast-hinterland connections (e.g., Abungu and Mutoro 1993).

A few researchers have transcended the debate over origins and chart a processual account of the development of Swahili society. The most thoughtful of these initiatives (H. Wright 1993) argues that long-distance trade alone was not sufficient to promote the rise of sociopolitical hierarchies. Instead, trade promoted inequalities between communities, leading to instability and conflict, which in turn promoted the rise of states through competition; this, of course, is the peer-polity interaction model of state formation (Renfrew and Cherry 1986). In this particular context, Islam promoted a cultural and ideological unity that counteracted divisive economic competition (H. Wright 1993).

At last it seems that some coastal archaeologists are escaping from simplistic models of state formation that pay undue attention to the question of origins and assume that international trade must be the engine that drives the development of sociopolitical complexity. After rejecting these models, it becomes possible to explore explanations of state formation that emphasize social agency, power, and ideology. A focus on these variables both at the coast and in western Uganda will not allow a formulation of a single all-embracing theory of state formation in East Africa. Yet the discussion may help us to gain a better understanding of the archaeological record in both regions. In so doing, we may balance anthropological theory against historical contingency to produce a new perspective on tropical African state formation that may serve to guide further research.

Agency, Power, and the Dual-Processual Theory

Processual archaeology proceeded from the premise that culture was an adaptive system that underwent changes through time, as a result of either external inputs (for example, climatic change or demographic shifts) or internal forces (such as technological developments) that were rooted in one part of the cultural system, which in turn caused changes throughout the system as a result of positive feedback mechanisms. This approach is nicely illustrated by the flow diagrams of state formation commonly encountered in prehistory textbooks (see Brumfiel 1992 for further discussion).

By contrast, postprocessual archaeology (I use this phrase very loosely to refer to the wide variety of archaeologies whose advocates see themselves as being other than "processual"), or at least some manifestations of it, has placed a greater emphasis on the individual within society. This individual is not merely a cog in a cultural wheel but an active participant, whose actions produce and reproduce culture. Different individuals in a society may pursue the same or different goals by a variety of means. Thus, it is the activities of individuals within a particular geographic and historical context that produce, reproduce, and change culture. Among the goals that individuals may pursue are wealth, status, and power. Wealth refers to the accumulation of material possessions; status to the respect, or lack thereof, that one is accorded by other members of the society; and power to the capacity to control the labor and activities of others. Wealth, status, and power are often, but not necessarily, linked. A priest, for example, may have high status but little wealth; his or her power may be evident in some domains but circumscribed in others. In striving for these goals, individuals will use the means at their disposal to attempt to influence, control, or subvert the governing institutions of society (Blanton et al. 1996:2). These "means" are various sources of social power, which Mann (1986) classifies as military, economic, political, and ideological.

In his examination of the concept of power, Mann (1986) also makes several other useful distinctions relevant here. In particular, he distinguishes between the distributive and collective aspects of power and between authoritative and diffused power. Distributive power refers to the power exercised by one person over others, whereas collective power refers to cooperation between individuals that allows them to enhance their control over others or over nature (Mann 1986:6, citing Parsons 1960:199–225). Both these aspects of power must be institutionalized in some way in the culture in which power is exercised. Distributive power correlates to a large extent with authoritative power, which is "actually willed by groups and institutions. It comprises definite commands and conscious obedience" (Mann 1986:8). Diffused power spreads through a population in a less overt manner. Relations of power result from common interest or are part of the natural or moral order of society. Mann (1986) uses the example of the diffused power of capitalism, which has largely defeated the authoritative power of the trade unions. Thus, at a risk of oversimplification, we may create a dichotomy between power in its distributive and authoritative aspects on the one hand, and power in its collective and diffused aspects on the other hand. Blanton et al. (1996:2) recognize this dichotomy under the rubric of "exclusionary" (or "network") and "corporate" power strategies. These authors then discuss how these strategies may operate and be manifested in the archaeological record, thereby providing a point of departure for the present discussion of state formation in East Africa.

Exclusionary strategies are commonly founded upon exchange relationships established between individuals from different ethnic groups. Thus, they focus on long-distance networks of exchange that involve the flow of prestige goods; they are wealth financed rather than staple financed (Earle 1987). Individuals strive to acquire wealth and status through their exotic ties, which they then attempt to convert into authoritative and distributive power within their own society. Since, in theory at least, any individual may pursue long-distance social and economic ties, this strategy is inherently unstable. Therefore, the challenge that successful individuals must meet is to attract followers and institutionalize their authority at home, while maintaining monopoly ties with other elites abroad so that they alone have access to sources of wealth.

Blanton et al. (1996:5) argue that there are two major avenues by which individuals meet this challenge: patrimonial rhetoric and prestige-goods systems. Patrimonial rhetoric invokes and promotes ties between individuals and groups that both emphasize corporate membership (for example, clans and extended families) and institutionalize distributive power (for example, gender hierarchies and conical lineages). Such rhetoric may be invisible in the archaeological record unless it is given material expression in a form that can be read by archaeologists (DeMarrais, Castillo, and Earle 1996). Prestige-goods systems are, by their nature, much more apparent in the archaeological record. Here, elites attempt to attract followers by creating a demand for prestige goods and then controlling their production, exchange, and distribution. Thus, prestige goods may be woven into the fabric of societal reproduction by being substituted for common goods, such as livestock, in contexts such as bridewealth payments or other rites of passage. In order to maintain control of these prestige-goods systems, elites are likely to foster the production of items that are labor-intensive or involve complex technology, since in these contexts they may employ their distributive and authoritative power to harness social and economic resources to which others do not have access (Brumfiel and Earle 1987). Thus, prestige-goods systems may well promote technological innovation in the production of exotic goods rather than agricultural tools and other instruments of staple production (Blanton et al. 1996:5). The other challenge that elites face is to maintain their monopoly of long-distance relationships with other elites. Blanton et al. (1996:5) suggest that this is facilitated by the use of a symbolic vocabulary which they term an "international style," which "facilitates cross-cultural exchanges and reconfirms the elite's legitimacy vis-à-vis other elites."

Corporate strategies, as one might expect, emphasize the collective rather than the individual. They employ the collective and diffused aspects of power. Discussion of the material basis and expression of corporate power strategies in the archaeological literature may be traced to Renfrew's (1974) "group-oriented chiefdoms." These chiefdoms commonly make use of monuments that appear to affirm group solidarity and require major inputs of corporate labor for their construction. They are financed by the production of a surplus of staple goods, such as food crops, rather than by prestige goods. This staple finance is characterized by vertical relations of production and exchange, as opposed to the horizontal relations among elites that are the hallmark of wealth finance and exclusionary power strategies (Kristiansen 1991:22). Thus, in corporate strategies elites promote an ideology of corporate unity, in which they may eschew symbols of individual wealth, such as the ownership and display of prestige goods. Instead, elites appropriate surplus production to build monuments to ancestors or gods, with whom they communicate on behalf of the people. Thus, elites are accorded status and permitted to exercise power, at least in situations where they have no recourse to coercion, because of their organizational skills (P. Wilson 1988:121–122) and their ritual powers. These ritual (or ideological [Mann 1986]) sources of power are employed in perpetuating the well-being of the society as a whole in relation to both the spirit world and material existence. Thus, elites who employ corporate power strategies may be responsible for impressive monuments in the archaeological record without leaving any obvious traces of their own existence, such as burials containing prestige goods or dwellings that are more substantial than those of commoners (Blanton et al. 1996). Similarly, technological innovation is likely to focus on ways in which subsistence production may be intensified rather than on the development of prestige goods.

This discussion of exclusionary and corporate power strategies raises the question of which circumstances are likely to favor the use of one set of strategies rather than another. Blanton et al. (1996:7) point out that "there is a loose association of the corporate strategy with environmental situations providing the potential for substantial agricultural development and of the network strategy with more marginal environments." Clearly, in marginal environments, trade in prestige goods and the development of an international style may be a more feasible power strategy than any attempt to promote and appropriate surplus production of staples. However, a priori there would seem to be no reason why exclusionary strategies would not also succeed in agriculturally fertile core areas. Nevertheless, we may envisage a core/periphery model equated respectively with corporate and exclusionary power strategies. Furthermore, it seems likely that polities founded upon the two different kinds of power strategies would be antagonistic and therefore temporally or spatially separated (Blanton et al. 1996:7).

Dual-Processual Theory and East African State Formation

Blanton et al. (1996) term their formulation of exclusionary and corporate "political economies," which may succeed each other across space and through time, a "dual-processual theory"—a perhaps grandiloquent formulation that attempts to fuse social theory with processual archaeology. These authors apply their theory to the Mesoamerican past. Here, obviously, we are concerned with the goodness-of-fit and explanatory potential of the theory when applied to East African data.

Readers who have come this far will no doubt recognize that correlations can be made between corporate power strategies and western Uganda on the one hand, and exclusionary strategies and the Swahili coast on the other. But does the application of the theory offer any explanatory potential beyond simply matching features of the theory to the archaeological record? It is possible that the elucidation of where the theory does not fit may be more illuminating than seeing where it does fit and may offer directions for future research.

Western Uganda

The Bunyoro-Kitara region, wherein are found the earthworks and other sites that represent the earliest evidence of complex societies, was sparsely inhabited by farmers in the 1st millennium AD (Robertshaw 1994; Fig. 10.1). Immigration into the region from more populous fertile areas along the Lake Victoria shore and in the Western Rift probably occurred around AD 1000 or shortly thereafter (Reid 1991; Robertshaw 1994; Schoenbrun 1993a). Thus, Bunyoro-Kitara may have been a "peripheral" region at this time, at least when viewed at a macro-regional scale. Indeed, I have previously applied Igor Kopytoff's (1987) model of the internal African frontier to this situation and argued that early settlers in the region were constrained by a shortage of labor and thus sought to attract followers by a variety of means, including control over the distribution of iron tools and ritual power (Robertshaw

1999). Although it is not clear, at least in my own mind, whether the processes I have described may be identified as exclusionary or corporate in nature, we might expect such a periphery to be characterized by exclusionary strategies. Individuals would be striving to attract followers in a context in which overall population numbers and densities were low, and where there was probably little or no surplus production of agricultural crops. In such a situation, it would have been almost impossible to promote a corporate identity beyond that of the lineage. Thus, emergent elites may have harnessed their energies to the development of specialized skills and knowledge, such as ironworking and ritual practices, that both enhanced their status and permitted them to engage in some manner in prestige-goods systems, which in turn would facilitate marriage contracts and other mechanisms to increase the size of their communities.

Archaeological evidence for this initial period of settlement is as yet scanty. However, the only two sites from this period to have been investigated in any detail do seem to contain evidence for the existence of prestige-goods systems. At Ntusi, there are glass beads from about the 13th century that must have reached the site through exchange networks stretching to the Indian Ocean over 1,000 miles distant (Reid 1991). Similarly, there is evidence of craft specialization in the production of ivory goods (Reid 1991) which must, by their very nature, have served non-utilitarian or ritual functions and were most likely manufactured for exchange in prestige-goods systems and perhaps to create an "international style." However, at Ntusi there are also earthworks, known as *bwogero* or dams (Sutton 1985), which might equate better with corporate power strategies. These earthworks are undated and may well date to later occupations of the site.

Certainly, this is the case at Munsa, where the earthen trenches were constructed several centuries after initial use of the hill at the center of the site (Robertshaw 1997). Burials are among the earliest features at this site, dating to about the 11th century. Found in most of the adult burials are glass beads or copper or iron bracelets and beads (Robertshaw 1997). These artifacts could be construed as evidence for prestige-goods systems and exclusionary power strategies involving individual markers of elite status—in this instance jewelry presumably worn in life as well as in death.

The relatively small-scale, simple chiefdoms founded upon exclusionary political economies, proposed for the initial period of settlement of Bunyoro-Kitara (Robertshaw 1997), were replaced by the 15th century, if not before, by larger polities founded upon corporate political economies. This scenario appears to be the easiest way to interpret the earthworks, whose construction at Munsa, Kibengo (Robertshaw 2001), and Bigo (Posnansky 1969:135) dates to about the 15th or 16th century. These are by far the largest earthworks in the region (Lanning 1953) and their construction clearly required substantial labor forces. Schmidt (1990) does cautiously suggest that individual earthworks may have been extended at various times in more recent centuries. From the limited dating evidence available, however, this would not seem to be true of Munsa (Robertshaw 1997).

The earthworks are associated with comparatively little occupation debris except at the very center of each site (we can state this with confidence only for Bigo and Munsa), and there is little to suggest the existence of elite individuals. Certainly there is no clear evidence for prestige-goods systems; indeed, not one glass bead or other exotic item has been found at Bigo (Posnansky 1969). Similarly, at Munsa glass beads were recovered only in earlier burials. Thus, the elites remain hidden archaeologically. Instead, we can envisage the workings of corporate power strategies wherein labor was mobilized to build monuments that expressed group solidarity and reaffirmed the social order. Moreover, at least at Munsa, the earthworks were dug around a hill on whose summit were located the burials of an earlier elite whose power had been built through exclusionary strategies. Thus, the Munsa earthworks not only expressed group solidarity in material form but also encircled and metaphorically captured the power and legitimacy of earlier elites.

Furthermore, at the time the earthworks were constructed at this site, large pits were dug at its center. We presume that the primary function of these pits was grain storage. Thus, it appears that surplus food production may have been collected by the elites and stored on the site, perhaps to be redistributed during famines. This would accord with our knowledge of corporate power strategies, which are characterized by surplus food production and vertical relations of inequality. There is also substantial evidence for ironworking at Munsa, again at the center of the site, suggesting, perhaps, elite control of the production of agricultural tools, though the single excavated furnace apparently precedes the construction of the earthworks by a century or two (Robertshaw 1997).

If, as we have proposed, the western Ugandan earthworks are indicative of corporate power strategies, then we must explain the shift away from earlier exclusionary strategies. Tentatively, we may suggest that some of the earlier elites were indeed successful at attracting followers and that in time this led to agricultural intensification and surplus food production (see also Sutton 1993), encouraging elite appropriation of the surplus and the promulgation of ideologies of corporate identity that transcended the lineage or clan. Historical research also points to a growth in the numbers of cattle, as well as new, more inclusive forms of ritual (Tantala 1989). Cattle continue to dominate the faunal assemblage at Munsa (Reid, pers. comm.) and, to a lesser extent, at Bigo. Thus, a successful subsistence economy may have transformed Bunyoro-Kitara from a peripheral area into a core area, in which corporate power strategies facilitated the development of larger polities (complex chiefdoms?) than had existed previously. The role of possible environmental changes in this process is under investigation (Robertshaw and Taylor 2000), but the change may coincide with the end of the Little Ice Age. Studies of neighboring regions, such as the Lake Victoria environs and the Western Rift, are also required to see whether there were corresponding changes, particularly in long-distance exchange networks, elsewhere in the macro-region in which Bunyoro-Kitara is situated.

Two other topics merit consideration in our attempt to apply Blanton et al.'s dual-processual theory to western Uganda. These are, firstly, the role of the Cwezi shrine sites and, secondly, the abandonment of the earthworks and the establishment of the later Nyoro state. Various shrines to members of the Cwezi dynasty are scattered through Bunyoro-Kitara. Such shrines, some of which are still active centers of ritual activity, represent the only sites to be identified with the Cwezi "empire," whose existence has been discounted by many historians. Thus, for example, Mubende Hill is said to have been the first capital of the Cwezi empire (Nyakatura 1973) and has a shrine dedicated to the supposed founder of the empire at which penitents sought various favors, particularly fertility and wealth, with the aid of a resident spirit-medium (Lanning 1966). Excavations at this site revealed a village with numerous pits containing grindstones and pottery, as well as bones from a wide variety of animals including cattle; there was little evidence for the existence of a prestige-goods system (Lanning 1966; Robertshaw 1994:108). With calibrated radiocarbon dates in the late 13th and 14th centuries, settlement at the site is earlier than the construction of the earthworks at Munsa and elsewhere (Robertshaw 1994:108).

The continued ritual importance of this site for centuries after its initial occupation suggests that in some sense it was (and still is) a place of power. However, to categorize the site within the exclusionary/corporate dichotomy is problematic. On the one hand, the fact that important Nyoro coronation rituals were held here indicates that members of the Bito dynasty sought both to derive legitimacy from the shrine and its Cwezi spirits and to validate the site as a symbol of Nyoro ethnic identity, thereby encapsulating it within corporate power strategies. On the other hand, it is clear that the spirit-mediums resident at this and other shrines enjoyed a great deal of independence within the Nyoro state. It seems that the shrines served as symbolic, and perhaps on occasion actual, centers of resistance to the imposition of Bito authority (Berger 1981). In this respect, it may be argued that spirit-mediums were harnessing ritual authority as part of exclusionary power strategies in opposition to the Nyoro state. Therefore, we may point to the existence of competition between individualizing elites and the corporate political economy of the Nyoro state. Here, then, we may recognize the existence of a dynamic struggle between individuals and groups which employed, respectively, exclusionary and corporate power strategies. We can thus easily comprehend how the eventual triumph of one side might have transformed the region's political economy if British colonialism had not intervened. Moreover, in the historical context of the 14th century, what we may be observing at Mubende Hill is an exclusionary strategy founded upon ideological (ritual) sources of power that preceded the establishment of the later corporate polities responsible for the construction of the earthworks.

What about the establishment of the later Nyoro state? Here we have relevant ethnographic and historical data but little archaeological evidence. We know that the earthworks were abandoned and it has been suggested that there was a concomitant shift from nucleated to more dispersed settlement patterns (Robertshaw 1994). The historical evidence indicates that the ruling dynasty of the Nyoro state, the Bito, came from the region immediately north of Bunyoro, and that they were in some manner ignorant of the traditions of cattle keeping (Beattie 1960; Nyakatura 1973). In terms of dual-processual theory, the ethnographic data (see especially Beattie 1960, 1971) are best interpreted as documenting a political economy founded upon corporate power strategies. What precipitated the changes while maintaining a framework of corporate strategies? Historians have proposed various theories (e.g., Steinhart 1984; Oliver 1977). Given the paucity of archaeological data, it may be wise to profess our own ignorance, while suggesting that answers may lie in competition between elites struggling within a context of climatic shifts and of events and historical processes occurring beyond the borders of Bunyoro.

The Swahili Coast

Perched on the "edge" of Africa in a region where many areas are rather marginal for agriculture and where livestock are prone to numerous diseases, the coast is easily perceived as a peripheral region. Here, then, we would a priori expect exclusionary power strategies to be the modus operandi. (Of course, this may be assailed as a landlubber's perspective. By contrast, one might view coastal settlements as situated in close proximity to a bounteous ocean teeming with fish and marine mammals and criss-crossed by international trade routes.)

Indeed, examination of the archaeological record points to exclusionary power strategies in which elites sought to acquire control over the exchange and distribution of prestige goods, while creating an "international style" founded upon the ideology of Islam and aspects of Asian material culture, including architecture and fine ceramics. The existence of such an "international style" does not, of course, imply the presence of foreign colonists on the East African coast; indigenous African entrepreneurs would cultivate this style in order to legitimize their elite status with their trading partners around the Indian Ocean and, presumably, to impress the members of their local communities. Moreover, in accord with the technological implications of exclusionary strategies, as discussed above, there is evidence for considerable craft production at an early date on Swahili sites—for example in iron and in shell beads (Chittick 1974, 1984)—as well as for technological innovation. Indeed, recent research has discovered the oldest crucible steel in the world at the site of Galu on the Kenya coast (C. Kusimba 1993; Kusimba, Killick, and Creswell 1994; Fig. 10.1), and actual crucibles, probably for smelting copper, have been reported from Manda (Chittick 1984:212).

As we have seen, there is compelling evidence for exclusionary power strategies in the latter part of the 1st millennium AD leading to the development of competing towns along the East African coast (H. Wright 1993). As coastal populations increased and the apparatus of state-level societies was established, however, we might predict a shift toward corporate power strategies within the context of larger polities. Certainly, this dynamic is evident in various regions of Mesoamerica (Blanton et al. 1996). Does it occur on the East African coast also?

The period of the 11th through the 13th centuries is marked by rapid population increase concomitant with notable growth in the number and size of settlements. Thus, it is in this period that we might expect a shift to corporate power strategies. Several lines of evidence suggest that this shift did indeed occur. Particularly notable is the shift to Islam's becoming the religion of the masses rather than one practiced only by the elite, as may well have been the case previously. Horton (1987:319) remarks that "the widespread and deliberate conversion of East African coastal communities to Islam...took place during the eleventh century." This process of Islamization occurred first in the larger settlements, as is evident from a flurry of mosque construction and the appearance of Islamic tombs (see H. Wright 1993:669 for a summary of the evidence). Thus, Islam was converted from an aspect of "international style" that served to distinguish elites from commoners into a symbol of larger corporate identity.

In addition, there is evidence for greater investment in public architecture and monumental building in this period. The so-called sea walls at Manda were greatly expanded (Chittick 1984), while at Kilwa the Great Mosque was constructed (Chittick 1974). Other sites along the coast also document increased building in stone, particularly of mosques (see H. Wright 1993).

While such work may be indicative of a concern with corporate identity and hence, the application of corporate power strategies, it would appear that there was no associated shift from wealth-based to staple-based finance. The towns that thrived in this period seem to have been those entrepots through which most trade goods passed. Thus, prestige-goods systems still flourished, as is evident not only from the wealth of imported ceramics, beads, and other items but also from the local minting of coins at Kilwa

(Chittick 1974; Fig. 10.2), Mogadishu (Chittick 1982a; Fig. 10.2), and perhaps other towns. The theoretical dichotomy between exclusionary strategies and wealth-based finance on the one hand, and corporate strategies and staple-based finance on the other, seems to break down when applied to the Swahili of the first half of the 2nd millennium AD. Clearly there are economic, ecological, and geographic factors that may make the Swahili case unusual, if not unique. It is also possible, however, that the transition from exclusionary to corporate power strategies did not reach its conclusion because of the interference of the Portuguese at the beginning of the 16th century. Although such speculation is inherently unsatisfactory, we might argue that, in the absence of Portuguese interference, a gradual shift from wealth-based to some form of staple-based finance might have eventually occurred. It is intriguing, therefore, that the state centered upon Great Zimbabwe began to fragment in the mid-15th century (Huffman 1995). This suggests that, even without Portuguese interference, the gold trade, on which the wealth of Kilwa and, to a lesser degree, other coastal towns depended, might have collapsed. At that point, a change to staple-based finance would have presumably represented one possible adaptation to changing circumstances.

Conclusion

The sociopolitical context in which East African archaeology has been undertaken has led, when addressing many issues in the region's prehistory, almost inexorably to a concern with origins, including state formation. Debate over exotic versus indigenous origins has been misconstrued as being alternative explanations for the rise of states. The identification of origins is decidedly not the same as the explanation of the process of state formation. Now that the origins debate has been recognized as the red herring that it is, or at least now that it has been flogged like the proverbial dead horse, archaeologists have at last begun to turn their attention to the study of the processes of state formation.

I have argued here that sociological perspectives that emphasize the active role of individuals in seeking, attaining, and consolidating power hold considerable promise in understanding this process. Power may be derived from a variety of sources and may be manifested and exercised in various ways. Similarly, power may be materialized and given expression in what constitutes the archaeological record. The archaeological record, however, is not simply a text from which we can readily excerpt the sentences and chapters concerning power. We must first develop appropriate epistemological and methodological tools. Here I chose to follow Blanton et al. (1996) in drawing a distinction between exclusionary (network) and corporate power strategies, the former founded upon wealth-based finance and prestige-goods systems, and the latter upon staple-based finance and public works (monuments). The scheme has heuristic value in offering explanations for such apparent "mysteries" as the invisibility of elites in western Uganda and the varied pace of technological innovation in different regions. Moreover, the concern with social agency and power creates a rubric through which we may comprehend the effects on a society of external forces—for example, climatic change or the diffusion of technology. Archaeologists may thereby escape both the sterile search for origins and the tyranny of single-factor explanations such as "climate change" or "population increase" that promote simplistic reductionism. Consideration of social agency may not only lead to the development of models to explain the process of state formation but may also suggest answers to some of archaeology's other Big Questions.

II

East African Archaeology: A Southern African Perspective

Peter Mitchell

When in 1947 the First Pan-African Congress on Prehistory met in Nairobi it initiated a series of meetings that continue to bring together archaeologists and others involved in the reconstruction of Africa's past. In that immediate postwar period a particularly close linkage was perceived between the prehistories of southern and East Africa: Stone Age cultural assemblages from East Africa were, for example, described as "Wilton," after the typesite of southern Africa's own Holocene microlithic tradition (L. Leakey 1931). Furthermore, the basic chronostratigraphic frameworks for the Quaternary of both regions had been tied together by Van Riet Lowe's (1929) and Smuts's (1932) southward extension of L. Leakey's (1929) pluvial hypothesis, which correlated presumed periods of higher rainfall in Africa with periods of glacial advance in the northern hemisphere. The discrediting of this pluvial scheme (Flint 1959) was followed by the 1965 Burg-Waterstein conference (Bishop and Clark 1967), which encouraged the development of more regionally focused cultural taxonomies that, though much needed, have perhaps impeded longer distance comparisons. While the institutionalization of apartheid in South Africa and Namibia after 1948 and Southern Rhodesia's unilateral declaration of independence in 1965 contributed to the isolation of those working in southern Africa, more positively the proliferation of research increasingly directed archaeologists' attention to the complexities of the data and theoretical problems of their own areas. Research contributions from different parts of the continent have been brought together in successive conference proceedings and edited volumes (e.g., Clark and Brandt 1984; Shaw et al. 1993; Sutton [ed.] 1994/95; Pwiti and Soper 1996; Connah 1998; S. McIntosh 1999; van der Veen 1999; Blench and MacDonald 2000), as well as in the Cambridge and UNESCO histories of Africa, but only a few archaeologists have recently felt comfortable enough with the archaeological records of both regions to essay either a general synthesis (e.g., Phillipson 1977, 1994) or more specific comparisons (e.g., Connah 2001).

It is thus with some trepidation, and conscious of my own limited first-hand acquaintance with the archaeological record of East Africa, that I offer here a southern African perspective on recent research in Kenya, Tanzania, and Uganda. As I comment on the individual chapters, I attempt to isolate some of the themes that run through and between the individual contributions, themes which, I believe, speak to the present and future practice of archaeology north and south of the Zambezi. Beginning with S. B. Kusimba and C. M. Kusimba's investigation in Chapter 1 of hunter-gatherer mobility strategies, I consider studies of technological organization and the relationship between Later Stone Age (LSA) archaeology (including rock art) and hunter-gatherer ethnography (cf. Mabulla, Chapter 3 this volume). Karega-Munene's discussion of pastoralism in Chapter 2 not only invites comparison with the rapidly developing subject of pastoralist origins in southern Africa, but, like Wandibba's chapter (4) on the ethnoarchaeology of pottery, raises the issue of how far ethnicity may be evident in material culture, an issue that goes to the heart of both Iron Age research in southern Africa and studies there of the relations between foragers and pastoralists.

The embeddedness of artifact production within a matrix of social and ideological relations is something stressed not only by Wandibba, but also by Mapunda (Chapter 5) and by Kusimba and Killick (Chapter 7) in their respective contributions on iron technology. Though less investigated from an ethnoarchaeological standpoint south of the Zambezi, the connections between ironworking and Iron Age worldviews have been explored by several authors (e.g., Collett 1993; Whitelaw 1994/95), while D. Miller (1996) has undertaken extensive metallurgical analyses of Iron Age metal artifacts that provide a comparison with Kusimba and Killick's study.

The significance of iron production as a basis for political power is stressed both by Mapunda and by Kusimba and Killick, while Kessy (Chapter 8) identifies local trade as an important factor in urban and state development on the East African coast.

Brought within the purview of Blanton et al.'s (1996) general model for state formation by Robertshaw in Chapter 10, comparisons can be sought with the relative importance in southern Africa of indigenous factors and external Indian Ocean coast–oriented trade in the rise of such states as Mapungubwe and Great Zimbabwe.

Running through many of the preceding chapters is a further theme that is perhaps the most important of all, namely the responsibility of contemporary archaeologists not only to the archaeological record but also to the communities among which, or for which, they work, whether in the field of ethnoarchaeology (Mabulla, Chapter 3 this volume) or that of cultural heritage management and the conservation of archaeological sites (Musiba and Mabulla, Chapter 9 this volume). Closely tied to the development of histories that are free of the racist biases of the past, as well as to issues of ecotourism and the generation of funding for archaeological research, this theme of responsibility is one of increasing interest and debate in southern, just as in East African archaeology.

Kusimba and Kusimba's analysis in Chapter 1 of lithic assemblage variability at two Kenyan localities—Lukenya Hill and Kisio Rock Shelter—provokes several comparisons with LSA archaeology in southern Africa, two of which I consider here, and a third below. Focusing first on the late Pleistocene period represented at Lukenya Hill (S. Kusimba 2001), shared features of the southern and East African archaeological records at this time include a general rarity of sites and a tendency for them to concentrate in or close to areas of greater topographic diversity. In southern Africa ecological factors have been held responsible for both patterns, with paleoenvironmental indicators suggesting that the prevalence of cold, dry conditions at the Last Glacial Maximum reduced ecological productivity and concentrated settlement into areas of greatest ecological diversity (J. Deacon 1984). As Kusimba and Kusimba indicate, more recent discussion of this period in the southern African literature has questioned the validity of previously postulated contrasts between Pleistocene and Holocene lifeways, and specifically the association, during the former period, of large game hunting, high mobility, and large group size (H. Deacon 1972). Plant foods may have held a key role in the subsistence strategies of both periods, with changes in the distribution of plant food staples largely responsible for shifts in the distribution of human populations through the most recent glacial-interglacial cycle (H. Deacon 1993).

With paleoenvironmental reconstructions becoming increasingly fine grained, we can begin to inquire not only how subsistence strategies altered in relation to successive shifts in climatic and ecological conditions but also how they varied across space, thus moving away from a monolithic view of late Pleistocene adaptations. That both Hadzabe (Mabulla, Chapter 3 this volume) and Kalahari Bushman (Lee 1979) ethnography demonstrate that plant food–based adaptations are just as feasible in dry grasslands as those based on "big game hunting" is apposite here, as is the possibility that Pleistocene LSA adaptations in the Lukenya Hills area differed from or were linked to those known in more upland areas, such as the Central Rift Valley (Ambrose 1992). From a southern African perspective, this recalls Parkington's (1990) cautions about reconstructing prehistoric settlement-subsistence systems from partial settlement distributions (sensu Gamble 1984), as well as work by Klein (1984) and Opperman (1987) that suggests much greater continuity in hunting patterns across the Pleistocene/Holocene boundary in some areas than in the Cape Fold Mountain Belt. Nevertheless, the Pleistocene record from southern Africa still has nothing with which to parallel Lukenya Hill site GvJm46, interpreted by Marean (1990) as a mass-drive site for killing a now extinct small alcelaphine.

Despite their prominence as sources of archaeological materials, the use of rock shelters by hunter-gatherers has received little ethnographic or ethnoarchaeological study. Mabulla's contribution (Chapter 3) in this respect is thus an important aspect of his detailed and highly informative chapter on Hadzabe land-use patterns. His identification of separate female/male activity areas for the manufacture of beads and arrows not only recalls similar observations among Kalahari Bushmen, but also brings to mind Wadley's (1987) identification of this kind of structured use of space in mid-Holocene levels at Jubilee Shelter near Johannesburg. That Hadzabe construct fences and other structures within rock shelters to demarcate sleeping, cooking, and working areas provides ethnographically grounded evidence with which to interpret the stakeholes found in some rock shelter excavations, such as at Sehonghong, Lesotho (Carter, Mitchell, and Vinnicombe 1988), for which a comparable, though less detailed, oral tradition was recorded by P. Vinnicombe (pers. comm.). Mabulla's evidence also recalls the brush-defined living areas found in Holocene contexts at Big Elephant Shelter, Namibia (Clark and Walton 1962), as well as the bed-and-ash pattern characteristic of many Western Cape rock shelters (e.g., Parkington and Poggenpoel 1987). His further observation that Hadzabe use rock shelters on a seasonal basis for protection from the elements and from predators is a useful reminder against archaeologists' temptation to see rock shelters as central to rather than one component of a settlement system, as is his caution that most material is discarded immediately outside the dripline. Bolahla rock shelter in southern Lesotho is one of the few in southern Africa at which talus deposits have been systematically investigated and shown to contain stratigraphically consistent patterns of change in artifact deposition (Mitchell, Parkington, and Yates 1994).

Mabulla identifies Hadzabe perception of their landscape and its history as an important aspect of his research. In southern Africa Janette Deacon (1988) was one of the first archaeologists to address this issue. Using the extensive ethnographic record of the now extinct /Xam Bushmen of the Northern Cape Province collected in the later 19th century by Wilhelm Bleek and Lucy Lloyd, she was able to show that some features of the local landscape known to be of mythological significance were also marked by concentrations of rock engravings. More recently, Solomon (1997) and

Ouzman (1998) have explored the relation between landscape and rock art from a phenomenological perspective, while Ouzman and Wadley (1997) have combined rock art and excavated data to investigate the significance—as a "place"—of Rose Cottage Cave in the eastern Free State. What makes a given rock shelter a particularly significant place may be difficult to establish, though Mabulla identifies, perhaps not surprisingly, its degree of protection and the possibilities afforded by its outlook for surveying the landscape for game as important physical criteria. Many rock shelters in the Eyasi Basin are painted but there seems no evidence at present that ritual activities are undertaken inside them, nor do contemporary Hadzabe paint (Lim 1992). Nevertheless, Mabulla records their claim to authorship of prehistoric art within their territory, a claim that suggests ethnographic data might be used to explore the meaning of this art, just as has been done in southern Africa (Lewis-Williams and Dowson 1999).

Ethnoarchaeological studies of contemporary hunter-gatherer groups have, of course been undertaken in the Kalahari—one thinks of key studies by such workers as John Yellen (1977) and the late Susan Kent (1993)—but tracing the connections between them and the deeper, prehistoric past has been less intensively undertaken. Smith and Lee's (1997) study thus marks a welcome return to this subject in southern African archaeology in helping to establish the extent to which contact with pastoralists, Iron Age farmers, and European settlers has transformed Kalahari hunter-gatherers to the point that analogies with the LSA past are of negligible value. Mabulla's contention that in East Africa such contacts do not preclude ethnographic studies from contributing to the development of general principles and processes that affect all hunter-gatherer societies, past and present, sits more comfortably with the views of scholars such as Kent (1992) and Solway and Lee (1990) than with the argument that foragers are inevitably marginalized and consigned to a subservient position when they engage with food-producing societies (Wilmsen 1989). Here I turn to the third major focus of Kusimba and Kusimba's chapter, noting that Kisio Rock Shelter has clear evidence for occupation by people who combined intensive use of a variety of small bovids and ground game with access to trade beads and iron artifacts. As the authors point out, ethnohistorically documented Wasanye and Waata foragers provide a plausible authorship for these archaeological residues and thus one interpretation for their Kisio site, though this explanation is in need of testing elsewhere in the Tsavo area (cf. Kusimba and Kusimba 2000). Parallels with the southern African literature are easy to find: Denbow (1999), van der Ryst (1998), and S. Hall and Smith (2000) all discuss the development of exchange links between hunter-gatherers and farmers, while Wadley (1996) emphasizes the possibilities for assimilation and disruption of forager social relations that such contacts may have produced. Kusimba and Kusimba also note that cultural change may have been a two-way process, with food producers opting to abandon cultivation and/or live-stock keeping in favor of foraging and/or occupational specializations that included hunting and the supply of other bush products: three Khoe-speak-ing, but physically negroid groups—the Dama of Namibia, the Kwadi of Angola, and the so-called River Bushmen of northern Botswana—may illus-trate this process in southern Africa (Barnard 1992).

Karega-Munene's chapter (2) does an admirable job of deconstructing the history of the nomenclature that has grown up around the archaeologi-cal cultures now generally referred to as Pastoral Neolithic. Much of the empirical evidence that he then discusses calls to mind contemporary debates surrounding the introduction of pastoralism into southern Africa. The importance of knowing what it is that radiocarbon dates are dating is one of these (Bousman 1998). In particular, Sealy and Yates (1994, 1996) have shown that most early claims for the presence of sheep in southern Africa are misleading since direct AMS dating of the sheep bones themselves establishes that they have migrated downward within rock shelter deposits or that original stratigraphic interpretations were at fault (but cf. Henshilwood 1996). With the exception of some of those associated with Kansyore ware, all of the radiocarbon determinations listed by Karega-Munene for the Pastoral Neolithic older than 3000 BP have been run on bone apatite, which is generally considered an unreliable medium, or on charcoal that, in the light of the southern African experience, may or may not be reli-ably associated with remains of domestic livestock. An AMS dating program might help clarify the spread of livestock rearing into East Africa, while simultaneously offering a more informed idea of where to look for the prox-imate sources of the sheep, goats, and cattle concerned.

The absence to date of any direct evidence for cultivation at Pastoral Neolithic sites is also intriguing; Robertshaw and Collett's (1983) arguments to the contrary depend entirely on indirect lines of argument. The parallel here with southern African Khoekhoe pastoralists is close since ethnohis-toric sources suggest the only plant they may have cultivated was cannabis (Elphick 1977). In both cases too, at least as far as south-central Namibia and the Western Cape Province of South Africa are concerned, we are looking at pastoralists for whom symbiotic exchange relationships with cereal produc-ers were impossible: Iron Age farming communities were absent from the areas in which pastoralists lived. As both Bower (1997) and R. McIntosh (1997) have commented, this makes the prehistoric African pastoralist record strikingly different from the subsistence ecology of any ethnograph-ically pastoralist community. Symbiotic exchanges between pastoralists and foragers may have existed, as they do in parts of East Africa today, but com-petition for wild resources with forager groups is also likely, at least in areas best suited for keeping livestock. The progressive confinement of foragers to areas marginal for a pastoral way of life has, for example, been identified as a strong theme in the archaeology of the Western Cape (Parkington and Hall 1987), with ethnically quite distinct forager and pastoralist populations identified in the material culture record (Smith et al. 1991). Debate continues between the proponents of this argument and the view that what the Dutch and other Europeans observed in the 16th and 17th centuries AD was a single socioeconomic continuum in which some groups held large numbers of livestock and a dominant political position over others temporarily without herds for reasons of theft and disease (see Mitchell 2002: chapter 9, for fuller discussion with references).

As Karega-Munene indicates, the diversity of ceramic wares identified in the East African Pastoral Neolithic also remains poorly understood. Interestingly, this too is a phenomenon that also is now becoming apparent south of the Zambezi. Here, between ca. 2100 and 1500 BP, archaeologists are no longer only confronted with the earliest Iron Age pottery in the eastern half of the subcontinent (Whitelaw 1998) and Cape coastal ware from sites like Die Kelders (Schweitzer 1979) in the southern and southwestern Cape. From northern Botswana, the Matopo Hills of western Zimbabwe, and almost as far south as Johannesburg we have Bambata ware, interpreted by Huffman (1994) as Iron Age in origin, though found almost exclusively in LSA rock shelter contexts (for alternative interpretations of Bambata ware see N. Walker 1983; Reid, Sadr, and Hanson-James 1998). In southeastern southern Africa Mazel (1992; but cf. 1999) has made a strong case that thin-walled undecorated ceramics found in LSA rock shelter contexts may predate the introduction of heavily decorated, thicker-walled Iron Age pottery, while in the Eastern Cape other undecorated pottery comes from Uniondale rock shelter (Leslie 1989). Still further confusing the situation, finger-nail impressed ceramics from Geduld, north-central Namibia, and Buffelskom in the foothills of the Soutpansberg Mountains 1500 km to the southeast add another dimension to the variability of these early pottery traditions (Smith and Jacobson 1995; S. Hall and Smith 2000). The tenuousness of the correlations made in East Africa and described by Karega-Munene should serve as a caution to southern African researchers against assigning all of these wares, in the first instance, to distinct cultural if not ethnolinguistic entities.

The processes by which pottery and domestic livestock entered southern and East Africa thus form a potentially fruitful area for the interchange of ideas between archaeologists working in the two parts of the continent. Bower's (1991) "trickle-and-splash" model, for example, suggests that before 3000 BP livestock (though not perhaps dairy products) formed only a small part of the total diet among East African stockkeepers, raising the possibility that sheep and later cattle were taken up by foragers for ecological, subsistence, and/or social reasons that remain to be explored; an argument that finds a southern African parallel in the work of Kinahan (1991) in the central Namib desert (but see Smith, Nates, and Jacobsen 1996). The possibility that late Holocene foragers were moving toward a delayed returns economy (Jerardino 1996; S. Hall 2000) may provide a social and/or economic context for the introduction of ceramics and sheep, just as in East Africa the presence of pottery-using "aqualithic" groups in the Lake Turkana region (Phillipson 1977) may signal the presence of communities receptive to the possibilities that stock rearing offered for wealth accumulation and countering subsistence risk. The "splash" component of Bower's (1991) model, evident from around 3000 BP, sees the development of specialized pastoral economies in East Africa, perhaps linked to movements of people from further north. A similar two-stage interpretation may prove attractive in southern Africa, where cattle seem a distinctly later introduction than sheep in the Western Cape (Klein and Cruz-Uribe 1989), and both Henshilwood (1996) and Sadr (1998) have suggested that the development of pastoralism, as a socially and economically distinct lifestyle, was a much later phenomenon than the introduction of sheep and pottery. Sadr's (1998) admittedly controversial proposal that the historic Khoekhoen only moved south from northern Botswana to enter the Cape ca. 1200–900 BP might provide the "splash" needed for a southern African application of Bower's model. Facilitating but also constraining the "trickles" and "splashes" of livestock movement into and between East and southern Africa, we should also bear in mind the role played by animal diseases and the distributions of their vectors or host populations; Gifford-Gonzalez's (2000) innovative paper on the distribution of some of these infections south of the Sahara should act as a spur to much further work in this field.

A major theme of current East African research (e.g., Karega-Munene, Chapter 2 this volume) is that similarities and differences in material culture reflect not only cultural and linguistic divisions but also a range of other relationships between the producers and consumers of pottery and, we might add, other kinds of artifacts. Wandibba's chapter (4) on ceramic ethnoarchaeology in Kenya provides much hard evidence in support of this contention and invites comparison with recent ethnoarchaeological work in Cameroon, which seeks to examine the meaning of ceramic style at all levels of artifact production and consumption (Gosselain et al. 1996). Both this work and Mapunda's study of the sociology of iron production in Tanzania offer important insights into the spatial and gender organization of craft activities. In southern Africa comparatively little detailed ethnoarchaeological research of this kind has been undertaken among agricultural communities (but see, for example, Krause 1985; and references cited in Lane 1998a) and the opportunities for carrying it out may now be disappearing quickly as urbanization and market penetration proceed and traditional knowledge is lost. They are, however, opportunities that should be seized in order to flesh out, from a more archaeologically directed perspective, the information recorded by 19th-century travelers and settlers and 20th-century ethnographers.

The cautions raised by Karega-Munene, Wandibba, and Mapunda against making direct correlations between material culture and ethnicity have a particular resonance in southern African Iron Age studies, where the dominant approach tends to emphasize precisely this kind of identification. As outlined by Tom Huffman (1989) ceramic style is part of an "integrated and repetitive code of cultural symbols [that], to be used and understood,...has to be learned by a group of people speaking the same language" (Huffman and Herbert 1994/95:31). It follows then that, unless there is clear evidence for the production of pottery for market exchange, differences in ceramic style connote differences in ethnic affiliation and that the movement of peoples from one area to another can thus be traced fairly directly in the archaeological record. But missing from arguments that equate ceramic style with ethnicity to the exclusion of other factors (such as trade, intercommunity marriage, social class, or political position; cf. Mapunda, Chapter 5 this volume) is the post-processualist recognition that material culture has an active part in and does not only passively reflect social life (Hodder 1982). Arguing the same point for the Late Iron Age of KwaZulu-Natal M. Hall and Mack (1983) suggest that the emphasis on equating pots with people is not unrelated to the past political environment in southern Africa, in which minority governments emphasized the search for tribal diversity and classification (M. Hall 1984a). Since, however, Early Iron Age societies were, at the very least, divided along lines of age and gender and in some areas seem to have been stratified politically from the middle of the 1st millennium AD (Whitelaw 1994/95), competing interests in the use of material symbols were surely present. The challenge must rather be whether we as archaeologists can pick them up since, as Binford (1962) remarked four decades ago, cultural systems are differentially organized and all artifacts and other products of human activity carry potential information on all aspects of those cultural systems.

In a parallel spirit Lane (1994/95, 1998b) critiques the other principal model employed by Iron Age archaeologists in southern Africa, Huffman's (1989, 1996a) cognitive-structural models for understanding Iron Age settlement patterns. The spatio-temporally more widespread of these identifies the Central Cattle Pattern, first formulated by Kuper (1980), as a model for the organization of settlement space determined by attitudes relating to the symbolic value of cattle in acquiring wealth and women and to a patrilineal kinship system that reveres male ancestors. This model has now been widely recognized south of the Limpopo at sites dating to the 1st and 2nd millennia AD. Yet, as Lane points out, several issues have been neglected in the rush to apply it. Among these are (1) the general validity of the 19th/20th-century ethnographies employed and the historical specificity of the analogies drawn from them (cf. M. Hall 1984b); (2) a failure to consider the possibility that contact with forager communities may be reflected not only at the genetic and linguistic levels but also at the symbolic (e.g., Tesele 1994; Hammond-Tooke 1998); and (3) the implication that the basic ideology and settlement system of southern African Iron Age communities persisted with little alteration over some two millennia of demographic growth, expansion, migration, and socioeconomic change (M. Hall 1986; Segyobe 1993). If we query the structuralist focus on a single, generalized, idealized model of settlement and social structure and a Childean view of archaeological cultures, then the opportunity exists to try and make sense of variety, rather than uniformity, in the architectural layout, symbolic organization, and material culture of Iron Age settlements, including the potential role of structuring principles other than those reflected in the Central Cattle Pattern (e.g., Sekgarametso 1995). Several social practices are apparent in the Early Iron Age but unrecorded in most of the subcontinent ethnographically (Maggs 1994/95). That this is so reinforces the case for important social changes having taken place among farming communities south of the Limpopo over the past two millennia.

Huffman and Herbert's (1994/95) suggestion, based on parallel linguistic and ceramic design arguments, that the Sotho/Tswana- and Nguni-speaking peoples of southern Africa only migrated there from East Africa around the end of the 1st millennium AD, identifies southern Tanzania in particular as an important area for a collaborative program of Iron Age research between southern and East African based–workers. The value of such a program might, however, in the light of the points just made, go beyond the specific dimensions of their hypothesis to initiate a broader exchange of ideas, bringing a concern with the symbolic organization of social space more fully into East African archaeology, while encouraging southern African workers to question the ethnicity/style equation within a culturally more varied setting (cf. Hodder 1982; Moore 1986; Saetersdal 1999).

Robertshaw's discussion of the applicability to East Africa of Blanton et al.'s (1996) model of state formation raises many of the same general issues. In southern Africa the emergence of state-level societies has been traced from late 1st/early 2nd millennium AD sites, such as Schroda and then Bambandyanalo, in the Limpopo Valley, through the nearby site of Mapungubwe, to Great Zimbabwe and its successors (Pikirayi 2001). It has been argued that a central element of this process was the development of a new kind of settlement pattern, expressive of the establishment of sacred kingship, a state bureaucracy, and a class system, including the physical segregation of the king's household and royal burials on a hilltop, the use of stone walling to delineate elite areas of a settlement, and the presence of an area set aside for premarital initiation schools (Huffman 1996a). State formation processes among Nguni- and Sotho/Tswana-speaking peoples in the 18th and 19th centuries developed along different lines, although a new settlement pattern did characterize both the Zulu state and some of its offshoots (Mitchell 2002).

Robertshaw's adoption of Blanton et al.'s (1996) distinction between exclusionary and corporate power strategies might, I suggest, prove helpful in understanding variability among such state formation processes south of the Zambezi, just as much as in East Africa, not least because it focuses attention on issues of power and ideology that are already present, explicitly or implicitly, in studies of the Zimbabwe Tradition (Garlake 1973a; M. Hall 1987; Huffman 1996a; Pikirayi 2001). Can we, for example, see exclusionary strategies of power being pursued (as Robertshaw suggests for the Swahili towns) more strongly early on in the Shashe-Limpopo Basin (Schroda and Bambandanyalo)? And did corporate ones, emphasizing the sacred role of the king in interceding through his ancestors with God to ensure rain and prosperity, become more important thereafter, marked by the construction of stone-walled enclosures and elite shifts to hilltop locations at Mapungubwe and Great Zimbabwe? Were exclusionary strategies more important in southern Africa, as they were in Mesoamerica (Blanton et al. 1996), in ecologically more marginal areas (the Limpopo Valley, the eastern Kalahari), rather than in those with greater potential for agricultural production (the Zimbabwe Plateau)? How far do we find evidence for Later Iron Age elites developing an international style that, as Blanton et al. (1996) argue, would have reconfirmed their legitimacy vis-à-vis other elites? Did the exotic ceramics and iron gongs at Great Zimbabwe (Garlake 1973b) help create this legitimacy by making reference to elite practices on the Swahili coast on the one hand and in the Zambian/Katangan Copperbelt area on the other? And was competitive emulation between emerging elites also an important factor in the spread of the Zimbabwe Tradition itself, from its initial focus in the Shashe-Limpopo Basin, and the incorporation within it of local Gumanye, Harare, and Musengezi communities in the central and northern reaches of the Zimbabwe Plateau?

In emphasizing social agency, power, and ideology, Robertshaw thus questions the dominant role often accorded external trade in understanding African state formation, and in particular the development of complex polities south of the Zambezi. The limitations of such single factor explanations have been taken up in recent syntheses of Swahili archaeology (C. Kusimba 1999a; Horton and Middleton 2000) and are promoted here in the chapters of Kessy (8) and of Kusimba and Killick (7). The first stresses the importance of trading networks among and within Iron Age societies (Pemba and Zanzibar), alongside archaeologists' longer standing interest in documenting external trade connections. Kessy's detailed consideration of both settlement location and resource distribution strengthens the argument he makes that systems of exchange and the sociopolitical structures to support them must already have been in place *before* the initiation of trade with the Middle East or across the Indian Ocean. If correct, the identification of bananas, originally a Southeast Asian cultigen, in a mid-1st millennium BC context in Cameroon (Mbida et al. 2000) greatly extends the antiquity of such systems of interaction between Africa and other parts of the Indian Ocean. At the same time, the work of Chami (2001) points to at least off-shore coastal voyaging by East Africans themselves prior to the introduction of iron.

Differential ownership of key resources (such as salt and iron production) provides an internal motor for the development of social stratification. Kusimba and Killick, in Chapter 7, concentrate on the part played by iron-working in particular in the emergence of the Swahili city-states, especially insofar as iron may have been produced on a large scale for exchange both into the hinterland and across the Indian Ocean. Their detailed analysis of artifacts and slags from several sites on the Kenyan coast and studies by Killick (1990), C. Kusimba (1993), Mapunda (1995a, Chapter 5 this volume), and Schmidt (1997b) provide a solid basis for understanding East African ironworking technology. As previously noted, the work of D. Miller (e.g., 1996) offers a southern African counterpart to this. His conclusions from Iron Age sites in Botswana's Tsodilo Hills parallel Kusimba and Killick's recognition in the Galu and Ungwana samples of both hot and cold forging, but not of quenching or tempering.

Looking at these chapters from a southern African standpoint leads one to consider whether the production of iron or other basic necessities such as salt has not been undervalued in explanations of state formation that emphasize trade in gold, ivory, cloth, and beads between emerging polities and the East African coast. The significance of cattle and transhumant beef production in the rise of Great Zimbabwe has, of course, been argued by Garlake (1978), but what of control over access to or the production of iron among the southernmost Nguni, who in the 16th and 17th centuries AD did little smelting (Derricourt 1977), or on South Africa's highveld, where charcoal was difficult to come by (Maggs 1976)? Perhaps too we need to consider in more detail how far specialized mining, metalworking, and saltmaking communities, such as those reported by van der Merwe and Scully (1971), Evers (1979), and Maggs (1992), were able to play an important part in local and regional politics.

Before concluding this chapter with a discussion of some of the points raised by Musiba and Mabulla in their study of tourism's impact on the ecology and cultural heritage of the Ngorongoro Crater, I want to turn tables and pick up on some of the areas of research less strongly represented in the preceding chapters. Perhaps reflecting the emphasis on the relatively recent (Iron Age/Pastoral Neolithic) past, paleoenvironmental change and its impact on human communities is not a focus of any of the contributions (but note Robertshaw's suggestion that the end of the Little Ice Age was implicated in the development of larger polities in Uganda's Bunyoro-Kitara region, and Mapunda's references to the hydrological history of Lake

Tanganyika for our understanding of settlement changes in Ufipa). Here the possibly better documented climatic record for southern Africa allows one to suggest that East African archaeologists working in the Holocene should make more thorough use of ecological data. Huffman (1996b), for example, has been able to link shifts in Iron Age settlement distributions with changes in rainfall over the last 2000 years, arguing, for example, that the collapse of Mapungubwe and simultaneous rise of Great Zimbabwe coincided with the beginning of drier conditions in the Little Ice Age, while a subsequent warmer, wetter interval facilitated 17th-century Iron Age settlement of South Africa's highveld grasslands.

Huffman (1996b) also makes the point that high rainfall in southern Africa in the latter part of the 18th century AD encouraged the widespread adoption of maize within a context of population growth. When severe droughts hit shortly thereafter (from around AD 1800), a severe imbalance of people and resources developed that, along with accelerating competition for trade with Europeans, helped precipitate the *Mfecane*. Might archaeological data help establish the cultural and climatic context within which maize was introduced and spread in East Africa (cf. Stahl 2001)? And what of the ecological context for the adoption of earlier cultigens— bananas, Southeast Asian yams—or the ecological consequences of their cultivation? As Reid (1997) points out, a lack of paleoenvironmental data hinders the construction of explanations of state formation in the Interlacustrine area, even though both archaeological (Robertshaw, Chapter 10 this volume) and historical linguistic (e.g., Schoenbrun 1998) researches are proceding apace. The same is, of course, self-evidently true for modeling the spread and development of Iron Age farming communities from the start, still too heavily dependent in many areas upon ceramics, rather than a broader range of cultural evidence that includes detailed subsistence data.

Mention of maize and its introduction inevitably draws attention to the arrival on the East African coast of the Portuguese, but, as Horton (1997) points out, though much attention has been given to historical sources in the study of the origins of the Swahili towns and the Interlacustrine states, the archaeology of colonialism on the East African coast has been neglected. This is in marked, though partly understandable, contrast to the situation in South Africa, where studies of the mutual effects on colonizer and colonized of European settlement form one of archaeology's fastest growing subdisciplines (M. Hall 1993, 2000; Schrire 1995). East Africa prior to the late 19th century AD was witness to two different colonizers—the Portuguese and the Omani Arabs. Comparative investigation of the two, and of both with the impact of Portuguese, Dutch, and British colonization further south, might be of interest, in, for example, the field of religion, or the establishment and maintenance of slave-run plantation economies.

179

One area of archaeological research where explicit comparisons have already been made between East and southern Africa is that of rock art, with Lewis-Williams (1986) having attempted to extend the shamanistic hypothesis fundamental to present understanding of Bushman rock art to that of central Tanzania (but see Lim 1992). Though perhaps less widespread or numerous than the rock art of southern Africa, paintings and engravings are found in several regions of Kenya, Tanzania, and Uganda (Lim 1997) and have, depending on style and location, affiliations with modern hunter-gatherer, pastoralist, and agricultural communities. Dating rock art is as much a problem in East Africa as elsewhere, but in southern Africa a considerable literature has developed on how changes in the distribution of the art and its imagery recorded and formed part of the transformation of hunter-gatherer societies in the wake of their interaction with pastoralist, Iron Age, or European neighbors (e.g., Campbell 1987; Loubser and Laurens 1994; S. Hall and Smith 2000). Given the ethnographic information available for the Sandawe (Ten Raa 1971; Lim 1992) and the possibility noted by Mabulla (Chapter 3) that similar data can be obtained from the Hadzabe, does scope exist for similar studies in East Africa?

Whether in East Africa, southern Africa, or elsewhere, archaeologists increasingly recognize a responsibility to the descendants of those whose past lives they study, a responsibility particularly incumbent where archaeologists come from abroad or belong to communities and traditions very different from those among whom they carry out their research. Mabulla's contribution to this volume emphasizes the threats posed to the cultural survival of the Hadzabe foragers in Tanzania's Eyasi Basin by habitat destruction, competition for resources by pastoralist and agropastoralist neighbors, and attempts by the Tanzanian government and international development organizations to encourage them to become sedentary farmers. Similar problems have confronted hunter-gatherer groups in both Botswana and Namibia. In all three countries the fact that foragers are few and lack a strong political voice is critical, allowing their concerns to be overshadowed by the interests of others in development projects (Smith et al. 2000). The Kalahari Peoples Fund (Lee 1979) provides one southern African instance where concerned anthropologists have acknowledged that their relationship to those among whom they have conducted their research should extend to offering support in their contemporary sociopolitical situation. But as Musiba and Mabulla make plain, such concerns are far from exclusive to the archaeology of forager societies and sustainable ecotourism, including tourism aimed at archaeological sites, has both a cultural and an economic value of great potential to many of East Africa's communities (cf. Mabulla 2000).

As African states continue to restructure themselves economically and attempt to address the most basic health, educational, and other needs of their populations, archaeologists throughout the continent face many of the same problems, among them those identified by C. Kusimba (1996c), Mabulla (1996b), Abungu and Abungu (1998), and the contributors to Schmidt and McIntosh (1996): how to teach and remain abreast of new theoretical and methodological developments; how to carry out research at more than the most basic level of rescue projects; how to conserve monuments and sites, particularly when they are or should be open to the public; how to manage increasingly large volumes of finds in museums that are understaffed and underfunded; and how to undertake all of these tasks in a situation of static or declining funds. Here, surely, is where cooperation among African researchers can bear fruit, through pooling research experience, through sharing access to analytical facilities (in southern Africa, the examples of the Quaternary Dating Unit in Pretoria and the Stable Isotopes Laboratory in the University of Cape Town's Archaeology Department come to mind), and through the exchange of ideas and information regarding the preservation and presentation of their countries' cultural heritage. The development of community-based museums in Botswana (Phaladi 1998), the establishment of the Richtersveld National Park in South Africa, the land of which is communally owned by the indigenous Nama pastoralists (Douglas 1997), and the development of community-based wildlife management programs such as Zimbabwe's Campfire Project (Holt-Biddle 1994) may all provide insights for the revamped Ngorongoro Conservation Authority urged by Musiba and Mabulla (Chapter 10). Experience elsewhere of conserving rock art while presenting it to the public (e.g., Loubser 1991), might also, if developed in such a community-based way, provide useful suggestions for preserving the paintings of East Africa, many of which are rapidly disappearing (M. Leakey 1983). Whether in these ways, through sharing the experience of developing effective legislation regarding monitoring of development impacts on the cultural environment, joint research projects (for example, field investigation of Huffman and Herbert's [1994/95] hypothesis regarding Nguni and Sotho/Tswana origins in southern Tanzania), or institutionalized academic exchanges, cooperation between the different regions of Africa is increasingly to be looked for in the decades to come.

References

Abungu, G. H. O. 1989. Communities on the River Tana, Kenya: An Archaeological Study of Relations between the Delta and River Basin, 700-1890. Ph.D. dissertation, Archaeology Department, Cambridge University, Cambridge.

Abungu, G. H. O., and L. Abungu. 1998. Saving the Past in Kenya: Urban and Monument Conservation. *African Archaeological Review* 15:221-224.

Abungu, G. H. O., and H. W. Mutoro. 1993. Coast-Interior Settlements and Social Relations in the Kenya Coastal Hinterland. In *The Archaeology of Africa: Food, Metals and Towns*, ed. T. Shaw, P. Sinclair, B. Andah, and A. Okpoko, pp. 694-704. New York: Routledge.

Aikman, D. I., and S. M. Cobb. 1989. Water Development in the Ngorongoro Conservation Area. *Ngorongoro Conservation and Development Project Technical Report 8*. Nairobi: IUCN Regional Office for Eastern Africa.

Allen, J. de Vere. 1984. Witu and Swahili Historians. In *State Formation in Eastern Africa*, ed. A. I. Salim, pp. 216-249. Nairobi: Heinemann.

———. 1993. *Swahili Origins*. London: James Currey.

Al-Maamiry, A. H. 1980. *Oman and East Africa*. 2nd ed. New Delhi: Lancer.

Ambrose, S. H. 1982. Archaeological and Linguistic Reconstructions of History in East Africa. In *The Archaeological and Linguistic Reconstruction of African History*, ed. C. Ehret and M. Posnansky, pp. 104-157. Berkeley: University of California Press.

———. 1984. The Introduction of Pastoral Adaptations to the Highlands of East Africa. In *From Hunters to Farmers: The Causes and Consequences of Food Production in Africa*, ed. J. D. Clark and S. A. Brandt, pp. 212-239. Berkeley: University of California Press.

———. 1985. Excavations at Masai Gorge Rock Shelter, Naivasha. *Azania* 20:29-67.

———. 1986. Hunter-Gatherer Adaptations to Non-marginal Environments: An Ecological and Archaeological Assessment of the Dorobo Model. *Sprache und Geschichte in Afrika* 7:11-42.

———. 1992. The Pleistocene Cultural Sequence at Enkapune ya Muto. *Nyame Akuma* 37:38-39.

Århem, K. 1985a. *The Maasai and the State: The Impact of Rural Development Policies on a Pastoral People in Tanzania.* IWGIA Document 52. Copenhagen.

———. 1985b. *Pastoral Man in the Garden of Eden: The Maasai of the Ngorongoro Conservation Area, Tanzania.* Uppsala Research Reports in Cultural Anthropology. Uppsala, Sweden: University of Uppsala, Department of Cultural Anthropology in cooperation with Scandinavian Institute of African Studies.

Bachmann, H. G. 1982. *The Identification of Slags from Archaeological Sites.* Institute of Archaeology Occasional Paper 6. London: University of London.

Bakari, M. B. 1981. *Customs of the Swahili People.* Berkeley, CA: University of California Press.

Baker, S. W. 1866. *The Albert N'yanza, Great Basin of the Nile and Exploration of the Nile Sources.* London: Macmillan.

Barbour, J. 1989. Western Bantu: Avalogoli. In *Kenyan Pots and Potters*, ed. J. Barbour and S. Wandibba, pp. 41-46. Nairobi: Oxford University Press.

Barbour, J., and S. Wandibba (eds.). 1989. *Kenyan Pots and Potters.* Nairobi: Oxford University Press.

Barendsen, G. W., E. S. Deevy, and L. J. Gralenski. 1957. Yale Natural Radiocarbon Measurements III. *Science* 126:908-918.

Barnard, A. 1992. *Hunters and Herders of Southern Africa: A Comparative Ethnography of the Khoisan Peoples.* Cambridge: Cambridge University Press.

Barndon, R. 1992. Traditional Iron Working among the Fipa: An Ethnoarchaeological Study from Southwestern Tanzania. M.A. thesis, University of Bergen, Norway.

Barnicot, N. A., F. J. Benett, J. C. Woodburn, T. R. E. Pilkington, and A. Antonis. 1972. Blood Pressure and Serum Cholesterol in the Hadza of Tanzania. *Human Biology* 44:87-116.

Barthelme, J. W. 1984. Early Evidence for Animal Domestication in Eastern Africa. In *From Hunters to Farmers: The Causes and Consequences of Food Production in Africa*, ed. J. D. Clark and S. A. Brandt, pp. 200-205. Berkeley: University of California Press.

———. 1985. *Fisher-Hunters and Neolithic Pastoralists in East Turkana, Kenya.* BAR International Series 254. Oxford: British Archaeological Reports.

Baud-Bovy, M., and F. Lawson. 1977. *Tourism and Recreation Development: A Handbook of Physical Planning.* London: Architectural Press.

Beattie, J. 1960. *Bunyoro: An African Kingdom.* New York: Holt, Rinehart and Winston.

———. 1971. *The Nyoro State.* Oxford: The Clarendon Press.

Begley, S. 1993. The Meaning of Junk: What's Good Science. *Newsweek* (March 22): 62-64.

Bell, R. H. V. 1986. Traditional Use of Wildlife Resources within Protected Areas. In *Conservation and Wildlife Resources in Africa*, ed. R. H. V. Bell and E. McShane-Caluzi, pp. 297-315. Washington, DC: Peace Corps.

Bennett, F. J., N. A. Barnicot, J. C. Woodburn, M. S. Pereira, and B. E. Henderson. 1973. Studies on Viral, Bacterial, Ricettsial and Treponemal Diseases in the Hadza of Tanzania and a Note on Injuries. *Human Biology* 45:243-272.

Bennett, N. R. 1969. France and Zanzibar. In *Eastern African History*, ed. D. F. McCall, N. R. Bennett, and B. Joffrey, pp. 148-175. New York: Praeger.

Berger, I. 1981. *Religion and Resistance.* Tervuren, Belgium: Musée Royal de l'Afrique Centrale.

Berry, S. 1993. *No Condition Is Permanent: The Social Dynamics of Agrarian Change in Sub-Saharan Africa.* Madison: University of Wisconsin Press.

Bettinger, R. L. 1991. *Hunter-Gatherers: Archaeological and Evolutionary Theory.* New York: Plenum.

Binford, L. R. 1962. Archaeology as Anthropology. *American Antiquity* 28:217-225.

———. 1978. *Nunamiut Ethnoarchaeology.* New York: Academic Press.

———. 1980. Willow Smoke and Dog's Tails: Hunter-Gatherer Settlement Systems and Archaeological Site Formation. *American Antiquity* 45:4-20.

———. 1983. *In Pursuit of the Past: Decoding the Archaeological Record.* New York: Thames and Hudson.

Bishop, W. W., and J. D. Clark (eds.). 1967. *Background to Evolution in Africa.* Chicago, IL: University of Chicago Press.

Blackburn, R. H. 1973. Okiek Ceramics: Evidence for Central Kenya Prehistory. *Azania* 8:55-70.

Blanton, R. E., G. M. Feinman, S. A. Kowalewski, and P. N. Peregrine. 1996. A Dual-Processual Theory for the Evolution of Mesoamerican Civilization. *Current Anthropology* 37:1-14.

Blench, R. M., and K. C. MacDonald (eds.). 2000. *The Origins and Development of African Livestock: Archaeology, Genetics, Linguistics and Ethnography.* London: UCL Press.

Blurton-Jones, N., K. Hawkes, and P. Draper. 1993. Differences between Hadza and !Kung Children's Work: Affluence or Practical Reason? In *Key Issues in Hunter-Gatherer Research*, ed. E. S. Burch and L. J. Ellana, pp. 189-215. Providence, RI: Berg.

Blurton-Jones, N., L. C. Smith, J. F. O'Connell, K. Hawkes, and C. L. Kamuzora. 1992. Demography and Density Population of Savanna Foragers. *American Journal of Physical Anthropology* 89:159-181.

Bousman, C. B. 1998. The Chronological Evidence for the Introduction of Domestic Stock into Southern Africa. *African Archaeological Review* 15:133-150.

Bower, J. R. F. 1973. Seronera: Excavations at a Stone Bowl Site in the Serengeti National Park, Tanzania. *Azania* 8:71-104.

———. 1991. The Pastoral Neolithic of East Africa. *Journal of World Prehistory* 5:49-82.

———. 1997. Eastern African Pastoralists. In *Encyclopedia of Precolonial Africa*, ed. J. O. Vogel, pp. 205-210. Walnut Creek, CA: AltaMira Press.

Bower, J. R. F., and C. M. Nelson. 1978. Early Pottery and Pastoral Cultures of Central Rift Valley, Kenya. *Man* 13:554-566.

Bower, J. R. F., C. M. Nelson, A. F. Waibel, and S. Wandibba. 1977. The University of Massachusetts Later Stone Age/Pastoral Neolithic Comparative Study in Central Kenya: An Overview. *Azania* 12:119-46.

Brady, J. R. 1950. *Commerce and Conquest in East Africa*. Salem, MA: Essex Institute.

Britton, S. G. 1982. The Political Economy of Tourism in the Third World. *Annals of Tourism Research* 9:339-358.

Brock, B., and P. W. Brock. 1963. Iron-Working amongst the Nyiha of Southwestern Tanganyika. *South African Archaeological Bulletin* 18:97-100.

Bronson, B. 1986. The Making and Selling of Wootz, a Crucible Steel of India. *Archeomaterials* 1(1): 13-51.

Brooks, A. S., and P. Robertshaw. 1990. The Glacial Maximum in Tropical Africa: 22,000-12,000 B.P. In *The World at 18,000 B.P.* Vol. 2: *Low Latitudes*, ed. C. Gamble and O. Soffer, pp. 120-169. London: Unwin Hyman.

Brown, J. 1966. The Excavations of a Group of Burial Mounds in Ilkek near Gilgil, Kenya. *Azania* 1:59-77.

———. 1969. Some Polished Axes from East Africa. *Azania* 4:160-166.

———. 1972. Potting in Ukambani. *Method and Tradition* 1(2): 22-28.

———. 1989a. Southern Nilotic: Pokot. In *Kenyan Pots and Potters*, ed. J. Barbour and S. Wandibba, pp. 53-58. Nairobi: Oxford University Press.

———. 1989b. Samburu Dorobo (Mathews). In *Kenyan Pots and Potters*, ed. J. Barbour and S. Wandibba, pp. 77-80. Nairobi: Oxford University Press.

———. 1989c. Central Bantu: Agikuyu. In *Kenyan Pots and Potters*, ed. J. Barbour and S. Wandibba, pp. 86-90. Nairobi: Oxford University Press.

Brumfiel, E. M. 1992. Breaking and Entering the Ecosystem: Gender, Class, and Faction Steal the Show. *American Anthropologist* 94:551-567.

Brumfiel, E. M., and T. K. Earle. 1987. Specialization, Exchange, and Complex Societies. In *Specialization, Exchange and Complex Societies*, ed. E. M. Brumfiel and T. K. Earle, pp. 1-9. Cambridge: Cambridge University Press.

Buchanan, F. 1807. *A Journey from Madras through the Countries of Mysore, Lanara, and Malabar*, 3 vols. London: W. Bulmer.

Bunn, H. T., L. Bartram, and E. Kroll. 1988. Variability in Bone Assemblage Formation from Hadza Hunting, Scavenging, and Carcass Processing. *Journal of Anthropological Archaeology* 7:412-457.

Burch, E. S., Jr. 1994. The Future of Hunter-Gatherer Research. In *Key Issues in Hunter-Gatherer Research*, ed. E. S. Burch, Jr., and L. J. Ellana, pp. 441-455. Providence, RI: Berg.

Burkitt, C. M. 1925. *Prehistory: A Study of Early Cultures in Europe and the Mediterranean Basin*. Cambridge: Cambridge University Press.

Butler, R. W. 1989. Alternative Tourism: Pious Hope or Trojan Horse. *World Leisure and Recreation* 31(4): 9-16.

Campbell, C. 1987. Art in Crisis: Contact Period Rock Art in the South-eastern Mountains of Southern Africa. M.A. thesis, University of the Witwatersrand, Johannesburg.

Campbell, K., and H. Hofer. 1995. People and Wildlife: Spatial Dynamics and Zones of Interaction. In *Serengeti II: Dynamics, Management, and Conservation of an Ecosystem*, ed. A. R. E. Sinclair and P. Arcese, pp. 534-567. Chicago, IL: University of Chicago Press.

Carr, P. J. (ed.). 1994. *The Organization of North American Prehistoric Chipped Stone Tool Technologies*. Archaeological Series 7. Ann Arbor, MI: International Monographs in Prehistory.

Carter, P. L., P. J. Mitchell, and P. Vinnicombe. 1988. *Sehonghong: The Middle and Later Stone Age Industrial Sequence at a Lesotho Rock-Shelter*. BAR International Series 406. Oxford: British Archaeological Reports.

Casson, L. 1989. *The Periplus Maris Erythraei*, text with introduction, translation, and commentary. Princeton, NJ: Princeton University Press.

Caton Thompson, G. 1931. *The Zimbabwe Culture: Ruins and Reactions*. Oxford: The Clarendon Press.

Chakrabarti, D. K. 1992. *The Early Use of Iron in India*. Delhi: Oxford University Press.

Chami, F. A. 1988. The Coastal Iron Age Site in Kisarawe, Tanzania. M.A. thesis, Department of Anthropology, Brown University, Providence, RI.

———. 1992. Limbo: Early Iron-Working in South-eastern Tanzania. *Azania* 27:45-52.

———. 1994a. *The Tanzanian Coast in the First Millennium AD: An Archaeology of the Iron-Working, Farming Communities*. Studies in African Archaeology 7. Uppsala, Sweden: Societas Archaeologica Upsaliensis.

———. 1994b. New Chronology for the First Millennium AD Sites on the Coast of Eastern Africa: Early Urban Settlements; A Conceptual Problem. Paper read at the World Archaeology Intercongress, Mombasa, Kenya.

———. 1997. The Ancient Cultural Sequences for the Coast of East Africa. In *The Development of Urbanism in Africa from a Global Perspective*, ed. P. Sinclair, H. Mutoro, and G. Abungu. London: Routledge. In press.

———. 1998. A Review of Swahili Archaeology. *African Archaeological Review* 15(3): 199-221.

———. 1999. Roman Beads from the Rufiji Delta, Tanzania: First Incontrovertible Link with *Periplus*. *Current Anthropology* 40(2): 237-241.

———. 2001. Chicken Bones from a Neolithic Limestone Cave Site, Zanzibar: Contact between East Africa and Asia. In *People, Contact and the Environment in the African Past*, ed. F. A. Chami, G. Pwiti, and C. Radimilahy, pp. 84-97. Dar es Salaam, Tanzania: DUP.

———. 2002a. Kaole and the Swahili World. In *Southern Africa and the Swahili World*, ed. F. Chami and G. Pwiti, pp. 1-14. Studies in the African Past 2. Dar es Salaam, Tanzania: University of Dar es Salaam.

———. 2002b. People and Contacts in the Ancient Western Indian Ocean Seaboard or Azania. *Man and Environment* 27(1): 33-44.

Chami, F. A., and E. Kessy. 1995. Archaeological Work at Kisiju, Tanzania, 1994. *Nyame Akuma* 43:38-45.

Chami, F.A., and B. B. Mapunda. 1997. The 1996 Archaeological Reconnaissance North of the Rufiji Delta. *Nyame Akuma* 48:67-78.

Chami, F.A., and P. Msemwa. 1997a. The Excavation of Kwale Island, South of Dar-es-Salaam. *Nyame Akuma* 48:45-56.

———. 1997b. A New Look at Culture and Trade on the Azanian Coast. *Current Anthropology* 38(4): 673-677.

Chapman, S. 1967. Kantsyore Island. *Azania* 2:165-91.

Childe, V. G. 1953. *New Light on the Most Ancient East*. New York: Praeger.

Childs, S. T. 1991. Transformations: Iron and Copper Production in Central Africa. In *Recent Advances in Archaeometallurgical Research*, ed. P. Glumac, pp. 33-46. MASCA Research Papers in Science and Archaeology 8. Philadelphia, PA: University of Pennsylvania Museum of Archaeology and Anthropology.

——— (ed.). 1994. *Society, Culture and Technology in Africa*. MASCA Research Papers in Science and Archaeology, Supplement to Volume 11. Philadelphia, PA: University of Pennsylvania Museum of Archaeology and Anthropology.

Chittick, H. N. 1958-62. Recent Discoveries in Tanganyika. In *Actes du IV Congrès panafricain du prehistoire et de l'étude du quaternaire*. Musée Royal de l'Afrique Central 3: 215-223.

———. 1966. Unguja Ukuu: The Earliest Imported Pottery and an Abbasid Dinar. *Azania* 1:161-163.

———. 1967. Discoveries in the Lamu Archipelago. *Azania* 2:37-67.

———. 1974. *Kilwa: An Islamic Trading City on the East African Coast*. Nairobi: British Institute in Eastern Africa.

———. 1975a. An Early Salt Working Site on the Tanzanian Coast. *Azania* 10:151-153.

———. 1975b. The Peopling of the East African Coast. In *East Africa and the Orient*, ed. N. H. Chittick and R. Rotberg, pp. 16-43. New York: Africana Publishing House.

———. 1977a. Pre-Islamic Trade and Ports of the Horn. In *Proceedings of the VII Panafrican Congress of Prehistory and Quaternary*, ed. R. E. L. Leakey and B. A. Ogot. Nairobi: Longman.

———. 1977b. The East African Coast. Madagascar and the Indian Ocean. In *Cambridge History of Africa* 3. *From c. 1050 to 1600*, ed. R. Oliver, pp. 183-231. Cambridge: Cambridge University Press.

———. 1982a. Mediaeval Mogadishu. *Paideuma* 28:45-62.

———. 1982b. Reconnaissance in Coastal Tanzania. *Nyame Akuma* 20:57-58.

———. 1984. *Manda: Excavations at an Island Port on the Kenya Coast*. Memoir 9. Nairobi: British Institute in Eastern Africa.

Clarfield, G. 1989. Eastern Nilotic: Samburu Dorobo (Ndoto). In *Kenyan Pots and Potters*, ed. J. Barbour and S. Wandibba, pp. 80-85. Nairobi: Oxford University Press.

Clark, J. D. 1950. A Note on the Pre-Bantu Inhabitants of Northern Rhodesia and Nyasaland. *South African Journal of Science* 47:80-85.

———. 1962. The Spread of Food Production in Sub-Saharan Africa. *Journal of African History* 3:211-228.

———. 1967. The Problem of Neolithic Culture in Sub-Saharan Africa. In *Background to Evolution in Africa*, ed. W. W. Bishop and J. D. Clark, pp. 601-627. Chicago, IL: University of Chicago Press.

———. 1974. *Kalambo Falls Prehistoric Site*. Vol. 2: *The Later Prehistoric Cultures*. Cambridge: Cambridge University Press.

Clark, J. D., and S. A. Brandt (eds.). 1984. *From Hunters to Farmers: The Causes and Consequences of Food Production in Africa*. Berkeley, CA: University of California Press.

Clark, J. D., and J. Walton. 1962. A Late Stone Age Site in the Erongo Mountains, South West Africa. *Proceedings of the Prehistoric Society* 28:1-16.

CNPPA/IUCN. 1976. *The Biosphere Reserve and Its Relationship to National and International Conservation Efforts*. Report to Unesco. Gland, Switzerland: IUCN.

Coetzee, J. A., and E. M. Van Zinderen Bakker. 1989. Paleoclimatology of East Africa during the Last Glacial Maximum: A Review of Changing Theories. In *Quaternary and Environmental Research on East African Mountains*, ed. W. C. Mahaney, pp. 189-198. Rotterdam: A. Balkema.

Cohen, M. 1970. A Reassessment of the Stone Bowl Cultures of the Rift Valley, Kenya. *Azania* 5:27-38.

Cole, S. 1963. *The Prehistory of East Africa*. London: Weidenfield and Nicolson.

Collett, D. P. 1993. Metaphors and Representations Associated with Precolonial Iron-Smelting in Eastern and Southern Africa. In *The Archaeology of Africa: Foods, Metals and Towns*, ed. T. Shaw, P. J. J. Sinclair, B. W. Andah, and A. Okpoko, pp. 499-511. London: Routledge.

Collett, D. P., and P. T. Robertshaw. 1980. Early Iron Age and Kansyore Pottery: Finds from Gogo Falls, South Nyanza. *Azania* 15:133-145.

———. 1983a. Pottery Traditions of Early Pastoral Communities in Kenya. *Azania* 18:107-125.

———. 1983b. Problems in the Interpretation of Radiocarbon Dates: The Pastoral Neolithic of East Africa. *African Archaeological Review* 1:57-74.

Connah, G. 1987. *African Civilizations*. Cambridge: Cambridge University Press.

———. 1991. The Salt of Bunyoro: Seeking the Origins of an African Kingdom. *Antiquity* 65:479-494.

———. 1996. *Kibiro: The Salt of Bunyoro, Past and Present*. Memoir 13. Nairobi: British Institute in Eastern Africa.

———. 2001. *African Civilizations: An Archaeological Perspective*. Cambridge: Cambridge University Press.

———. (ed.). 1998. *Transformations in Africa: Essays on Africa's Later Past*. Leicester: Leicester University Press.

Cronk, L. 1991. Wealth, Status, and Reproductive Success among the Mukogodo of Kenya. *American Anthropologist* 93:345-360.

Cronk, L., and D. B. Dickson. 2001. Public and Hidden Transcripts in the East African Highlands: A Comment on Smith (1998). *Journal of Anthropological Archaeology* 20:113-121.

Curtin, P., S. Feierman, L. Thompson, and J. Vansina. 1978. *African History*. London: Longman.

David, N., R. Heimann, D. Killick, and M. Wayman. 1989. Between Bloomery and Blast Furnace: Mafa Iron-Smelting Technology in North Cameroon. *African Archaeological Review* 7:183-208.

D.D.Y. 1957. Cotton in Ufipa. In *Tanganyika Territory, District Book for the Ufipa District, Western Province*, vol. 1, pp. 20-28. Dar es Salaam, Tanzania: Government Printer.

Deacon, H. J. 1972. A Review of the Post-Pleistocene in South Africa. *South African Archaeological Society Goodwin Series* 1:26-45.

––––. 1976. *Where Hunters Gathered: A Study of Holocene Stone Age People in the Eastern Cape*. Claremont: South African Archaeological Society.

––––. 1993. Planting an Idea: An Archaeology of Stone Age Gatherers in South Africa. *South African Archaeological Bulletin* 48:86-93.

––––. 1995. Two Late Pleistocene/Holocene Archaeological Depositories from the Southern Cape, South Africa. *South African Archaeological Bulletin* 50:121-131.

Deacon, H. J., and J. Deacon. 1999. *Human Beginnings in Southern Africa: Uncovering the Secrets of the Stone Age*. Walnut Creek, CA: AltaMira Press.

Deacon, J. 1984. *The Later Stone Age of Southernmost Africa*. BAR International Series 213. Oxford: British Archaeological Reports.

––––. 1988. The Power of a Place in Understanding Southern San Rock Engravings. *World Archaeology* 20:129-140.

De Barros, P. 1990. Changing Paradigms, Goals, and Methods in the Archaeology of Francophone West African. In *A History of African Archaeology*, ed. P.T. Robertshaw, pp. 155-172. London: James Currey.

DeMarrais, E., L. J. Castillo, and T. Earle. 1996. Ideology, Materialization, and Power Strategies. *Current Anthropology* 37:15-31.

Denbow, J. R. 1990. Congo to Kalahari: Data and Hypotheses about the Political Economy of the Western Stream of the Early Iron Age. *African Archaeology Review* 8:139-175.

––––. 1999. Material Culture and the Dialectics of Identity in the Kalahari: AD 700-1700. In *Beyond Chiefdoms: Pathways to Complexity in Africa*, ed. S. K. McIntosh, pp. 110-123. Cambridge: Cambridge University Press.

de Rosemond, C. C. 1943. Iron Smelting in the Kahama District. *Tanganyika Notes and Records* 16:79-84.

Derricourt, R. 1977. *Prehistoric Man in the Ciskei and Transkei*. Cape Town: Struik.

Devereux, W. C. 1968. *A Cruise in the "Gordon."* London: Dowson of Pall Mall.

Dobbs, C. M. 1914. A Stone Bowl and Ring Discovered in Sotik. *Journal of the East African and Uganda Natural History Society* 4:145-146.

––––. 1918. A Stone Bowl in Sotik. *Journal of the East African and Uganda Natural History Society* 6:265-267.

Douglas, R. 1997. Parks, Peace and Prosperity. *Africa: Environment and Wildlife* 5(4): 30-39.

Earle, T. 1987. Chiefdoms in Archaeological and Ethnohistorical Perspective. *Annual Reviews in Anthropology* 16:279–308.

Edington, J. M., and M. A. Edington. 1977. *Ecology and Environmental Planning.* London: Chapman and Hall.

———. 1990. *Ecology, Recreation and Tourism.* Cambridge: Cambridge University Press.

Ehrenreich, R. M. 1995. Early Metalworking: A Heterarchical Analysis of Industrial Organization. In *Heterarchy and the Analysis of Complex Societies*, ed. R. M. Ehrenreich, C. L. Crumley, and J. E. Levy. Archaeological Papers of the American Anthropological Association 6.

Ehret, C. 1967. Cattle-Keeping and Milking in Eastern and Southern African History: The Linguistic Evidence. *Journal of African History* 8:1–17.

———. 1968. Sheep and Central Sudanic Peoples in Southern Africa. *Journal of African History* 9:213–221.

———. 1971. *Southern Nilotic History: Linguistic Approaches to the Study of the Past.* Evanston, IL: Northwestern University Press.

———. 1974. *Ethiopians and East Africans: The Problem of Contacts.* Nairobi: East African Publishing House.

———. 1982. The First Spread of Food Production to Southern Africa. In *The Archaeological and Linguistic Reconstruction of African History*, ed. C. Ehret and M. Posnansky, pp. 158–181. Berkeley, CA: University of California Press.

———. 1998. *An African Classical Age: Eastern and Southern Africa in World History, 1000 B.C. to A.D. 400.* Charlottesville, VA: University Press of Virginia.

Elenga, H., D. Schwartz, and A. Vincens. 1994. Pollen Evidence of Late Quaternary Vegetation and Inferred Climate Change in Congo. *Palaeogeography, Palaeoclimatology, Palaeoecology* 109:345–356.

Elenga, H., A. Vincens, and D. Schwartz. 1991. Presence d'Elements Forestiers Montagnards sur les Plateaux Batéké (Congo) au Pléistocène Supérieur: Nouvelles Données Palynologiques. *Paleoecology of Africa* 22:239–252.

Elphick, R. 1977. *Kraal and Castle: Khoikhoi and the Founding of White South Africa.* Johannesburg: Ravan Press.

Evers, T. M. 1979. Salt and Soapstone Bowl Factories at Harmony, Letaba District, North-East Transvaal. *South African Archaeological Society Goodwin Series* 3:94–107.

Fagan, B., and J. Yellen. 1968. Ivuna: Ancient Salt-Working in Southern Tanzania. *Azania* 3:1–43.

Fage, J. D. (ed.). 1978. *Cambridge History of Africa.* Vol. 2, *From c. 500 B.C.–A.D. 1050.* Cambridge: Cambridge University Press.

Faugust, P. M., and J. E. G. Sutton. 1966. The Egerton Cave on the Njoro River. *Azania* 1:149–153.

Fawcett, W. B., and A. LaViolette. 1990. Iron Age Settlement around Mkiu, South-Eastern Tanzania. *Azania* 25:19–25.

Field, C. R., G. Moll, and C. Ole Sonkoi. 1988. Livestock Development in the Ngorongoro Conservation Area. *Ngorongoro Conservation and Development Project Technical Report 7*. Nairobi: IUCN Regional Office for Eastern Africa.

Fisher, R. B. 1911. *Twilight Tales of the Black Baganda*. New York: Marshall Brothers; rpt. 1970, London: Frank Cass.

Flint, R. F. 1959. Pleistocene Climates in East and Southern Africa. *Bulletin of the Geological Society of America* 70:343-374.

Freeman-Grenville, G. S. P. 1962. *The East African Coast: Select Documents from the First to the Earlier Nineteenth Century*. Oxford: The Clarendon Press.

———. 1988. *The Swahili Coast, 2nd to the 19th Centuries*. London: Variorum Reprints.

Frosbrooke, H. 1990. Ngorongoro at Crossroads. *Kakakuona: Magazine of the Tanzanian Wildlife Protection Fund* 2(1).

Gabel, C. 1969. Six Rock Shelters on the Northern Kavirondo Shore of Lake Victoria. *African Historical Studies* 2:205-254.

Gamble, C. S. 1984. *The Palaeolithic Settlement of Europe*. Cambridge: Cambridge University Press.

Gamble, C. S., and A. W. Boisimier (eds.). 1991. *Ethnoarchaeological Approaches to Mobile Campsites: Hunter-Gatherer and Pastoralist Case Studies*. Ann Arbor, MI: International Monographs in Prehistory.

Garlake, P. S. 1973a. Excavations at the Nhunguza and Ruanga Ruins in Northern Mashonaland. *South African Archaeological Bulletin* 27:107-143.

———. 1973b. *Great Zimbabwe*. London: Thames and Hudson.

———. 1978. Pastoralism and Zimbabwe. *Journal of African History* 19(4): 479-493.

Geo: Un Nouveau Monde la Terre. 1989. *Tanzanie: Guide Tanzanien, des parcs et réserves*. Geo 130(32).

Georgiadis, N. 1995. Population Structure of Wildebeest: Implications for Conservation. In *Serengeti II: Dynamics, Management, and Conservation of an Ecosystem*, ed. A. R. E. Sinclair and P. Arcese, pp. 473-479. Chicago, IL: University of Chicago Press.

Gibbons, A. 1997. Back to Africa. *Science* 276:535-536.

Gifford, D. P., G. L. Isaac, and C. M. Nelson. 1980. Evidence for Predation and Pastoralism at Prolonged Drift: A Pastoral Neolithic Site in Kenya. *Azania* 15:57-108.

Gifford-Gonzalez, D. P. 1985. Faunal Assemblages from Masai Gorge Rock Shelter and Marula Rock Shelter. *Azania* 20:69-88.

———. 2000. Animal Disease Challenges to the Emergence of Pastoralism in Sub-Saharan Africa. *African Archaeological Review* 17:95-139.

Gifford-Gonzalez, D. P., and J. Kimengich. 1984. Faunal Evidence for Early Stock-Keeping in the Central Rift of Kenya: Preliminary Findings. In *Origin and Early Development of Food-Producing Cultures in North-Eastern Africa*, ed. L. Krzyzaniak and M. Kobusiewicz, pp. 457-471. Poznan: Polish Academy of Sciences.

Gill, M. N. 1981. The Potters' Mark: Contemporary and Archaeological Pottery of the Kenyan South-Eastern Highlands. Ph.D. dissertation, Department of Anthropology, Boston University.

Gosselain, O. P., A. Livingstone Smith, H. Wallaert, G. Williams Ewe, and M. Van der Linden. 1996. Preliminary Results of Fieldwork Done by the "Ceramic and Society Project" in Cameroon, December 1995-March 1996. *Nyame Akuma* 46:11-17.

Gramly, R. M. 1972. Report on the Teeth From Narosura. *Azania* 7:87-91.

———. 1975. Pastoralists and Hunters: Recent Prehistory in Southern Kenya and Northern Tanzania. Ph.D. dissertation, Department of Anthropology, Harvard University.

Grant, J. A. 1864. *A Walk Across Africa*. London: Blackwood.

Gray, J. M. 1975. A Portuguese Inscription and the Uroa Coin Hoard: Some Discoveries in Zanzibar. *Azania* 10:123-131.

———. 1977. The Hadimu and Tumbatu of Zanzibar. *Tanzania Notes and Records* 81:135-153.

Gregory, J. W. 1896. *The Great Rift Valley*. London: Frank Cass.

———. 1921. *The Rift Valleys and Geology of East Africa*. London: Seeley, Service.

Greig, R. C. H. 1937. Iron Smelting in Fipa. *Tanganyika Notes and Records* 4:77-81.

Gribbin, J., and J. Cherfas. 1982. *The Monkey Puzzle: Are Apes Descended From Man?* Aylesbury, U.K.: Triad Paladin.

Håland, R. 1993. Excavations at Dakawa, an Early Iron Age Site in East-Central Tanzania. *Nyame Akuma* 40:47-57.

Håland, R., and C. S. Msuya. 2000. Pottery Production, Iron Working, and Trade in the Early Iron Age: The Case of Dakawa, East-Central Tanzania. *Azania* 35:75-105.

Haberyan, K. A., and R. E. Hecky. 1987. The Late Pleistocene and Holocene Stratigraphy and Paleolimnology of Lakes Kivu and Tanganyika. *Paleogeography, Paleoclimatology, Paleoecology* 61:169-197.

Hall, M. J. 1984a. The Burden of Tribalism: The Social Context of Southern African Iron Age Studies. *American Antiquity* 49:455-467.

———. 1984b. The Myth of the Zulu Homestead: Archaeology and Ethnography. *Africa* 54:65-79.

———. 1986. The Role of Cattle in Southern African Agropastoral Societies: More Than Bones Alone Can Tell. *South African Archaeological Society Goodwin Series* 5:83-87.

———. 1990. Hidden History: Iron Age Archaeology in Southern Africa. In *A History of African Archaeology*, ed. P. Robertshaw, pp. 59-77. Portsmouth, NH: Heinemann.

———. 1993. The Archaeology of Colonial Settlement in Southern Africa. *Annual Review of Anthropology* 22:177-200.

———. 1996. *Archaeology Africa*. London: James Currey.

———. 2000. *Archaeology and the Modern World*. London: Routledge.

Hall, M. J., and K. Mack. 1983. The Outline of an Eighteenth Century Economic

System in South-East Africa. *Annals of the South African Museum* 91:163–194.

Hall, S. L. 2000. Burial Sequence in the Later Stone Age of the Eastern Cape Province, South Africa. *South African Archaeological Bulletin* 55:137–146.

Hall, S. L., and B. Smith. 2000. Empowering Places: Rock Shelters and Ritual Control in Forager-Farmer Interactions. *South African Archaeological Society Goodwin Series* 8:30–46.

Hammond-Tooke, W. D. 1998. Selective Borrowing? The Possibility of San Shamanistic Influence on Southern Bantu Divination and Healing Practices. *South African Archaeological Bulletin* 53:9–15.

Hanby, J. P, J. D. Bygott, and C. Parker. 1995. Ecology, Demography, and Behavior of Lions in Two Contrasting Habitats: Ngorongoro Crater and the Serengeti Plains. In *Serengeti II: Dynamics, Management, and Conservation of an Ecosystem*, ed. A. R. E. Sinclair and P. Arcese, pp. 315–331. Chicago, IL: University of Chicago Press.

al-Hassan, F. A. 1987. Demographic Archaeology. *Advances in Archaeological Method and Theory* 1:49–103.

al-Hassan, F. A., and D. R. Hill. 1986. *Islamic Technology*. Cambridge and Paris: Cambridge University Press/UNESCO.

Hawkes, K., J. F. O'Connell, and N. G. Blurton-Jones. 1991. Hunting Income Patterns among the Hadza: Big Game, Common Gods, Foraging Goals and the Evolution of the Human Diet. *Philosophical Transactions of the Royal Society of London* 334:243–250.

Headland, T., and L. Reid. 1989. Hunter-Gatherers and Their Neighbors from Prehistory to the Present. *Current Anthropology* 30:43–66.

Henshilwood, C. 1996. A Revised Chronology for Pastoralism in Southernmost Africa: New Evidence of Sheep at c. 2000 B.P. from Blombos Cave, South Africa. *Antiquity* 70:945–949.

———. 1997. Identifying the Collector: Evidence for Human Processing of the Cape Dune Mole-*Bathyergus suillus*, from Blombos Cave, Southern Cape, South Africa. *Journal of Archaeological Science* 24:659–662.

Herbert, E. W. 1993. *Iron, Gender, and Power: Rituals of Transformation in African Societies*. Bloomington, IN: Indiana University Press.

Herbich, I. 1981. Luo Pottery: Socio–Cultural Context and Archaeological Implications (An Interim Report). Seminar Paper 155. Nairobi: Institute of African Studies, University of Nairobi.

———. 1987. Learning Patterns, Potter Interaction and Ceramic Style among the Luo of Kenya. *African Archaeological Review* 5:193–204.

———. 1989. River-Lake Nilotic: Luo. In *Kenyan Pots and Potters*, ed. J. Barbour and S. Wandibba, pp. 27–40. Nairobi: Oxford University Press.

Hitchcock, R. K. 1982. The Ethnoarchaeology of Sedentism: Mobility Strategies and Site Formation among Foraging and Food Producing Populations in the Eastern Kalahari Desert, Botswana. Ph.D. dissertation, Department of Anthropology, University of New Mexico, Albuquerque, NM.

Hitchcock, R. K., and J. I. Ebert. 1989. Modeling Kalahari Hunter-Gatherer Subsistence and Settlement Systems: Implications for Development Policy and Land Use Planning. *Anthropos* 84:447-462.

Hivernel, F. M. M. 1978. An Ethnoarchaeological Study of Environmental Use in the Kenya Highlands. Ph.D. dissertation, University of London.

Hobley, C. W. 1895. Upon a Visit to Tsavo and the Taita Highland. *Geographical Journal* 5:545-561.

———. 1912. The Wa-Langulu or Ariangulu of the Taru Desert. *Man* 12:18-21.

———. 1913. Stone Axe. *Journal of the East African and Ugandan Natural History Society* 3:60-61.

———. 1929. *Kenya from Chartered Company to Crown Colony*. London: Frank Cass.

Hodder, I. 1982. *Symbols in Action: Ethnoarchaeological Studies of Material Culture*. Cambridge: Cambridge University Press.

Holis, A. C. 1909. A Note of the Graves of Wanyika. *Man* 9:145.

Holl, A. 1990. West African Archaeology: Colonialism and Nationalism. In *A History of African Archaeology*, ed. P. Robertshaw, pp. 296-308. London: James Currey.

Holland, M. D. 1991. Investigation before Conservation. *The Courier: An ACP-EEC Publication* 125.

Holt-Biddle, D. 1994. Campfire: An African Solution to an African Problem. *Africa: Environment and Wildlife* 2(1): 33-35.

Homewood, K. M., and W. A. Rodgers. 1991. *Maasailand Ecology: Pastoralist Development and Wildlife Conservation in Ngorongoro, Tanzania*. Cambridge: Cambridge University Press.

Horton, M. C. 1984. The Settlement of the Northern Swahili Coast. Ph.D. dissertation, Archaeology Department, Cambridge University, Cambridge.

———. 1985. Archaeological Survey of Zanzibar. *Azania* 20:167-71.

———. 1986. Asiatic Colonization of the East African Coast: The Manda Evidence. *Journal of the Royal Asiatic Society* 2:201-213.

———. 1987. Early Muslim Trading Settlements on the East African Coast: New Evidence from Shanga. *Antiquaries Journal* 67:290-322.

———. 1990. The *Periplus* and East Africa. *Azania* 25:95-99.

———. 1991. Origins of Islam in East Africa. *Archaeological Report, Leverhulme Project*. Nairobi: British Institute in Eastern Africa.

———. 1996. *Shanga: A Muslim Trading Community on the East African Coast*. Nairobi: British Institute in Eastern Africa.

———. 1997. Eastern African Historical Archaeology. In *Encyclopedia of Precolonial Africa: Archaeology, History, Languages, Cultures, and Environments*, ed. J. O. Vogel, pp. 549-554. Walnut Creek, CA: AltaMira Press.

Horton, M. C., H. M. Brown, and W. A. Oddy. 1986. The Mtambwe Hoard. *Azania* 21:115-213.

Horton, M. C., and M. C. Clark. 1985. *Zanzibar Archaeological Survey 1984-1985*. Zanzibar: Zanzibar Ministry of Information, Culture and Sports.

Horton, M. C., and J. Middleton. 2000. *The Swahili: The Social Landscape of a Mercantile Society*. Oxford: Blackwells.

Horton, M. C., and N. Mudida. 1993. Exploitation of Marine Resources: Evidence for the Origin of the Swahili Communities of East Africa. In *The Archaeology of Africa: Food, Metals and Towns*, ed. T. Shaw, P. Sinclair, B. Andah, and A. Okpoko, pp. 673–693. New York: Routledge.

Huffman, T. N. 1989. Ceramics, Settlements and Late Iron Age Migrations. *African Archaeological Review* 7:155–182.

———. 1994. Toteng Pottery and the Origins of Bambata. *Southern African Field Archaeology* 3:3–9.

———. 1995. Ideological Unity and Political Fragmentation in the Zimbabwe Kingdoms. Paper presented at the second biennial meeting of the Complex Societies Group, San Bernardino, CA.

———. 1996a. *Snakes and Crocodiles: Power and Symbolism in Ancient Zimbabwe*. Johannesburg: Witwatersrand University Press.

———. 1996b. Archaeological Evidence for Climatic Change During the Last 2000 Years in Southern Africa. *Quaternary International* 33:55–60.

Huffman, T. N., and R. K. Herbert. 1994/95. New Perspectives on Eastern Bantu. *Azania* 29/30:27–36.

Ingrams, W. H. 1967. *Zanzibar, Its History and Its People*. 2nd ed. London: Frank Cass.

IUCN. 1976. *Proceedings of a Regional Meeting on the Creation of a Coordinated System of National Parks and Reserves in Eastern Africa*. Morges, Switzerland: IUCN.

———. 1978. *Categories, Objectives and Criteria for Protected Areas*. Gland, Switzerland: IUCN.

———. 1980. *World Conservation Strategy: Living Resource Conservation for Sustainable Development*. Gland, Switzerland: IUCN/UNEP/WWF.

———. 1984. Categories, Objectives and Criteria for Protected Areas. In *National Parks, Conservation and Development: The Role of Protected Areas in Sustaining Society*, ed. J. A. McNeely and K. R. Miller. Washington, DC: IUCN/Smithsonian Institution Press.

Jerardino, A. 1996. Changing Social Landscapes of the Western Cape Coast of Southern Africa over the Last 4500 Years. Ph.D. dissertation, University of Cape Town, Cape Town.

Jochim, M. A. 1976. *Hunter-Gatherer Subsistence and Settlement: A Predictive Model*. New York: Academic Press.

Juma, A. M. 1996. The Swahili and the Mediterranean Worlds: Pottery of the Late Roman Period from Zanzibar. *Antiquity* 70:148–154.

K. W. [Tito Winyi]. 1935. The Kings of Bunyoro-Kitara. *Uganda Journal* 3:155–160.

Kaare, B. T. M. 1989. The Hadzabe and Tanzanian State: Problems of Transformation in a Hunting and Gathering Community. M.A. thesis, University of Dar es Salaam, Tanzania.

———. 1993. The Impact of Modernization Policies on the Hunter-Gatherer Hadzabe: The Case of Education and Language Policies of Post-

Independence Tanzania. In *Key Issues in Hunter-Gatherer Research*, ed. E. S. Burch, Jr., and L. J. Ellana, pp. 315-331. Providence, RI: Berg.

Karega-Munene. 1993. Neolithic/Iron Age Subsistence Economies in the Lake Victoria Basin of East Africa. Ph.D. dissertation, Archaeology Department, Cambridge University, Cambridge.

——. 1996. The East African Neolithic: An Alternative View. *African Archaeological Review* 13:247-254.

——. 2002. *Holocene Foragers, Fishers and Herders of Western Kenya*. BAR International Series 1037. Oxford: British Archaeological Reports.

Karoma, N. J. 1996. The Deterioration and Destruction of Archaeological and Historical Sites in Tanzania. In *Plundering Africa's Past*, ed. P. R. Schmidt and R. J. McIntosh, pp. 191-201. Bloomington, IN: Indiana University Press.

Kent, S. 1992. The Current Forager Controversy: Real versus Ideal Views of Hunter-Gatherers. *Man* 27:45-70.

——. 1993. Variability in Faunal Assemblages: The Influence of Hunting Skill, Sharing, Dogs and Mode of Cooking on Faunal Remains at a Sedentary Kalahari Community. *Journal of Anthropological Archaeology* 12:323-385.

——. 1996. *Cultural Diversity among Twentieth Century Foragers: An African Perspective*. Cambridge: Cambridge University Press.

——. 1998. Hunting Variability at a Recently Sedentary Kalahari Village. In *Cultural Diversity among Twentieth-Century Foragers: An African Prespective*, ed. S. Kent, pp. 125-156. Cambridge: Cambridge University Press.

Killick, D. J. 1990. Technology in Its Social Setting: Bloomery Iron-Working at Kasungu, Malawi, 1860-1940. Ph.D. dissertation, Department of Anthropology, Yale University, New Haven, CT.

Kinahan, J. 1991. *Pastoral Nomads of the Central Namib Desert*. Windhoek: New Namibia Books.

Kingdon, J. 1982. *East African Mammals: An Atlas of Evolution in Africa*. New York: Academic Press.

Kirkman, J. S. 1964. *Men and Monuments on the East African Coast*. London: Lutterworth.

——. 1974. *Fort Jesus: A Portuguese Fortress on the East African Coast*. Oxford: Oxford University Press.

Kirknaes, J. 1989. *Mhunzi*. Copenhagen, Denmark: Villadsen & Christensen.

Kirwin, L. 1986. Rhapta, Metropolis of Azania. *Azania* 21:99-114.

Kiyaga-Mulindwa, D. 1993. The Iron Age Peoples of East-Central Botswana. In *The Archaeology of Africa: Food, Metals, and Towns*, ed. T. Shaw, P. Sinclair, B. Andah, and A. Okpoko, pp. 386-390. New York: Routledge.

Klein, R. G. 1984. Later Stone Age Faunal Samples from Heuningneskrans Shelter (Transvaal) and Leopard's Hill Cave (Zambia). *South African Archaeological Bulletin* 39:109-116.

——. 1989. Biological and Behavioral Perspectives on Modern Human Origins in Southern Africa. In *The Human Revolution: Behavioral and Biological*

Perspectives on the Origin of Modern Humans, eds. P. Mellars and C. Stringer, pp. 529–546. Princeton, NJ: Princeton University Press.

Klein, R. G., and K. Cruz-Uribe. 1989. Faunal Evidence for Prehistoric Herder-Forager Activities at Kasteelberg, Western Cape Province, South Africa. *South African Archaeological Bulletin* 44:82–97.

Knauft, B. M. 1991. Violence and Sociality in Human Evolution. *Current Anthropology* 32:391–428.

Kohl-Larsen, L., and M. Kohl-Larsen. 1958. *Die Bilderstrasse Africas*. Kassel: Erich Roth Verlag.

Kopytoff, I. 1987. The Internal African Frontier: The Making of African Political Culture. In *The African Frontier: The Reproduction of Traditional African Societies*, ed. I. Kopytoff, pp. 3–84. Bloomington, IN: Indiana University Press.

Kramer, C. 1985. Ceramic Ethnoarchaeology. *Annual Review of Anthropology* 14:77–102.

———. 1994. A Tale of Two Cities: Ceramic Ethnoarchaeology in Rajasthan. In *Living Traditions: Studies in the Ethnoarchaeology of South Asia*, ed. B. Allchin, pp. 307–322. Oxford and New Delhi: IBH Publishing and PVT.

Kratz, C. 1989. Southern Nilotic: Okiek. In *Kenyan Pots and Potters*, ed. J. Barbour and S. Wandibba, pp. 64–74. Nairobi: Oxford University Press.

Krause, R. A. 1985. *The Clay Sleeps: An Ethnoarchaeological Study of Three African Potters*. Tuscaloosa: University of Alabama Press.

Kristiansen, K. 1991. Chiefdoms, States, and Systems of Social Evolution. In *Chiefdoms: Power, Economy and Ideology*, ed. T. Earle, pp. 16–43. Cambridge: Cambridge University Press.

Kroll, E., and T. Douglas (eds.). 1991. *The Interpretation of Archaeological Spatial Patterning*. New York: Plenum.

Kuper, A. 1980. Symbolic Dimensions of the Southern Bantu Homestead. *Africa* 50:8–23.

Kusimba, C. M. 1993. The Archaeology and Ethnography of Iron Metallurgy on the Swahili Coast. Ph.D. dissertation, Department of Anthropology, Bryn Mawr College, Bryn Mawr, PA.

———. 1996a. The Social Context of Iron Forging on the Kenya Coast. *Africa* 66(3): 386–410.

———. 1996b. Spatial Organization at Swahili Archaeological Sites in Kenya. In *Proceedings of the 10th Congress of the Panafrican Association*, ed. G. Pwiti and R. Soper, pp. 703–714. Harare: University of Zimbabwe Publications.

———. 1996c. Archaeology in Africa's Museums. *African Archaeological Review* 13:165–170.

———. 1997. Swahili and Coastal City-States. In *Encyclopedia of Africa: Archaeology, History, Languages, Cultures, and Environments*, ed. J. Vogel, pp. 507–512. Walnut Creek, CA: AltaMira Press.

———. 1999a. *The Rise and Fall of Swahili States*. Walnut Creek, CA: AltaMira Press.

———. 1999b. Material Symbols among the Precolonial Swahili of the East African Coast. In *Material Symbols in Prehistory*, ed. J. Robb, pp. 318-341. Carbondale, IL: Southern Illinois University Press.

Kusimba, C. M., D. Killick, and R. G. Creswell. 1994. Indigenous and Imported Metals at Swahili Sites on the Coast of Kenya. In *Society, Culture, and Technology in Africa*, ed. S. T. Childs, pp. 63-77. MASCA Research Papers in Science and Archaeology, Supplement to Volume 11. Philadelphia, PA: University of Pennsylvania Museum of Archaeology and Anthropology.

Kusimba, C. M., and S. B. Kusimba. 1998-2000. Field Notes, Tsavo Archaeological Research Project. Unpublished mss.

———. 2000. Hinterlands and Cities: Archaeological Investigations of Economy and Trade in Tsavo, Southeastern Kenya. *Nyame Akuma* 54:13-24.

Kusimba, S. B. 1999. Hunter-Gatherer Land Use Patterns in Later Stone Age East Africa. *Journal of Anthropological Archaeology* 18:165-200.

———. 2001. The Pleistocene Later Stone Age in East Africa: Excavations and Lithic Assemblages from Lukenya Hill. *African Archaeological Review* 18:77-123.

Lane, P. 1994/95. The Use and Abuse of Ethnography in Iron Age Studies of Southern Africa. *Azania* 29/30:51-64.

———. 1998a. Ethnoarchaeological Research—Past, Present and Future Directions. In *Ditswa Mmung: The Archaeology of Botswana*, ed. P. Lane, A. Reid, and A. Segobye, pp. 177-205. Gaborone: The Botswana Society.

———. 1998b. Engendered Spaces, Bodily Practices in the Iron Age of Southern Africa. In *Gender in African Prehistory*, ed. S. Kent, pp. 179-204. Walnut Creek, CA: AltaMira Press.

Lange, G. 1991. A Seed of Wild Finger Millet from Gogo Falls. In *Gogo Falls: Excavations at a Complex Archaeological Site East of Lake Victoria*, ed. P. Robertshaw. Appendix. *Azania* 26:191-192.

Lanning, E. C. 1953. Ancient Earthworks in Western Uganda. *Uganda Journal* 17(1): 51-62.

———. 1966. Excavations at Mubende Hill. *Uganda Journal* 30(2): 153-163.

LaViolette, A. 1996. Report on Excavations at the Swahili Site of Pujini, Pemba Island, Tanzania. *Nyame Akuma* 46:72-83.

Leakey, L. S. B. 1929. An Outline of the Stone Age of Kenya. *South African Journal of Science* 26:749-757.

———. 1931. *The Stone Age Cultures of Kenya Colony*. Cambridge: Cambridge University Press.

———. 1936. *Stone Age Africa: An Outline of Prehistory in Africa*. London: Oxford University Press.

Leakey, L. S. B., and S. Cole (eds.). 1952. *Proceedings of the Pan-African Congress on Prehistory, 1947*. Oxford: Blackwell.

Leakey, L. S. B., and W. E. Owen. 1945. *A Contribution to the Study of the Tumbian Culture in East Africa*. Occasional Papers 1. Nairobi: Coryndon Memorial Museum.

Leakey, M. D. 1943. Notes on the Ground and Polished Stone Axes of East Africa. *Journal of the East Africa Natural History Society* 17:182-195.

————. 1945. Report on the Excavations at Hyrax Hill, Nakuru, Kenya Colony, 1937-1938. *Transactions of the Royal Society of South Africa* 30:271-409.

————. 1966. Excavations of Burial Mounds in Ngorongoro Crater. *Tanzania Notes and Records* 66:123-135.

————. 1979. Footprints Frozen in Time. *National Geographic Magazine* 155(4): 446-457.

————. 1983. *Africa's Vanishing Art: The Rock Paintings of Tanzania.* New York: Doubleday.

Leakey, M. D., and R. L. Hay. 1979. Pliocene Footprints in the Laetoli Beds at Laetoli, Northern Tanzania. *Nature* 278:317-323.

Leakey, M. D., and L. S. B. Leakey. 1950. *Excavations at the Njoro River Cave: Stone Age Cremated Burials in Kenya Colony.* Oxford: The Clarendon Press.

Leakey, R. 1991. Tourism and Environment in East Africa. BBC1 Radio (broadcast Feb. 18).

Lee, R. B. 1979. *The !Kung San: Men, Women and Work in a Foraging Society.* Cambridge: Cambridge University Press.

————. 1992. Art or Science? The Crisis in Hunter-Gatherer Studies. *American Anthropologist* 94:31-54.

Lee, R. B., and R. Daly. 1999. *The Encyclopedia of Hunters and Gatherers.* New York: Cambridge University Press.

Lee, R. B., and I. DeVore. 1968. Problems in the Study of Hunter-Gatherers. In *Man the Hunter*, eds. R. B. Lee and I. DeVore, pp. 3-12. New York: Aldine.

Lent, P.C. 1974. Mother-Infant Relationships in Ungulates. In *The Behavior of Ungulates in Relation to Management*, ed. V. Geist and F. Walther, pp. 14-55. Morges, Switzerland: IUCN.

Leslie, M. 1989. The Holocene Sequence from Uniondale Rock Shelter in the Eastern Cape. *South African Archaeological Society Goodwin Series* 6:17-32.

Lewicki, T. 1969. *Arabic External Sources for the History of Africa to the South of the Sahara.* Oddzial Krakowie Prace Komisji Orientalistycznej 9. Wroclaw: Polska Akademia Nauk.

Lewis-Williams, J. D. 1986. Beyond Style and Portrait: A Comparison of Tanzanian and Southern African Rock Art. In *Contemporary Studies on Khoisan*, part 2, ed. R. Vossen and K. Keuthmann, pp. 95-139. Hamburg: Helmut Buske Verlag.

Lewis-Williams, J. D., and T. A. Dowson. 1999. *Images of Power.* Johannesburg: Southern Books.

Lim, L. I. 1992. A Site-Oriented Approach to Rock Art: A Study from Usandawe, Central Tanzania. Ph.D. dissertation, Department of Anthropology, Brown University, Providence, RI.

————. 1993. A Site-Oriented Approach to Rock Art: A Case Study from Usandawe, Kondoa District. Paper presented at the International Congress in Honor of Dr. Mary D. Leakey, Arusha, Tanzania.

————. 1997. Eastern African Rock Art. In *Encyclopedia of Precolonial Africa*, ed. J. O. Vogel, pp. 362-368. Walnut Creek, CA: AltaMira Press.

Livingstone, D. A. 1965. Sedimentation and the History of Water Level Change in Lake Tanganyika. *Limnology and Oceanography* 10:607–610.

Loubser, J. N. H. 1991. The Conservation of Rock Paintings in Australia and Its Applicability to South Africa. *Navorsinge van die Nasionale Museum (Bloemfontein)* 7:113–143.

Loubser, J. N. H., and G. Laurens. 1994. Depictions of Domestic Ungulates and Shields: Hunter/Gatherers and Agro-pastoralists in the Caledon River Valley Area. In *Contested Images: Diversity in Southern African Rock Art Research*, ed. T. A. Dowson and J. D. Lewis-Williams, pp. 83–118. Johannesburg: Witwatersrand University Press.

Lubbock, J. 1872. *Prehistoric Times as Illustrated by Ancient Remains and the Manners and Customs of Modern Savages*. London: William and Northgate.

Lynch, B. M., and L. H. Robbins. 1979. Cushitic and Nilotic Prehistory: New Archaeological Evidence from North-West Kenya. *Journal of African History* 20:319–328.

Mabulla, A. Z. P. 1996a. Middle and Later Stone Age Land-Use and Lithic Technology in the Eyasi Basin, Tanzania. Ph.D. dissertation, Department of Anthropology, University of Florida, Gainesville.

———. 1996b. Tanzania's Endangered Heritage: A Call for a Protection Program. *African Archaeological Review* 13:197–214.

———. 2000. Strategy for Cultural Heritage Management (CHM) in Africa: A Case Study. *African Archaeological Review* 17:211–233.

MacIver, D. R. 1906. *Medieval Rhodesia*. London: Macmillan.

Mackinnon, J., K. Mackinnon, C. Graham, and J. Thorsell. 1986. *Managing Protected Areas in the Tropics*. Cambridge: IUCN.

Maddin, R., J. D. Muhly, and T. S. Wheeler. 1977. How the Iron Age Began. *Scientific American* 23(4): 122–131.

Maggs, T. O'C. 1976. *Iron Age Communities of the Southern Highveld*. Pietermaritzburg: Natal Museum.

———. 1992. My Father's Hammer Never Ceased Its Song Day and Night: The Zulu Ferrous Metalworking Industry. *Natal Museum Journal of Humanities* 4:65–87.

———. 1994/95. The Early Iron Age in the Extreme South: Some Patterns and Problems. *Azania* 29/30:171–186.

Mann, M. 1986. *The Sources of Social Power*, vol. 1. *A History of Power from the Beginning to A.D. 1760*. Cambridge: Cambridge University Press.

Manyesha, H. A. 1988. Parokia ya Kirando Kale Mpaka Siku Hizi. Manuscript prepared to commemorate a centenary (1888–1988) of Christianity at Kirando.

Mapunda, B. B. 1991. Iron-Working along the Lower Ruhuhu River Basin, Southern Tanzania: Report and Tentative Conclusions. M.A. paper, Department of Anthropology, University of Florida, Gainesville.

———. 1995a. An Archaeological View of the History and Variation of Iron Working in Southwestern Tanzania. Ph.D. dissertation, Department of Anthropology, University of Florida, Gainesville.

———. 1995b. Iron Age Archaeology in Southeastern Lake Tanganyika Region, Southwestern Tanzania. *Nyame Akuma* 43:46–57.

Marean, C. W. 1990. Late Quaternary Paleoenvironments and Faunal Exploitation in East Africa. Ph.D. dissertation, Department of Anthropology, University of California, Berkeley.

———. 1992a. Hunter to Herder: Large Mammal Remains from the Hunter–Gatherer Occupation at Enkapune ya Muto Rock Shelter. *African Archaeological Review* 10:65–127.

———. 1992b. Implications of Late Quaternary Mammalian Fauna from Lukenya Hill (South-Central Kenya) for Paleoenvironmental Change and Faunal Extinctions. *Quaternary Research* 37:239–255.

———. 1997. Hunter-Gatherer Foraging Strategies in Tropical Grasslands: Model Building and Testing in the East African Middle and Later Stone Age. *Journal of Anthropological Archaeology* 16:189–225.

Marean, C., and D. Gifford-Gonzalez. 1991. Late Quaternary Extinct Ungulates of East Africa and Paleoenvironmental Implications. *Nature* 350:418–420.

Marshall, F. B. 1986. Aspects of the Advent of Pastoral Economies in East Africa. Ph.D. dissertation, Department of Anthropology, University of California, Berkeley.

———. 1990a. Cattle Herders and Caprine Flocks. In *Early Pastoralists of South-Western Kenya*, ed. P. Robertshaw, pp. 205–260. Memoir 11. Nairobi: British Institute in Eastern Africa.

———. 1990b. Origins of Specialized Pastoral Production in East Africa. *American Anthropologist* 92:873–894.

———. 1991. Mammalian Fauna from Gogo Falls. In *Gogo Falls: Excavations at a Complex Archaeological Site East of Lake Victoria*, ed. P. Robertshaw. Appendix 2. *Azania* 26:175–179.

Marshall, F. B., K. Stewart, and J. W. Barthelme. 1984. Early Domestic Stock at Dongodien in Northern Kenya. *Azania* 19:120–127.

Martin, E. B. 1978. *Zanzibar: Tradition and Revolution*. London: Hamilton.

Masao, F. T., and H. W. Mutoro. 1988. The East African Coast and the Comoro Islands. In *General History of Africa*, vol. 3. *Africa from the Seventh to the Eleventh Century*, ed. M. El Fasi, pp. 586–615. Berkeley: University of California Press.

May-Landgrebe, S. 1989. Tourismus und Dritte Welt: Planungen für ein Sozial- und umweltverträglisches Reisen: das Beispiel Kapverde. In *Tourismus- Umwelt-Gesellschaft: Wege zu einen Sozial- und umweltverträglisches Reisen*, ed. A. Steinecke. Bielefeld: IFKA Schriftenreihe.

Mazel, A. D. 1992. Early Pottery from the Eastern Part of Southern Africa. *South African Archaeological Bulletin* 47:3–7.

———. 1999. Nkolimahashi Shelter: The Excavation of Later Stone Age Rock Shelter Deposits in the Central Thukela Basin, KwaZulu-Natal, South Africa. *Natal Museum Journal of Humanities* 11:1–21.

Mbida, C. M., W. van Neer, G. Doutre Lepont, and L. Vrydagh. 2000. Evidence for

Banana Cultivation and Animal Husbandry during the First Millennium BC in the Forest of Southern Cameroon. *Journal of Archaeological Science* 27:151–162.

McBrearty, S. A. 1986. The Archaeology of the Muguruk Site, Western Kenya. Ph.D. dissertation, Department of Anthropology, University of Illinois, Urbana–Champaign.

McBrearty, S. A., and A. Brooks. 2000. The Revolution That Wasn't: A New Interpretation of the Origin of Modern Human Behavior. *Journal of Human Evolution* 39:453–563.

McDowell, W. 1981. Hadza Traditional Economy and Its Prospects from Development. Unpublished report, Ministry of Information and Culture, Dar es Salaam, Tanzania.

McIntosh, R. J. 1997. Agricultural Beginnings in Sub-Saharan Africa. In *Encyclopedia of Precolonial Africa*, ed. J. O. Vogel, pp. 409–418. Walnut Creek, CA: AltaMira Press.

McIntosh, S. K. (ed.). 1999. *Beyond Chiefdoms: Pathways to Complexity in Africa*. Cambridge: Cambridge University Press.

McNeely, J. A., and J. W. Thorsell. 1989. Jungles, Mountains, and Islands: How Tourism Can Help Conserve the Natural Heritage. *World Leisure and Recreation* 31(4).

Mehlman, M. J. 1977. Excavations at Nasera Rock, Tanzania. *Azania* 12:111–118.

——. 1979. Mumba-Hohle Revisited: The Relevance of a Forgotten Excavation to Some Current Issues in East African Prehistory. *World Archaeology* 11:80–94.

——. 1989. Later Quaternary Archaeological Sequences in Northern Tanzania. Ph.D. dissertation, Anthropology Department, University of Illinois, Urbana-Champaign.

Mellaart, J. 1965. *The Earliest Civilization of the Near East*. London: Thames and Hudson.

Merrick, H. V. 1973. Aspects of the Size and Shape Variation of the East African Stone Bowls. *Azania* 8:115–130.

Merrick, H. V., and F. H. Brown. 1984a. Obsidian Sources and Patterns of Source Utilization in Kenya and Northern Tanzania: Some Initial Findings. *African Archaeological Review* 2:129–152.

——. 1984b. Rapid Chemical Characterization of Obsidian Artifacts by Electron Microprobe Analysis. *Archaeometry* 26:230–236.

Merrick, H. V., F. H. Brown, and M. Connelly. 1990. Sources of the Obsidian at Ngamuriak and Other South–Western Kenyan Sites. In *Early Pastoralists of South-Western Kenya*, ed. P. Robertshaw. Memoir 11. Nairobi: British Institute in Eastern Africa.

Merritt, H. 1975. A History of the Taita. Ph.D. dissertation, Department of History, Indiana University, Bloomington.

Miller, D. 1996. *The Tsodilo Jewellery: Metal Work from Northern Botswana*. Cape Town: University of Cape Town Press.

Miller, J. 1969. *The Spice Trade of the Roman Empire*. Oxford: The Clarendon Press.

Mitchell, P. J. 1992. Last Glacial Maximum Hunter-Gatherers in Southern Africa as an Example of a High-Technology Foraging System. Paper presented at the Twelfth Biennial Conference of the Society of Africanist Archaeologists, Los Angeles, CA, March.

———. 2002. *Archaeology of Southern Africa*. Cambridge: Cambridge University Press.

Mitchell, P. J., J. E. Parkington, and R. Yates. 1994. Recent Holocene Archaeology in Western and Southern Lesotho. *South African Archaeological Bulletin* 49:33–52.

Moore, H. L. 1986. *Space, Text and Gender: An Anthropological Study of the Marakwet of Kenya*. Cambridge: Cambridge University Press.

Movius, H. L. (ed.). 1977. *Excavations of the Abri Pataud, Les Eyzies (Dordogne)*. American School of Prehistoric Research, Bulletin 30. Cambridge, MA: Peabody Museum Press.

Mturi, A. A. 1986. The Pastoral Neolithic of West Kilimanjaro. *Azania* 21:53–63.

Muriuki, G. 1974. *A History of the Kikuyu, 1500-1900*. Nairobi: Oxford University Press.

Musiba, C. M. 1995. To Conserve and Use or to Treat and Bury: Toward a Tanzanian Plan for Long-Term Conservation and Sustainable Use of Archaeological, Paleoanthropological and Paleontological Sites. Paper presented at the Bellagio Conference on Preservation and Use of Olduvai Gorge, Laetoli, Rock Art and Other Paleoanthropological Resources in Tanzania, Bellagio, Italy, May.

Musiba, C. M., M. Selvaggio, C. C. Magori, N. J. Karoma, and D. M. K. Kamamba. 2002. Merging Community Participation, Science Education, and Conservation of Cultural Heritage: The Role of Tanzania Field School in Anthropology. In *Proceedings of the International Conference on Teaching World Heritage and New Technologies of Information and Communication in Africa, Dakar, Senegal, October 15-17*. UNESCO Conference on World Heritage in the Digital Age, 30th Anniversary of the World Heritage Convention.

Mutoro, H. W. 1979. A Contribution to the Study of Cultural and Economic Dynamics of Historical Settlements of the East African Coast with Particular Reference to the Ruins of Takwa. M.A. thesis, University of Nairobi.

Mutundu, K. 1999. *Ethnohistoric Archaeology of the Mukogodo in North-Central Kenya: Hunter-Gatherer Subsistence and the Transition to Pastoralism in Secondary Settings*. Cambridge Monographs in African Archaeology 47. Oxford: Archaeopress.

Ndagala, D. K. 1988. Free or Doomed? Images of the Hadzabe Hunters and Gatherers of Tanzania. In *Hunters and Gatherers 1. History, Evolution, and Social Change*, ed. T. Ingold, D. Riches, and J. Woodburn, pp. 65–72. Oxford: Berg.

Ndagala, D. K., and N. Zengu. 1989. From the Raw to the Cooked: Hadzabe Perception of Their Past. In *Who Needs the Past?*, ed. R. Layton, pp. 51–54. London: Unwin Hyman.

Needham, J. 1980. The Evolution of Iron and Steel Technology in East and Southeast Asia. In *The Coming of the Age of Iron*, ed. T. A. Wertime and J. D. Muhly, pp. 507-542. New Haven, CT: Yale University Press.

Nelson, C. M., and J. Kimengich. 1984. Early Phases of Pastoral Adaptation in the Central Highlands of Kenya. In *Origin and Early Development of Food-Producing Cultures in North-Eastern Africa*, ed. L. Krzyzaniak and M. Kobusiewicz, pp. 481-487. Poznan: Polish Academy of Sciences.

Nelson, C. M., and M. Posnansky. 1970. The Stone Tools from the Re-excavation of Nsongezi Rock Shelter. *Azania* 5:119-172.

Nelson, M. C. 1992. The Study of Technological Organization. In *Advances in Archaeological Method and Theory*, vol. 3, ed. M. B. Schiffer, pp. 57-100. Tucson, AZ: University of Arizona Press.

Newitt, M. 1978. The Southern Swahili Coast in the First Century of European Expansion. *Azania* 13:111-126.

Ngorongoro Conservation Area (NCA). 1992. *NCA Annual Report*. Ngorongoro, Tanzania: NCA.

———. 1995. *NCA Research Priorities*. Ngorongoro, Tanzania: NCA.

Ngorongoro Ecological Monitoring Program (NEMP). 1989. *Ngorongoro Ecological Monitoring Program, Annual Report*. Ngorongoro, Tanzania: NCA.

Nicholls, C. S. 1971. *The Swahili Coast: Politics, Diplomacy and Trade on the African Littoral (1798-1856)*. London: George Allen and Unwin.

Notis, M. R., V. C. Pigott, P. E. McGovern, K. H. Liu, and C. P. Swann. 1986. The Metallurgical Technology: The Archaeometallurgy of Iron Steel. In *The Late Bronze Age and Early Iron Ages of Central Transjordan: The Baq'ah Valley Project, 1977-1981*, ed. P. E. McGovern, pp. 272-278. Monograph 65. Philadelphia, PA: University of Pennsylvania Museum of Archaeology and Anthropology.

Nurse, D., and T. Spear. 1985. *The Swahili: Reconstructing the History and Language of an African Society, 800-1500*. Philadelphia, PA: University of Pennsylvania Press.

Nyakatura, J. 1973. *Anatomy of an African Kingdom*, ed. G. N. Uzoigwe. Garden City, NY: Anchor-Doubleday.

Nyerere, J. K. 1968. *Nyerere on Socialism*. London: Oxford University Press.

———. 1974. *Freedom and Development*. New York: Oxford University Press.

O'Brien, T. P. 1939. *The Prehistory of Uganda Protectorate*. Cambridge: Cambridge University Press.

Obst, E. 1912. Von Mkalama in Land der Watindiga. *Mitteilungen der Geographischen Geselschaft in Hamburg* 26:2-27.

O'Connell, J. F., and K. Hawkes. 1988. Hadza Hunting, Butchering, and Bone Transport and Their Archaeological Implications. *Journal of Anthropological Research* 44(2): 113-161.

Odner, K. 1972. Excavations at Narosura, a Stone Bowl Site in the Southern Kenya Highlands. *Azania* 7:25-92.

Organisation for Economic Cooperation and Development (OECD). 1990. *Tourism*

Policy and International Tourism in OECD Member Countries: Evolution of Tourism in OECD Countries in 1987. Paris: OECD Tourism Committee.

Okpoko, A. I. 1991. Review of *A History of African Archaeology* by P. Robertshaw.

Olindo, P. M., I. Douglas-Hamilton, and P. Hamilton. 1988. The 1988 Tsavo Elephant Count. Unpublished report to the Kenya Wildlife Service, Nairobi.

Oliver, R. 1953. A Question about the Bacwezi. *Uganda Journal* 17:135-137.

———. 1965. The Problem of the Bantu Expansion. *Journal of African History* 7:361-376.

———. 1977. The East African Interior. In *Cambridge History of Africa 3. From c. 1050 to 1600*, ed. R. Oliver, pp. 621-669. Cambridge: Cambridge University Press.

Ominde, S. H. 1952. *The Luo Girl: From Infancy to Marriage*. London: Macmillan.

Omollo, J. O. 1988. An Ethno-Archaeological Study of the Ceramic Industry of the Luo of Nyakach Division, Kisumu District. B.A. dissertation, Department of History, University of Nairobi.

Onyango-Abuje, J. C. 1976. Reflections on Culture Change and Distribution during the Neolithic Period in East Africa. In *Hadith 6. History and Social Change in East Africa*, ed. B. A. Ogot. Nairobi: East African Publishing House.

———. 1977a. A Contribution to the Study of the Neolithic in East Africa with Particular Reference to Nakuru–Naivasha Basins. Ph.D. dissertation, Department of Anthropology, University of California, Berkeley.

———. 1977b. Crescent Island: Preliminary Report on Excavations at an East African Neolithic Site. *Azania* 12:147-159.

———. 1980. Temporal and Spatial Distribution of Neolithic Cultures in East Africa. In *Proceedings of the Eighth Panafrican Congress of Prehistory and Quaternary Studies*, ed. R. E. Leakey and B. A. Ogot, pp. 288-292. Nairobi: International Louis Leakey Memorial Institute for African Prehistory.

Opperman, H. 1987. *Later Stone Age Hunter-Gatherers of the Drakensberg Foothills*. BAR International Series 339. Oxford: British Archaeological Reports.

Opperman, H., and B. Hydenrych. 1990. A 22,000 Year Old Middle Stone Age Camp Site with Plant Food Remains from the North-East Cape. *South African Archaeological Bulletin* 45:93-99.

Ouzman, S. 1998. Towards a Mindscape of Landscape: Rock Art as Expression of World Understanding. In *The Archaeology of Rock Art*, ed. C. Chippindale and P. S. C. Taçon, pp. 30-41. Cambridge: Cambridge University Press.

Ouzman, S., and L. Wadley. 1990. A View from the South: Southern Africa before, during and after the Last Glacial Maximum. In *The World at 18,000 B.P. 2. Low Latitudes*, ed. C. Gamble and O. Soffer, pp. 214-225. London: Unwin Hyman.

———. 1996. What is an Eland? N!ao and the Politics of Age and Sex in the Paintings of the Western Cape. In *Miscast: Negotiating the Presence of the Bushmen*, ed. P. Skotnes, pp. 281-290. Cape Town: University of Cape Town Press.

———. 1997. A History in Paint and Stone from Rose Cottage Cave, South Africa. *Antiquity* 71:386-404.

Parkington, J. E., and C. Poggenpoel. 1987. Diepkloof Rock-Shelter. In *Papers in the Prehistory of the Western Cape, South Africa*, ed. J. E. Parkington and M. Hall, pp. 269–293. BAR International Series 332. Oxford: British Archaeological Reports.

Parry, W., and R. Kelly. 1987. Expedient Core Technology and Sedentism. In *The Organization of Core Technology*, eds. J. Johnson and C. Morrow, pp. 285–304. Boulder, CO: Westview.

Parsons, T. 1960. The Distribution of Power in American Society. In *Structure and Process in Modern Societies*, ed. T. Parsons. New York: Free Press.

Pearce, S., and M. Posnansky. 1963. The Re-excavation of Nsongezi Rock-Shelter, Ankole. *Uganda Journal* 27:85–94.

Perkin, S. 1995. Multiple Land Use in the Serengeti Region: The Ngorongoro Conservation Area. In *Serengeti II: Dynamics, Management, and Conservation of an Ecosystem*, ed. A.R.E Sinclair and P. Arcese, pp. 571–587. Chicago, IL: University of Chicago Press.

Perrott, R. A., and F. A. Street-Perrott. 1982. New Evidence for a Late Pleistocene Wet Phase in Northern Intertropical Africa. *Paleoecology of Africa* 14:57–75.

Phaladi, S. 1998. The Organisation of Archaeology. In *Ditswa Mmung: The Archaeology of Botswana*, ed. P. Lane, A. Reid, and A. Segobye, pp. 233–239. Gaborone: The Botswana Society.

Phillips, P. 1980. *The Prehistory of Europe*. London: Allen Lane.

Phillipson, D. W. 1977. *The Later Prehistory of Eastern and Southern Africa*. London: Heinemann.

———. 1979. Some Iron Age Sites in the Lower Tana Valley. *Azania* 14:155–160.

———. 1984. Aspects of Early Food Production in Northern Kenya. In *Origin and Early Development of Food-Producing Cultures in North-Eastern Africa*, ed. L. Krzyzaniak and M. Kobusiewicz, pp. 489–495. Poznan: Polish Academy of Sciences.

———. 1985. *African Archaeology*. Cambridge: Cambridge University Press.

———. 1994. *African Archaeology*, 2nd ed. Cambridge: Cambridge University Press.

Pikirayi, I. 1993. *The Archaeological Identity of the Mutapa State: Towards an Historical Archaeology of Northern Zimbabwe*. Uppsala, Sweden: Societas Archaeologica Upsaliensis.

———. 2001. *The Zimbabwe Culture*. Walnut Creek, CA: AltaMira Press.

Posnansky, M. 1962. The Neolithic Cultures of East Africa. In *Actes du IV Congrès panafricain du prehistoire et de l'étude du quaternaire*, ed. G. Mortelmans and J. Nenquin, pp. 273–281. Tervuren, Belgium: Musée Royal de l'Afrique Centrale.

———. 1966. Kingship, Archaeology and Historical Myth. *Uganda Journal* 30(1): 1–12.

———. 1967. Excavations at Lanet, Kenya, 1957. *Azania* 2:89–114.

———. 1969. Bigo bya Mugenyi. *Uganda Journal* 33(2): 125–150.

Posnansky, M., and J. W. Sikibengo. 1959. Ground Stone Axes and Bored Stones in Uganda. *Uganda Journal* 23:179–181.

Prime Minister and First President's Office (PMFPO). 1990. Proposed Education and Settlement Program for Nomadic Pastoral and Traditional Hunter-Gatherer Societies in Tanzania. Dar es Salaam, Tanzania.

———. 1992. Integrated Development Program for the Nomadic Pastoral and Traditional Hunting Communities of Tanzania. Dar es Salaam, Tanzania.

Prins, A. H. J. 1961. *The Swahili-Speaking Peoples of Zanzibar and the East African Coast (Arabs, Shirazi, and Swahili)*. London: International African Institute.

Procter, J. 1960. Did You See Me from Afar? *Tanganyika Notes and Records* 54:48-50.

Pwiti, G., and R. Soper (eds.). 1996. *Aspects of African Archaeology*. Harare: University of Zimbabwe Press.

Rangeley, W. H. J. 1963. The Earliest Inhabitants of Nyasaland. *Nyasaland Journal* 16(2): 35-42.

Raymond, R. 1984. *Out of the Fiery Furnace*. University Park, PA: Pennsylvania State University Press.

Reid, A. 1991. The Role of Cattle in the Later Iron Age Communities of Southern Uganda. Ph.D dissertation, Archaeology Department, Cambridge University, Cambridge.

———. 1997. Lacustrine States. In *Encyclopedia of Precolonial Africa*, ed. J. O. Vogel, pp. 501-507. Walnut Creek, CA: AltaMira Press.

Reid, A., K. Sadr, and N. Hanson-James. 1998. Herding Traditions. In *Ditswa Mmung: The Archaeology of Botswana*, ed. P. Lane, A. Reid, and A. Segobye, pp. 81-100. Gaborone: The Botswana Society.

Renfrew, C. 1972. *The Emergence of Civilisation: The Cyclades and the Aegean in the Third Millennium B.C.* London: Methuen.

———. 1974. Beyond a Subsistence Economy. The Evolution of Social Organization in Prehistoric Europe. In *Reconstructing Complex Societies: An Archaeological Colloquium*, ed. C. B. Moore, pp. 69-95. Bulletin of the American Schools of Oriental Research 20. Chicago: ASOR.

Renfrew, C., and J. J. Cherry (eds.). 1986. *Peer Polity Interaction and Socio-Political Change*. Cambridge: Cambridge University Press.

Rigby, P. 1985. *Persistent Pastoralists: Nomadic Societies in Transition*. London: Zed Books.

Robbins, L. H. 1984. Late Prehistoric Aquatic and Pastoral Adaptations West of Lake Turkana, Kenya. In *From Hunters to Farmers: The Causes and Consequences of Food Production in Africa*, ed. J. D. Clark and S. A. Brandt, pp. 206-211. Berkeley: University of California Press.

Roberts, A. 1993. Smelting Ironies: The Performance of a Tabwa Technology. Paper presented at 5th Stanley Conference on African Art: The Project for Advanced Study of Art and Life in Africa (PASALA), University of Iowa, March 5-6.

Robertshaw, P. 1990. The Development of Archaeology in East Africa. In *A History of African Archaeology*, ed. P. Robertshaw, pp. 78-94. London: James Currey.

———. 1991. Gogo Falls: Excavations at a Complex Archaeological Site East of Lake Victoria. *Azania* 26:63-195.

———. 1994. Archaeological Survey, Ceramic Analysis and State Formation in Western Uganda. *African Archaeological Review* 12:105-131.

———. 1995. The Last 200,000 Years (or Thereabouts) in East African Prehistory. *Journal of Archaeological Research* 3(1): 55-86.

———. 1997. Munsa Earthworks: A Preliminary Report. *Azania* 32:1-20.

———. 1999. Seeking and Keeping Power in Bunyoro-Kitara, Uganda. In *Beyond Chiefdoms: Pathways to Complexity in Africa*, ed. S. K. McIntosh, pp. 124-135. Cambridge: Cambridge University Press.

———. 2001. The Age and Function of the Ancient Earthworks of Western Uganda. *Uganda Journal* 47:20-33.

——— (ed.). 1990. *A History of African Archaeology*. Portsmouth, NH: Heinemann.

Robertshaw, P., and D. P. Collett. 1983. The Identification of Pastoral Peoples in the Archaeological Record: An Example from East Africa. *World Archaeology* 15:67-78.

Robertshaw, P., D. P. Collett, D. P. Gifford, and N. B. Mbae. 1983. Shell Middens on the Shores of Lake Victoria. *Azania* 18:1-43.

Robertshaw, P., and D. Taylor. 2000. Climate Change and the Rise of Political Complexity in Western Uganda. *Journal of African History* 41:1-28.

Robertshaw, P., and W. Wetterstrom. 1989. Plant Remains From Gogo Falls. *Nyame Akuma* 31:25-27.

Roscoe, J. 1923. *The Bakitara*. Cambridge: Cambridge University Press.

Rostoker, W., and B. Bronson. 1990. *Pre-Industrial Iron: Its Technology and Ethnology*. Archeomaterials Monograph 1. Philadelphia, PA: Archeomaterials.

Rostoker, W., and J. R. Dvorak. 1990. *Interpretation of Metallographic Structures*. New York: Academic Press.

Routledge, W. S., and K. Routledge. 1910. *With a Prehistoric People: The Akikuyu of British East Africa*. London: Arnold.

Rowly-Conwy, P. 2001. Time, Change, and the Archaeology of Hunter-Gatherers: How Original is the Original Affluent Society? In *Hunter-Gatherers: An Interdisciplinary Perspective*, ed. C. Panter-Brick, R. Layton, and P. Rowley-Conwy. New York: Cambridge University Press.

Runyoro, V. 1995. Long-Term Trends in the Herbivore Populations of the Ngorongoro Crater, Tanzania. In *Serengeti II: Dynamics, Management, and Conservation of an Ecosystem*, ed. A.R.E. Sinclair and P. Arcese, pp. 146-168. Chicago, IL: University of Chicago Press.

Sadr, K. 1998. The First Herders at the Cape of Good Hope. *African Archaeological Review* 15:101-132.

Saetersdal, T. 1999. Symbols of Cultural Identity: A Case Study from Tanzania. *African Archaeological Review* 16:121-135.

Sampson, G. 1998. Tortoise Remains from a Later Stone Age Rock Shelter in the Upper Karoo, South Africa. *Journal of Archaeological Science* 25(10): 985-1000.

——. 2000. Taphonomy of Tortoises Deposited by Birds and Bushmen. *Journal of Archaeological Science* 27:779-788.

Samuels, L. E. 1982. *Metallographic Polishing by Mechanical Methods.* Metals Park, OH: American Society of Metals.

Sassoon, H. 1967. New Views on Engaruka, Northern Tanzania: Excavations Carried Out for the Tanzania Government in 1964 and 1966. *Journal of African History* 8:201-217.

——. 1968. Excavations of a Burial Mound in Ngorongoro Crater, Dar-es-Salaam. *Tanzania Notes and Records* 69:15-32.

Schepartz, L. A. 1988. Who Were the Later Pleistocene East Africans? *African Archaeological Review* 6:57-72.

Schmidt, P. R. 1990. Oral Traditions, Archaeology and History: A Short Reflective History. In *A History of African Archaeology*, ed. P. Robertshaw, pp. 252-270. Portsmouth, NH: Heinemann.

——. 1996. Reconfiguring the Barongo: Reproductive Symbolism and Reproduction among a Work Association of Iron Smelters. In *The Culture and Technology of African Iron Production*, ed. P. R. Schmidt, pp. 74-127. Gainesville, FL: University Press of Florida.

——. 1997a. *Iron Technology in East Africa.* London: James Currey.

——. 1997b. *Iron Technology in East Africa: Symbolism, Science, and Archaeology.* Bloomington, IN: Indiana University Press.

Schmidt, P. R., N. J. Karoma, A. LaViolette, W. B. Fawcett, A. Z. Mabulla, L. N. Rutabanzibwa, and C. M. Saanane. 1992. *Archaeological Investigations in the Vicinity of Mkiu, Kisarawe District, Tanzania.* Dar es Salaam, Tanzania: Archaeology Unit, University of Dar es Salaam.

Schmidt, P. R., and R. McIntosh (eds.). 1996. *Plundering Africa's Past.* Bloomington, IN: Indiana University Press.

Schoenbrun, D. L. 1998. *A Green Place, A Good Place: Agrarian Change, Gender, and Social Identity in the Great Lakes Region to the 15th Century.* London: James Currey.

——. 1990. Early History in East Africa's Great Lakes Region: Linguistic, Ecological and Archaeological Approaches, ca. 500 B.C. to ca. A.D. 1000. Ph.D. dissertation, Department of Anthropology, University of California, Los Angeles.

——. 1993a. Cattle Herds and Banana Gardens: The Historical Geography of the Western Great Lakes Region, ca. AD 800-1500. *African Archaeological Review* 11:39-72.

——. 1993b. We Are What We Eat: Ancient Agriculture Between the Great Lakes. *Journal of African History* 34:1-34.

Scholz, C. A., and B. R. Rosendahl. 1988. Low Lake Stands in Lakes Malawi and Tanganyika, East Africa, Delineated with Multifold Seismic Data. *Science* 240:1645-1648.

Schrire, C. 1995. *Digging through Darkness: Chronicles of an Archaeologist.* Charlottesville, VA: University Press of Virginia.

Schweitzer, F. R. 1979. Excavations at Die Kelders, Cape Province, South Africa.

Annals of the South African Museum 78:101-233.

Scott, B. 1987. *Metallography of Ancient Metallic Artifacts*. London: Institute of Archaeology.

Sealey, J. C., and S. Pfeiffer. 2000. Diet, Body Size, and Landscape Use among Holocene People in the Southern Cape, South Africa. *Current Anthropology* 41:642-654.

Sealy, J. C., and R. Yates. 1994. The Chronology of the Introduction of Pastoralism to the Cape, South Africa. *Antiquity* 68:58-67.

———. 1996. Direct Radiocarbon Dating of Early Sheep Bones: Two Further Results. *South African Archaeological Bulletin* 51:109-110.

Segyobe, A. K. 1993. Representing the Past: Anthropological and Archaeological Discourse in Southern Africa. Paper presented at the Conference on Symbols of Change: Transregional Culture and Local Practice in Southern Africa, Berlin.

Sekgarametso, P. 1995. An Archaeological Survey of Ntsweng in Molepolole. BA dissertation, University of Botswana, Gaberone.

Shaw, T. 1977. Hunters, Gatherers and First Farmers in West Africa. In *Hunters, Gatherers and First Farmers beyond Europe: An Archaeological Survey*, ed. J. V. S. Megaw, pp. 69-125. Leicester: Leicester University Press.

Shaw, T., P. J. J. Sinclair, B. W. Andah, and A. Okpoko (eds.). 1993. *The Archaeology of Africa: Foods, Metals and Towns*. London: Routledge.

Shepherd, G. 1982. The Making of the Swahili, A View from the Southern End of the East African Coast. *Paideuma* 28:129-147.

Sherrif, A. 1987. *Slaves, Spices and Ivory in Zanzibar*. London: James Currey.

Shinnie, M. 1965. *Ancient African Kingdoms*. London: Edward Arnold.

Shinnie, P. 1960. Excavations at Bigo 1957. *Uganda Journal* 24(1): 16-28.

Shott, M. 1992. On Recent Trends in the Anthropology of Foragers: Kalahari Revisionism and its Archaeological Implications. *Man* 27:843-871.

Sinclair, P. J. J. 1991. Archaeology in Eastern Africa: An Overview of Current Chronological Issues. *Journal of African History* 32:179-219.

———. 1993. Urban Origins in Eastern Africa: Overview. Paper presented at the World Archaeology Intercongress, Mombasa, Kenya.

Smith, A. B. 1998. Keeping People on the Periphery: The Ideology of Social Hierarchies between Hunters and Herders. *Journal of Anthropological Archaeology* 17:201-215.

Smith, A. B., and L. Jacobson. 1995. Excavations at Geduld and the Appearance of Early Domestic Stock in Namibia. *South African Archaeological Bulletin* 50:3-14.

Smith, A. B., and R. B. Lee. 1997. Cho/ana: Archaeological and Ethnohistorical Evidence for Recent Hunter-Gatherer/Agropastoralist Contact in Northern Bushmanland, Namibia. *South African Archaeological Bulletin* 52:52-58.

Smith, A. B., C. Malherbe, M. Guenther, and P. Berens. 2000. *The Bushmen of Southern Africa: A Foraging Society in Transition*. Cape Town: David Philip.

Smith, A. B., K. Sadr, J. Gribble, and R. Yates. 1991. Excavations in the South-Western Cape, South Africa, and the Archaeological Identity of Prehistoric Hunter-Gatherers within the last 2000 Years. *South African Archaeological Bulletin* 46:71–90.

Smuts, J. C. 1932. Climate and Man in South Africa. *South African Journal of Science* 29:98–131.

Solomon, A. C. 1997. Landscape, Form and Process: Some Implications for San Rock Art Research. *Natal Museum Journal of Humanities* 9:57–73.

Solway, J., and R. B. Lee 1990. Foragers Genuine or Spurious? Situating the Kalahari San in History. *Current Anthropology* 31:109–146.

Soper, R. C. 1967. Iron Age Sites in North-Eastern Tanzania. *Azania* 2:19–36.

———. 1971a. A General Review of Early Iron Age of the Southern Half of Africa. *Azania* 5:5–37.

———. 1971b. Early Iron Age Pottery Types from East Africa: Comparative Analysis. *Azania* 6:39–52.

———. 1971c. Iron Age Archaeological Sites in the Chobi Sector of Murchison Falls National Park, Uganda. *Azania* 6:53–87.

———. 1982. Bantu Expansion into Eastern Africa. In *The Archaeological and Linguistic Reconstruction of African History*, ed. C. Ehret and M. Posnansky, pp. 223–238. Berkeley: University of California Press.

———. 1989. Eastern Bantu: Adavida. In *Kenyan Pots and Potters*, ed. J. Barbour and S. Wandibba, pp. 96–99. Nairobi: Oxford University Press.

Soper, R. C., and B. Golden. 1969. An Archaeological Survey of Mwanza Region, Tanzania. *Azania* 4:15–79.

Speke, J. H. 1863. *Journal of the Discovery of the Source of the Nile*. Edinburgh: Blackwood.

Stahl, A. B. 1984. A History and Critique of Investigations into Early African Agriculture. In *From Hunters to Farmers: The Causes and Consequences of Food Production in Africa*, ed. J. D. Clark and S. A. Brandt, pp. 9–21. Berkeley, CA: University of California Press.

———. 2001. *Making History in Banda: Anthropological Visions of Africa's Past*. Cambridge: Cambridge University Press.

Steinhart, E. I. 1980. From "Empire" to State: The Emergence of the Kingdom of Bunyoro-Kitara. In *The Study of the State*, ed. H. Claessen and P. Skalnik, pp. 353–370. The Hague: Mouton.

———. 1984. The Emergence of Bunyoro. In *State Formation in Eastern Africa*, ed. A. I. Salim, pp. 70–90. Nairobi: Heinemann.

Stewart, K. 1991. Fish Remains From Gogo Falls. In *Gogo Falls: Excavations at a Complex Archaeological Site East of Lake Victoria*, ed. P. Robertshaw. Appendix 3. *Azania* 26:179–180.

Stiles, D. 1979. Hunters of the Northern East African Coast. *Africa* 51:848–862.

———. 1980. Archaeological and Ethnographic Studies of Pastoral Groups of Northern Kenya. *Nyame Akuma* 17:20–24.

———. 1982. A History of Hunting Peoples on the Northern East African Coast.

Paideuma 28:165-174.

———. 1992. The Hunter-Gatherer Revisionist Debate. *Anthropology Today* 8:13-17.

Stiner, M. C., N. D. Munro, and T. A. Surovell. 2000. The Tortoise and the Hare: Small Game Use, the Broad Spectrum Revolution and Paleolithic Demography. *Current Anthropology* 41:39-73.

Sutton, J. E. G. 1964. A Review of Pottery from Kenya Highlands. *South African Archaeological Bulletin* 19:27-35.

———. 1974. The Aquatic Civilization of Middle Africa. *Journal of African History* 15:527-546.

———. 1977. The African Aqualithic. *Antiquity* 51:25-34.

———. 1980. Aquatic Reflections. In *Proceedings of the Eighth Panafrican Congress of Prehistory and Quaternary Studies*, ed. R. E. Leakey and B. A. Ogot, pp. 321-322. Nairobi: International Louis Leakey Memorial Institute for African Prehistory.

———. 1985. Ntusi and the "Dams." *Azania* 20:172-175.

———. 1990. *A Thousand Years of East Africa*. Nairobi: British Institute in Eastern Africa.

———. 1993. The Antecedents of the Interlacustrine Kingdoms. *Journal of African History* 34:33-64.

———. 1994/95. East Africa: Interior and Coast. *Azania* 29/30:227-231.

——— (ed.). 1994/95. The Growth of Farming Communities in Africa from the Equator Southwards. *Azania* 29/30:1-338.

Swai, B. 1984. Pre-Colonial States and European Merchant Capital. In *State Formation in East Africa*, ed. S. I. Salim, pp. 15-35. Nairobi: Heinemann.

Tantala, R. L. 1989. The Early History of Kitara in Western Uganda: Process Models of Religious and Political Change. Ph.D dissertation, University of Wisconsin, Madison, WI.

Tanzania Association of Archaeologists and Paleoanthropologists (TAAP). 1995. Bellagio Conference, Press Release: DTV and ITV. Dar es Salaam, Tanzania.

Taylor, S. J., and C. A. Shell. 1988. Social and Historical Implications of Early Chinese Iron Technology. In *The Beginning of the Use of Metals and Alloys*, ed. R. Maddin, pp. 205-221. Cambridge, MA: MIT Press.

Ten Raa, E. 1971. Dead Art and Living Society: A Study of Rock Paintings in a Social Context. *Mankind* 8:42-58.

Tesele, T. F. 1994. Symbols of Power: Beads and Flywhisks in Traditional Healing in Lesotho. B.A. (Honours) dissertation, University of Cape Town.

Thomas, J. 1988a. Neolithic Explanations Revisited: The Mesolithic-Neolithic Transition in Britain and South Scandinavia. *Proceedings of the Prehistoric Society* 54:59-66.

———. 1988b. *Re-thinking the Neolithic*. Cambridge: Cambridge University Press.

Thorbahn, P. 1979. Precolonial Ivory Trade of East Africa: Reconstruction of a Human-Elephant Ecosystem. Ph.D. dissertation, Department of Anthropology, University of Massachusetts, Amherst.

Thorp, C. R. 1996. A Preliminary Report on Evidence of Interaction between Hunter-Gatherers and Farmers along a Hypothesized Frontier in the Eastern Free State. *South African Archaeological Bulletin* 51:57–63.

Todd, J. A. 1985. Iron Production by the Dimi of Ethiopia. In *African Ironworking: Ancient and Traditional*, ed. R. Haaland and P. L. Shinnie, pp. 88–101. Oslo: Norwegian University Press.

Tremaine, M. 2003. Jewel in the Eco-Tourism Crown. *Msafiri* 43.

Tylecote, R. F. 1986. *The Prehistory of Metallurgy in the British Isles*. London: The Institute of Metals.

van der Merwe, N. J. 1969. *The Carbon-14 Dating of Iron*. Chicago, IL: University of Chicago Press.

———. 1980. The Advent of Iron in Africa. In *The Coming of the Age of Iron*, ed. T. Wartime and J. Muhly, pp. 463–506. New Haven, CT: Yale University Press.

———. 1991. Review of *A History Of African Archaeology* by P. Robertshaw. *Journal of Field Archaeology* 19:403–407.

van der Merwe, N. J., and R. T. K. Scully. 1971. The Phalaborwa Story: Archaeological and Ethnographic Investigation of a South African Iron Age Group. *World Archaeology* 3:178–196.

van der Ryst, M. 1998. *The Waterberg Plateau in the Northern Province in the Later Stone Age*. BAR International Series 715. Oxford: British Archaeological Reports.

van der Veen, M. (ed.). 1999. *The Exploitation of Plant Resources in Ancient Africa*. New York: Plenum.

van Lawick-Goodall, H., and J. van Lawick-Goodall. 1970. *Innocent Killers*. London: Collins.

Van Riet Lowe, C. 1929. Further Notes on the Archaeology of Sheppard Island. *South African Journal of Science* 26:665–683.

Vansina, J. 1990. *Paths in the Rainforest: Toward a History of Political Tradition in Equatorial Africa*. Madison: University of Wisconsin Press.

Verin, P. 1986. *The History of Civilization in North Madagascar*. Rotterdam: A. A. Balkema.

Vincent, A. S. 1985a. Plant Foods in Savanna Environments: A Preliminary Report of Tubers Eaten by the Hadza of Northern Tanzania. *World Archaeology* 17(2): 131–148.

———. 1985b. Wild Tubers as a Harvestable Resource in the East African Savannas: Ecological and Ethnographic Studies. Ph.D. dissertation, University of California.

von Mitzlaff, U. 1988. *Maasai-Frauen: Leben in einer patriachalischen Gesellschaft Feldforschung bei den Parakuyo, Tansania*. Munich: Trickster Wissenschaft Verlag.

Wadley, L. 1987. *Later Stone Age Hunter-Gatherers of the Southern Transvaal: Social and Ecological Interpretations*. BAR International Series 380. Oxford: British Archaeological Reports.

———. 1996. Changes in the Social Relations of Precolonial Hunter-Gatherers after

Agropastoral Contact: An Example from the Magaliesberg, South Africa. *Journal of Anthropological Archaeology* 15:205-217.

Wagner, D. B. 1994. *Iron and Steel in Ancient China*. Leiden: E. J. Brill.

Wagner, G. 1970. *The Bantu of Western Kenya*, vol. 2. Reprint, London: Oxford University Press.

Walker, J. N. 1995. *Late Pleistocene and Holocene Hunter-Gatherers of the Matopos: An Archaeological Study of Change and Continuity in Zimbabwe*. Uppsala, Sweden: Societas Archaeologica Upsaliensis.

Walker, N. J. 1983. The Significance of an Early Date for Pottery and Sheep in Zimbabwe. *South African Archaeological Bulletin* 38:88-92.

Walther, F. R. 1969. Flight Behavior and Avoidance of Predators in Thompson Gazelle (*Gazelle thompsoni*, Guenther 1884). *Behavior* 34:184-221.

Wandibba, S. 1977. An Attribute Analysis of the Ceramics of the Early Pastoralist Period from the Southern Rift Valley, Kenya. M.A. thesis, University of Nairobi.

———. 1980. The Application of Attribute Analysis to the Study of Later Stone Age/Neolithic Pottery Ceramics in Kenya (summary). In *Proceedings of the Eighth Panafrican Congress of Prehistory and Quaternary Studies*, ed. R. E. Leakey and B. A. Ogot, pp. 283-285. Nairobi: International Louis Leakey Memorial Institute for African Prehistory.

———. 1990. Ancient and Modern Ceramic Traditions in the Lake Victoria Basin of Kenya. *Azania* 25:69-78.

———. 1995. Seeking the Past in the Present: Archaeological Implications of Ethnographic Pottery Studies in Kenya. *KVHAA Conferences* 34:161-169.

Wayland, E. J. 1924. The Stone Age in Uganda. *Man* 24:124.

———. 1934. Rifts, Rivers, Rains, and Early Man in Uganda. *Journal of the Royal Anthropological Institute* 64:333-352.

Weaver, T., and D. Dale. 1978. Trampling Effects of Hikers, Motorcycles and Horses in Meadows and Forests. *Journal of Applied Ecology* 15:451-457.

Welbourn, A. 1989. Southern Nilotic: Endo. In *Kenyan Pots and Potters*, ed. J. Barbour and S. Wandibba, pp. 59-64. Nairobi: Oxford University Press.

Wembah-Rashid, J. 1969. Iron Workers of Ufipa. *Bulletin of the International Committee for Urgent Anthropological and Ethnological Research* 2:65-67.

Wetterstrom, W. 1991. Plant Remains From Gogo Falls. In *Gogo Falls: Excavations at a Complex Archaeological Site East of Lake Victoria*, ed. P. Robertshaw. Appendix 4. *Azania* 26:180-191.

White, F. 1983. *The Vegetation of Africa: A Descriptive Memoir to Accompany the UNESCO/AETFAT/UNSO Vegetation Map of Africa*. UNESCO Natural Resources Research Vol. 20. Paris: UNESCO.

Whitelaw, G. 1994/95. Towards an Early Iron Age Worldview: Some Ideas from KwaZulu-Natal. *Azania* 29/30:37-50.

———. 1998. Twenty-one Centuries of Ceramics in KwaZulu-Natal. In *Ubumba: Aspects of Indigenous Ceramics in KwaZulu-Natal*, ed. J. Addleson, J. Armstrong, B. Bell, I. Calder, and M. Mngwabe, pp. 3-12. Pietermaritzburg: Natal Museum Press.

Wijngaarden, Willem van, and V. W. P. van Engelen. 1985. *Soils and Vegetation of the Tsavo Area*. Nairobi: Geological Survey of Kenya.

Wilding, R. 1989. Coastal Bantu: WaSwahili. In *Kenyan Pots and Potters*, ed. J. Barbour and S. Wandibba, pp. 100-115. Nairobi: Oxford University Press.

Willis, R. 1968. The Fipa. In *Tanzania before 1900*, ed. A. D. Robert. Nairobi: East African Publishing House.

————. 1976. *On Historical Reconstruction from Oral-Traditional Sources: A Structuralist Approach*. The 12th Melville J. Herskovits Memorial Lecture Delivered under the Auspices of the Program of African Studies, Northwestern University, February 16.

————. 1981. *A State in the Making: Myth, History, and Social Transformation in Pre-colonial Ufipa*. Bloomington, IN: Indiana University Press.

Wilmsen, E. N. 1989. *Land Filled with Flies: A Political Economy of the Kalahari*. Chicago, IL: University of Chicago Press.

Wilmsen, E. N., and J. R. Denbow. 1990. Paradigmatic History of San-Speaking Peoples and Current Attempts at Revision. *Current Anthropology* 31:489-524.

Wilson, P. J. 1988. *The Domestication of the Human Species*. New Haven, CT: Yale University Press.

Wilson, T. H. 1982. Spatial Analysis of Settlement on the East African Coast. *Paideuma* 28:201-220.

Wise, R. 1958. Iron Smelting in Ufipa. *Tanganyika Notes and Records* 50:106-111.

Woodburn, J. C. 1964. The Social Organization of the Hadza of North Tanganyika. Ph.D. dissertation, Archaeology Department, Cambridge University, Cambridge.

————. 1968. Stability and Flexibility in Hadza Residential Groupings. In *Man the Hunter*, ed. R. B. Lee and I. DeVore, pp. 49-55. New York: Aldine.

————. 1972. Ecology, Nomadic Movements, and the Composition of the Local Group among Hunters and Gatherers: An East African Example and Its Implications. In *Man, Settlement, and Urbanism*, ed. P. J. Ucko, R. Tringham, and G. W. Dimbleby, pp. 193-206. London: Duckworth.

————. 1980. Hunters and Gatherers Today and Reconstruction of the Past. In *Soviet and Western Anthropology*, ed. E. Gellner, pp 95-117. New York: Columbia University Press.

————. 1988. African Hunter-Gatherer Social Organization: Is It Best Understood as a Product of Encapsulation? In *Hunters and Gatherers* 1: *History, Evolution, and Social Change*, ed. T. Ingold, D. Riches, and J. Woodburn, pp. 31-64. Oxford: Berg.

Wright, H. T. 1993. Trade and Politics on the Eastern Littoral of Africa, AD 800-1300. In *The Archaeology of Africa: Food, Metals and Towns*, ed. T. Shaw, P. Sinclair, B. Andah, and A. Okpoko, pp. 658-672. London: Routledge.

Wright, M. 1982. Towards a Critical History of Iron Makers in Sumbawanga District, Tanzania. History Seminar Papers, Department of History, University of Dar es Salaam.

————. 1985. Iron and Regional History: Report on Research Project in Southwestern Tanzania. *African Economic History* 14:147-65.

Wyckaert, R. P. 1914. Forgenos paiens et forgerons chretiens au Tanganyika. *Anthropos* 9:371-380.

Yellen, J. E. 1977. *Archaeological Approaches to the Present: Models for Reconstructing the Past.* New York: Academic Press.

Ylvisaker, 1982. The Ivory Trade in the Lamu Area. *Paideuma* 28:221-231.

Contributors

Felix Chami
Associate Professor
Archaeology Unit
University of Dar es Salaam
P.O. Box 35050
Dar es Salaam
Tanzania

Karega-Munene
Principal Research Scientist
Archaeology Division
National Museums of Kenya
P.O. Box 40658
Nairobi
Kenya

Emanuel T. Kessy
Assistant Lecturer
Archaeology Unit
University of Dar es Salaam
P.O. Box 35050
Dar es Salaam
Tanzania

David Killick
Associate Professor
Department of Anthropology
University of Arizona
Tucson, AZ 85721
USA

Chapurukha M. Kusimba
Associate Curator of Anthropology
Department of Anthropology
The Field Museum
1400 South Roosevelt Road at Lake
Shore Drive
Chicago, IL 60605
USA

Sibel B. Kusimba
Assistant Professor of Anthropology
Department of Anthropology
Northern Illinois University
DeKalb, IL 60115
USA

Audax A. P. Mabulla
Senior Lecturer and Coordinator
Archaeology Unit
University of Dar es Salaam
P.O. Box 35050
Dar es Salaam
Tanzania

Bertram B. B. Mapunda
Senior Lecturer
Archaeology Unit
University of Dar es Salaam
P.O. Box 35050
Dar es Salaam
Tanzania

Peter Mitchell
Lecturer in African Prehistory
School of Archaeology
University of Oxford
St Hugh's College
Oxford OX2 6LE
United Kingdom

Charles M. Musiba
Assistant Professor of Anthropology
Department of Sociology-
Anthropology
North Dakota State University
404-H Minard Hall, P.O. Box 5075
Fargo, ND 58105-5075
USA

Peter Robertshaw
Professor and Chair
Department of Anthropology
California State University at San
Bernardino
5500 University Parkway
San Bernardino, CA 92407-2397
USA

Simiyu Wandibba
Professor of Archaeology
Institute of African Studies
P.O. Box 30197
Nairobi
Kenya

Index